PSYCHOLOGY RESEARCH PROGRESS

ANTISOCIAL BEHAVIOR

ETIOLOGY, GENETIC AND ENVIRONMENTAL INFLUENCES AND CLINICAL MANAGEMENT

Psychology Research Progress

Additional books in this series can be found on Nova's website
under the Series tab.

Additional e-books in this series can be found on Nova's website
under the e-book tab.

PSYCHOLOGY RESEARCH PROGRESS

ANTISOCIAL BEHAVIOR

ETIOLOGY, GENETIC AND ENVIRONMENTAL INFLUENCES AND CLINICAL MANAGEMENT

JUSTINE H. GALLO
EDITOR

nova publishers
New York

For permission to use material from this book please contact us:
Telephone 631-231-7269; Fax 631-231-8175
Web Site: http://www.novapublishers.com

Library of Congress Cataloging-in-Publication Data

ISBN: 978-1-63321-521-4

Published by Nova Science Publishers, Inc. † New York

CONTENTS

PREFACE

Parents play a central role in the lives of their children. Parent-child interaction is a central variable in the etiology of antisocial behaviour. Research suggests that families of antisocial individuals are characterized by harsh and inconsistent discipline, little positive parental involvement and poor monitoring and supervision. Thus parents could create environments for unhealthy parent-child relationships with subsequent antisocial behaviour of their adolescents. This book discusses several topics that may lead to antisocial behavior. It describes the etiology, genetic and environmental influences, as well as clinical management of antisocial behavior.

Chapter 1 – Large-scale cooperation, or the willingness of individuals to incur costs in order to help others, is a defining trait of the human species. However, cooperation poses a theoretical puzzle: since it is individually costly to cooperate, it seems that natural selection should favor non-cooperation (defection). Recently, it has been proposed that coordinated, collective punishment by cooperators of defectors can allow cooperation to invade a population of defectors. Here, the authors address the fact that in this previous analysis, punishment was only available to cooperators; defectors had no ability to punish cooperators (i.e. antisocial punishment was not possible). In other models, the inclusion of antisocial punishment has been shown to undermine the ability of punishment to promote cooperation. Thus the authors examine the effect of allowing antisocial punishment on the emergence of cooperation. Their results suggest that coordinated punishment confers no competitive advantage when punishment is a strategy available to both cooperators and defectors. While coordinated prosocial punishers can invade a population of non-punishing defectors, they cannot invade a population of antisocial punishers. These results question the conclusion that coordinated punishment played a central role in the evolution of human cooperation, and highlight the importance of not arbitrarily excluding antisocial punishment strategies from evolutionary models.

Chapter 2 – Attention Deficit Hyperactivity Disorder (ADHD) and Substance Use Disorders (SUDs) are known to be important contributing factors in the development and exacerbation of various types of antisocial behavior. The treatment of patients who exhibit frequent antisocial behavior and suffer from these conditions is often experienced as challenging by therapists and usually produce very modest effects, if any at all. Recent advances in neuropsychology, however, may offer new perspectives concerning the efficacy of offender treatment in these patients.

This chapter will focus on two interesting new developments in offender treatment with patients suffering from ADHD and SUDs: Neurofeedback and the Relapse Early Warning And Response System (REWARS). Neurofeedback is a method of influencing the brain's activity by way of operant conditioning. REWARS is a daily test and intervention protocol for patients suffering from SUDs. It makes use of the attentional bias concerning stimuli that are related to the substance the subject is addicted to. This attentional bias is typically shown by the subject twelve to twenty-four hours before the onset of craving for the substance and subsequent relapse.

Both treatment methods will be explained extensively. Their empirical bases and implementability will also be discussed.

Chapter 3 – This chapter describes and analyzes delinquent and antisocial behavior in adolescence. The first section highlights the importance of defining the concept of delinquency when talking about minors. Data from both recent social research and government sources from different countries are presented. In the second section, the evolution of adolescent delinquent and antisocial behavior over the last few years is discussed and examined in both sexes and for different ages during the adolescent period. A third section includes the most relevant social and psychological explanatory models of adolescent delinquency provided by research in social sciences. The main important individual, family, school, and community risk factors studied in scientific literature are analyzed in depth in order to understand the origin, development and continuity of this kind of behavior in young people.

Chapter 4 – Is it what adult perpetrators of violence think or how they think that discriminates them most from non-violent members of the community? The research presented in this chapter investigated whether violent and criminal sentiments, attribution biases and/or violent grievance resolution strategies represented risk factors for aggressive behaviour. The participants were 546 adults comprising 105 violent offenders, 238 university students and 203 men and women from a community sample. The differences between offenders and non-offenders in violent attitudes was measured by the Violent and Criminal Sentiments Scale. The differences in attributional biases and problem solving was assessed by a set of measure designed for this study. The results showed that offenders were clearly different from non-offenders with the offenders endorsing significantly higher criminal and violent sentiments with an effect size of ^{2} =.46. The offenders also reported a significantly higher level of violence-based resolution strategies to end grievances than non-offenders. However, the surprising finding was that the adult male high-risk offenders did not demonstrate more pronounced hostile attributional biases than either adult men and women students or men and women from the community. The results imply that believing violence is acceptable and being prepared to use violence is more explanatory than how a person interprets the social behaviour of others. These findings have important implications for our understanding of why people behave aggressively and for the development of more effective intervention programs.

Chapter 5 – This chapter provides a review of the literature pertaining to the clinical presentation, epidemiology, etiology, prognosis and treatment of Oppositional Defiant Disorder (ODD) and antisocial behavior in children with Attention Deficit Hyperactivity Disorder (ADHD). The pervasive effects of ODD in children with ADHD may have an impact on their cognitive, behavioral, emotional and academic performances. ODD type behavior in ADHD school-aged children is characterized by talking back to adults, rejection by peers and failure in school. Followed into adolescence, some of these children may exhibit a significantly elevated risk for delinquent behaviors such as stealing and disobedient acts. The clinical presentation of antisocial behavior in adults is characterized by the progression of criminal behaviors and severe personality disturbance. A combination of genetic predispositions leading to cognitive deficits, combined with exposure to environmental risk factors contributes to the link between ADHD, ODD and antisocial behavior. Only in some cases, do children with ADHD continue to show these behaviors into adolescence and adulthood. Thus, there is generally a gradual decrease in antisocial behaviors and rates of dysfunctions and they may never be exhibited in later stages. An early intervention that aims to control the symptoms of ADHD and reduce the impact of antisocial and ODD type behavior at each developmental stage should be utilized. These interventions can consist of medication and a variety of psychosocial interventions, such as parent-child therapy, parent training, positive behavioral support, and collaborative problem solving.

Chapter 6 – In the chapter, theoretic, methodological, organizational aspects and regularities of course of drug dependence in persons under conditions of restraint of freedom will be considered. Pathogenetic aspects of deviant, delinquent and aggressive behavior associated with substance use will be studied. Social-psychological and subcultural aspects of behavior of drug addicted convicts will be described. Comparative analysis of factors contributing to formation of antisocial and asocial activity of the personality during drug use will be introduced. Variants of structure and dynamic of formation of remissions of drug dependence in convicts under penal system conditions and clinical dynamic of comorbid mental disorders will be distinguished. A special attention will be paid to principles of rehabilitation in convicts under specific conditions of penal system, study of predictors of breakdown and relapse in the process of course of remissions including young offenders as well to possibilities of clinical-mathematical prognosis of stability and length of remission. Measures of prevention of criminal behavior associated with drug dependence as well as breakdowns and relapses in convicts, issues of improvement of addictological help under current conditions of restraint of freedom will be defined.

Chapter 7 – Background: Parents play a central role in the lives of their children. Parent-child interaction is a central variable in the etiology of antisocial behaviour. Research suggests that families of antisocial individuals are characterized by harsh and inconsistent discipline, little positive parental involvement and poor monitoring and supervision. Thus parents could create environments for unhealthy parent-child relationships with subsequent antisocial behaviour of their adolescents.

Aim of the study is to systematically appraise studies which seek to examine the link between antisocial behaviour of adolescents and parental practices to manage the antisocial behaviour of their adolescents.

Methods: A comprehensive search was conducted to extract information regarding the topic. Ebscohost (Medline, CINAHL, PsycArticles), JSTOR and Pubmed for the period of 2003-2014. Two reviewers independently evaluated the methodological quality of the studies reviewed. Data was be extracted independently by two reviewers using the 'JBI data extraction tool'. The findings are summarized in narrative form.

Results: Eight studies were eligible for inclusion in this study. The majority of studies were longitudinal and included a study in Taiwan, New Zealand and the remainder in the USA. Parenting, in relation to antisocial behaviour of adolescents, was examined both genetically and environmentally. Parenting practices have an effect on the antisocial behaviour of adolescents. These parenting practices may also be transferred across generations. In particular, harsh, inconsistent parenting as well as low attachment levels between parent and adolescent, low parental control, low monitoring and low guidance all encouraged antisocial behaviour of adolescents and in some studies into young adulthood.

Conclusion: Positive and consistent parenting, father involvement and good parental role models reduced antisocial behaviour of adolescents.

In: Antisocial Behavior
Editor: Justine H. Gallo

ISBN: 978-1-63321-521-4

Chapter 1

Coordinated Punishment Does Not Proliferate When Defectors Can Also Punish Cooperators

Collin M. McCabe[1,*] ***and David G. Rand***[2]
[1]Department of Human Evolutionary Biology, Harvard University, Cambridge, MA, US
[2]Department of Psychology and Department of Economics, Yale University, New Haven, CT, US

Abstract

Large-scale cooperation, or the willingness of individuals to incur costs in order to help others, is a defining trait of the human species. However, cooperation poses a theoretical puzzle: since it is individually costly to cooperate, it seems that natural selection should favor non-cooperation (defection). Recently, it has been proposed that coordinated, collective punishment by cooperators of defectors can allow cooperation to invade a population of defectors. Here, we address the fact that in this previous analysis, punishment was only available to cooperators; defectors had no ability to punish cooperators (i.e. antisocial punishment was not possible). In other models, the inclusion of antisocial punishment has been shown to undermine the ability of punishment to promote cooperation. Thus we examine the effect of allowing antisocial punishment on the emergence of cooperation. Our results suggest that coordinated punishment confers no competitive advantage when punishment is a strategy available to both cooperators and defectors. While coordinated prosocial punishers can invade a population of non-punishing defectors, they cannot invade a population of antisocial punishers. These results question the conclusion that coordinated punishment played a central role in the evolution of human cooperation, and highlight the importance of not arbitrarily excluding antisocial punishment strategies from evolutionary models.

* Email address for correspondence: mccabe@fas.harvard.edu.

1. Introduction

Cooperation, operationally defined as paying costs to benefit others, is central to human existence and survival. Yet given that cooperation is individually costly, explaining why the selfish process of evolution would favor cooperation has been a major research focus for the last half-century. Evolutionary game theory, in particular using the Prisoner's Dilemma (PD), has been the central paradigm for studying the question. In a one-shot anonymous PD, and its n-player counterpart the Public Goods Game (PGG), cooperators always receive lower payoffs than non-cooperators (defectors), and thus natural selection favors defection. Numerous mechanisms for the evolution of cooperation, or alterations to the basic PD structure that can make cooperators out-earn defectors, have been proposed (Nowak, 2006; Rand & Nowak, 2013): direct reciprocity, where individuals interact repeatedly (Axelrod, 1984; Fudenberg & Maskin, 1990; Fudenberg, Rand, & Dreber, 2012; Nowak & Sigmund, 1992, 1993; Rand, Dreber, Ellingsen, Fudenberg, & Nowak, 2009; Trivers, 1971; van Veelen, García, Rand, & Nowak, 2012); indirect reciprocity, where individuals interact within groups and carry reputations (Milinski, Semmann, & Krambeck, 2002; Nakamura & Masuda, 2011; Nowak & Sigmund, 1998, 2005; Ohtsuki & Iwasa, 2006; Pfeiffer, Tran, Krumme, & Rand, 2012; Sommerfeld, Krambeck, Semmann, & Milinski, 2007; Wedekind & Milinski, 2000; Yoeli, Hoffman, Rand, & Nowak, 2013); kin selection, where individuals preferentially cooperate with related others (Hamilton, 1964; Holmes & Sherman, 1983; Jansen & van Baalen, 2006; Lieberman, Tooby, & Cosmides, 2007); structured interactions, where individuals are matched in non-random fashion such that cooperators are more likely to interact with other cooperators (Brandt, Hauert, & Sigmund, 2003; Fu et al., 2012; Hauert & Doebeli, 2004; Helbing, Szolnoki, Perc, & Szabó, 2010; Lindgren & Nordahl, 1994; Nowak & May, 1992; Ohtsuki, Hauert, Lieberman, & Nowak, 2006; Rand, Arbesman, & Christakis, 2011; Sekiguchi & Nakamaru, 2009; van Veelen et al., 2012); and multi-level (or group) selection, where competition and reproduction occurs at the level of the group as well as the level of the individual (Bowles, 2006; Bowles & Gintis, 2003; Boyd & Richerson, 1990; Choi & Bowles, 2007; J. Henrich, 2004; Paulsson, 2002; A. Traulsen & Nowak, 2006; Wilson, 1975).

Recently, an alternative possible route to cooperation has received considerable attention: the willingness for cooperators to pay to punish defectors (Almenberg, Dreber, Apicella, & Rand, 2011; Boyd & Richerson, 1992; Brandt et al., 2003; Condon & DeSteno, 2011; Fiery Cushman, Dreber, Wang, & Costa, 2009; FA Cushman & Macindoe, 2009; Denant-Boemont, Masclet, & Noussair, 2007; Dreber, Rand, Fudenberg, & Nowak, 2008; Egas & Riedl, 2008; Fehr & Fischbacher, 2004; Fehr & Gächter, 2000, 2002; Fowler, 2005; Fowler, Johnson, & Smirnov, 2005; Gächter, Renner, & Sefton, 2008; Hauert, Traulsen, Brandt, Nowak, & Sigmund, 2007; Hauser, Nowak, & Rand, 2014; Helbing et al., 2010; Joseph Henrich et al., 2010; Herrmann, Thoni, & Gächter, 2008; Houser, Xiao, McCabe, & Smith, 2008; Isakov & Rand, 2011; Janssen & Bushman, 2008; Jordan, McAuliffe, & Rand, 2014; M. Nakamaru & Iwasa, 2005; Nikiforakis, 2008; Nikiforakis & Mitchell, 2013; Ohtsuki, Iwasa, & Nowak, 2009; Ostrom, Walker, & Gardner, 1992; Powers, Taylor, & Bryson, 2012; Rand, Armao IV, Nakamaru, & Ohtsuki, 2010; Rand, Dreber, et al., 2009; Rand & Nowak, 2011; Rand, Ohtsuki, & Nowak, 2009; Rockenbach & Milinski, 2006; Sigmund, Hauert, & Nowak, 2001; Arne Traulsen, Röhl, & Milinski, 2012; Ule, Schram, Riedl, & Cason, 2009; Wu et al., 2009).

Numerous behavioral experiments demonstrate that many cooperators will pay to punish defectors, and that this can stabilize cooperation in the lab (Fehr & Fischbacher, 2003; Fehr & Gächter, 2000, 2002; Jordan et al., 2014; Ostrom et al., 1992; Ouss & Peysakhovich, 2013; Peysakhovich, Nowak, & Rand, 2014; Peysakhovich & Rand, 2013; Rand, Ohtsuki, et al., 2009; Rockenbach & Milinski, 2006). Complimenting this empirical work is a range of evolutionary models showing that allowing cooperators to punish defectors can facilitate the evolution of cooperation, in combination with some other mechanism (Boyd, Gintis, Bowles, & Richerson, 2003; Boyd & Richerson, 1992; Choi & Bowles, 2007; García & Traulsen, 2012; Hauert et al., 2007; Helbing et al., 2010; Joseph Henrich & Boyd, 2001; Hilbe & Traulsen, 2012; M. Nakamaru & Iwasa, 2005; M. Nakamaru & Iwasa, 2006; A. Traulsen, Hauert, De Silva, Nowak, & Sigmund, 2009). The general logic is that if defectors are punished, then the payoff advantage of defecting is negated and cooperators can outperform defectors; punishment itself is costly, creating a second order free-rider problem that some additional mechanism is required to address.

In the last few years, however, a body of evidence has begun to emerge challenging this positive role of punishment. Empirically, it has been shown that not only do cooperators punish defectors, but defectors also punish cooperators (Cinyabuguma, Page, & Putterman, 2006; Dreber et al., 2008; Ellingsen, Herrmann, Nowak, Rand, & Tarnita, 2012; Gächter & Herrmann, 2009, 2011; Gächter, Herrmann, & Thöni, 2010; Herrmann et al., 2008; Nikiforakis, 2008; Sylwester, Herrmann, & Bryson, (In press)). This 'antisocial punishment' has been ignored by nearly all previous theoretical models for the co-evolution of punishment and cooperation, which assume that only cooperators punish defectors. Punishment targeted at cooperators ('antisocial punishment') is excluded *a priori.*

Thus it is important to reconsider these models, and examine the consequences of allowing cooperators to be punished. Work in this vein has not been promising for punishment. When antisocial punishment, as well as indiscriminant punishment: (i) are added to the spatially structured model of (M. Nakamaru & Iwasa, 2005; M. Nakamaru & Iwasa, 2006) where agents are embedded in a lattice, the result is that defectors who punish cooperators are the only globally stable strategy (Rand et al., 2010); (ii) are added to the voluntary social dilemma model of (Hauert et al., 2007) where players can opt out of the game and be 'loners' who receive a fixed intermediate payoff, the result is that punishment no longer increases the level of cooperation in the steady state distribution for most parameter sets (although this result relies on loners being able to punish cooperators (García & Traulsen, 2012)); and (iii) are added to the exploration dynamics model of (A. Traulsen et al., 2009), where mutation rates are very high, again punishment no longer increases the state steady frequency of cooperation (regardless of whether the game is optional or compulsory) (Hauser et al., 2014). Similarly, when the intergroup conflict model of (Boyd et al., 2003) is extended such that defectors who receive punishment are allowed to retaliate, punishment is much less effective at promoting cooperation (Janssen & Bushman, 2008), and including defectors that punish cooperators in a group-structured model undermines the evolution of cooperation (Powers et al., 2012).

In this chapter, we extend these previous results by considering the role that antisocial punishment might play in a recently published model related to coordinated punishment (Boyd, Gintis, & Bowles, 2010) (hereafter abbreviated as BGB). BGB argue that coordinated, collective punishment can lead to establishment of cooperation as a stable strategy. In their model, cooperators are allowed to signal their intent to punish defectors before the game begins. This allows coordinated punishment to invade defection: punishers signal their intention to cooperate and punish defection, and then only follow through if enough others also signal. If too few others signal, then everyone defects; this allows the punishers to not be at a disadvantage when they are rare in a population otherwise made up of defectors.

As in most other models, BGB do not consider the possibility of antisocial punishment directed at cooperators. Here we consider the consequences of a modification to the defector strategy which exploits the signal given by would-be punishers: when punishers signal their intention to punish, they identify themselves to defectors as potential threats. Therefore our antisocial defectors punish those who signal, regardless of the signalers' subsequent behavior. This therefore prevents cooperative punishers from invading, because the cooperative punishers are once again at a disadvantage relative to a defector majority (since they are being punished for signaling, even if they do not subsequently cooperate and punish).

The chapter proceeds as follows. In Section 2, we give the details of the model. In Section 3 we present the results. In Section 4, we conclude.

2. METHODS

A. Original BGB Model

The BGB model consisted of n individuals playing a game with two parts. The first part was a single signaling stage. The second part was a repeated two-stage game in which players first decided whether to cooperate, and then decided whether to punish those who did not cooperate in the first stage.

In the signaling stage, individuals can choose to either signal, or not signal. Signaling carries a cost of signaling (q).

In the cooperation stage, individuals can choose to either cooperate or defect. If an individual cooperates, it incurs a cost of cooperation (c) and creates a benefit (b), which is divided amongst all n group members. If an individual defects, it incurs no cost and contributes no benefit to the group. The model also includes an error rate in cooperation (e), which accounts for the inability to cooperate given mistakes or extenuating circumstances which preclude cooperation, such that out of N possible instances of cooperation, $(1\text{-}e)N$ will result in cooperation, while eN will result instead in defection.

In the punishment stage, individuals can choose to punish or not punish. Punishers incur a cost (k) for each individual that defected in the previous stage, and inflict a cost (p) on each of these defecting individuals. Additionally, the model stipulates an advantage from coordinated punishment (a), such that the cost to punish decreases as the number of punishers increases if $a>1$ (if M is the number of punishers, the cost to punish is $Mk / [M^a]$).

The cycle of cooperation stage and punishment stage repeats T times.

BGB show that cooperation can invade defection by considering two strategies: the (cooperative) punisher (P) and the (defecting) non-punisher (N).

P players always signal in the signaling stage. Then in the cooperation and punishment stages, their behavior depends on the outcome of the signaling round. If a threshold number of players (τ+1) signaled in the signaling round, then P players will cooperate in every cooperation stage and punish all players that defected in the previous cooperation stage. If the threshold quorum was not met, P players will defect in every cooperation stage and not punishment.

N players do not signal in the signaling round, always defect in the first cooperation stage, and never punish. If the punishers chose to punish defectors in the first punishment stage (i.e. the threshold signaling quorum was met), then N players switch to cooperation for the remaining T-1 cooperation stages.

The model also includes assortment (or 'relatedness'). Where r is the average coefficient of relatedness among individuals in a group of n individuals, x is the frequency of punishers in the population, and j is the number of punishers among the other n-1 group members, the probability of encountering j punishers as a punisher is $\Pr(j|P)=r+(1-r)x$.

Thus the fitness of a punisher, $W_P(x)$ (Eq. 1.1) consists of four terms, first the baseline fitness, W_0, given as 1, then the cost q of signaling, then the benefits of cooperation minus the cost of punishing N defectors and erroneous defectors and the cost of being punished given erroneous defection in the first round (given that threshold quorum is met), and the benefits of cooperation minus the cost of punishing erroneous defectors and the cost of being punished given erroneous defection in all further (T-1) rounds in the game (given that threshold quorum is met):

$$
\begin{aligned}
W_P(x) &= W_0 - q \\
&+ \sum_{j=\tau}^{n-1} Pr(j|P)\left(-\frac{(e(j+1)+(n-1-j))k}{(j+1)^a} + (1-e)\left(\frac{b(j+1)}{n} - c\right)\right) \\
&+ (T-1)\sum_{j=\tau}^{n-1} Pr(j|P)\left((b-c)(1-e) - \frac{nek}{(j+1)^a} - ep\right)
\end{aligned}
\tag{1.1}
$$

Given r, x, and j as above, the probability of encountering j punishers as a non-punisher is $\Pr(j|N)=(1-r)x$. Thus the fitness of a non-punisher, $W_N(x)$ (Eq. 1.2) consists of three terms, first the baseline fitness, W_0, given again as 1, then benefit of all Ps' cooperation minus the cost of being punished in the first round (given that threshold quorum is met), and the benefits of cooperation minus the cost of being punished given erroneous defection in all further (T-1) rounds in the game (given that threshold quorum is met):

$$
\begin{aligned}
W_N(x) &= W_0 \\
&+ \sum_{j=\tau+1}^{n-1} Pr(j|N)\left(-p + \frac{(1-e)jb}{n}\right) \\
&+ (T-1)\sum_{j=\tau+1}^{n-1} Pr(j|N)\left((b-c)(1-e) - ep\right)
\end{aligned}
\tag{1.2}
$$

b. Extended Model Including Antisocial Punishment

We now extend the BGB model by altering the non-cooperative strategy to include antisocial punishment (creating a new strategy, the antisocial punisher A). Antisocial punishment in the extended model consists of incurring a cost to punish individuals that signaled in the signaling round of the game ("shooting the messenger") in all T punishment rounds. We assume that antisocial punishers incur the same cost of punishing (k) as did the original punishers, with the same punishment adjustment variable (a), to inflict the same cost of being punished (p) on other individuals, so that the punishment options were equal and opposite; however, the antisocial punishment was not restrained by any threshold variable (which could put rare A players at a disadvantage in P dominated groups).

Assuming the same parameters and probability distributions as before, the new fitness of a P player in the extended model, $W_{P*}(x)$ (Eq. 2.1), consists of the same four terms as before, in addition to one new term, the cost of being punished by A players in all rounds:

$$\begin{aligned} W_{P^*}(x) &= W_0 - q \\ &+ \sum_{j=\tau}^{n-1} Pr(j|P)\left(-\frac{(e(j+1)+(n-1-j))k}{(j+1)^a} + (1-e)\left(\frac{b(j+1)}{n} - c\right)\right) \\ &+ (T-1)\sum_{j=\tau}^{n-1} Pr(j|P)\left((b-c)(1-e) - \frac{nek}{(j+1)^a} - ep\right) \\ &+ T\sum_{j=0}^{n-2} Pr(j|P)(-p) \end{aligned} \tag{2.1}$$

The fitness of an A player, $W_A(x)$ (Eq. 2.2), consists of the same three terms as before, in addition to one new term, the cost of punishing all signalers (i.e. all P players) in all rounds:

$$\begin{aligned} W_A(x) &= W_0 \\ &+ \sum_{j=\tau+1}^{n-1} Pr(j|N)\left(-p + \frac{(1-e)jb}{n}\right) \\ &+ (T-1)\sum_{j=\tau+1}^{n-1} Pr(j|N)((b-c)(1-e) - ep) \\ &+ T\sum_{j=1}^{n-1} Pr(j|N)\left(-\frac{kj}{(n-j)^a}\right) \end{aligned} \tag{2.2}$$

3. RESULTS

We now explore the dynamic for these two different strategy sets. We use the same parameterization as in BGB: c=0.01, b=4c, p=q=k=1.5c, a=2, e=0.1, n=18, and T=25 (BGB argue that these values likely model the environment in which cooperation would have evolved in early *Homo* hunter-gatherers). We again follow BGB and examine two different coefficients of relatedness, r=0 (completely unrelated) and r=0.07 (BGB argue this represents the average relatedness of early *Homo* hunter-gatherer groups). Our analysis then varies the signalling threshold τ from 0 to n-1, and determines the evolutionary fixed points: x=0 and x=1 are always fixed points (because the model does not include mutation), as are values of x for which $W_P(x)=W_N(x)$ in the BGB model and $W_{P*}(x)=W_A(x)$ in the extended model.

Our analysis of the BGB model replicates BGB's results. We find a bifurcation at τ=1 in the unrelated case with r=0 (Fig. 1a), in which two interior (i.e. $0 < x < 1$) equilibria, one stable and one unstable, exist for all values of τ>1. In the case with relatedness r=0.07, no bifurcation occurs (Fig. 1b), and instead stable interior equilibria are present at all values of τ. Importantly, when τ<4, there is only a single stable interior equilibrium. Thus regardless of the where the population starts (including a case dominated by defectors), cooperation will evolve: P players can invade an N population when r=0.07 and τ<4. This finding was the main result of BGB, with which they argued that coordinated threshold punishment can drive the evolution of cooperation.

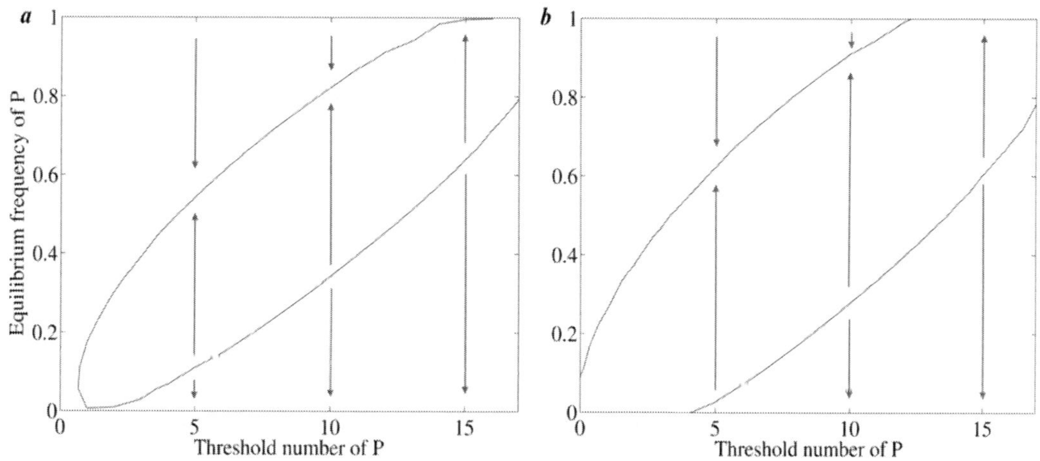

Figure 1. Flow diagrams of the original BGB model (P vs. N). Graphs plot the stable equilibrium frequencies of the P strategy as the threshold number of punishers varies from 0 to n-1 among populations of: *a.*) completely unrelated group members (r=0), and *b.*) average hunter-gatherer-related group members (r=0.07). Arrows indicate flow vectors; lines with converging flow vectors indicate stable equilibrium lines, and lines with diverging flow vectors indicate unstable equilibrium lines.

When analyzing the extended model, however, we see a very different result. For both r= 0 (Fig 2a) and r=0.07 (Fig 2b), P players can never invade A players. The unstable equilibrium ("dividing") line never drops below x=0.7, which provides no opportunity whatsoever for a rare punisher to invade a group of antisocial punishers. Similarly, however, there is no opportunity for a rare antisocial punisher to invade a group of punishers.

Conclusion

Here we have shown that coordinated punishment no longer allows cooperators to invade defectors if defectors can punish those who signal their willingness to sanction defectors. This punishment of signalers undermines the mechanism in the original BGB paper: signaling was only slightly costly because if a quorum was not met, the P players could avoid the costs of cooperation and punishment by just defecting themselves. However, if P players are punished for signaling, giving the signal again becomes highly costly. Furthermore, the A players' strategy of self-defense seems entirely psychologically plausible: if I were to tell you "I plan to punish you", which is effectively what the P players are doing to the N and A players in the signaling round, few would find it surprising if you preemptively punished me.

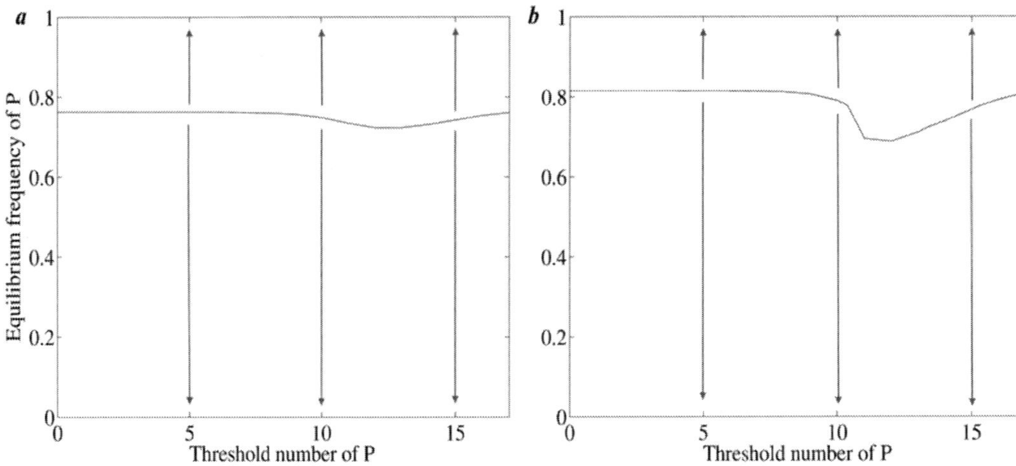

Figure 2. Flow diagrams of our extended model (P vs. A). Graphs plot the stable equilibrium frequencies of the P strategy as the threshold number of punishers varies from 0 to n-1 among populations of: *a.*) completely unrelated group members (r=0), and *b.*) average hunter-gatherer-related group members (r=0.07). Arrows indicate flow vectors; lines with converging flow vectors indicate stable equilibrium lines, and lines with diverging flow vectors indicate unstable equilibrium lines.

It is important to note that even against our antisocial A players, the cooperative punisher P strategy is still an equilibrium: a population dominated by P players cannot be invaded by A players. However, using the parameters that BGB argue are ecologically valid, the basin of attraction for the A players is much larger than that of the P players. Thus natural selection favors defection over cooperation.

Here we have provided yet another example of how adding antisocial punishment, an empirically demonstrated behavior which should not be ignored, dramatically changes the outcome of a model for the coevolution of cooperation and punishment. Our results show that this holds true whether punishment is solitary, as has been modeled in many previous studies, or it is coordinated among many individuals, as in the BGB model. Thus costly punishment is not a mechanism for the evolution of cooperation, and the great degree of cooperation observed among unrelated humans (Andreoni, Harbaugh, & Vesterlund, 2003; Balliet, Parks, & Joireman, 2009; Bateson, Nettle, & Roberts, 2006; Bolton, Katok, & Ockenfels, 2005; Burnham & Hare, 2007; Capraro, Jordan, & Rand, 2014; Dreber, Ellingsen, Johannesson, & Rand, 2013; Engel & Rand, 2014; Forsythe, Horowitz, Savin, & Sefton, 1994; Frank, Gilovich, & Regan, 1993a, 1993b; Goette, Huffman, & Meier, 2006; Gray, Ward, & Norton, 2012; Hallatschek & Nelson, 2008; Peysakhovich et al., 2014; Rand, Greene, & Nowak, 2012; Rand et al., 2014; Rapoport, 1965) is likely explained by forces other than costly punishment, perhaps such as repetition and reputation (Jordan, Rand, & Peysakhovich, Forthcoming).

ACKNOWLEDGMENTS

We thank Harvard University's Program for Evolutionary Dynamics for facilitating our research and collaboration, and specifically, Martin Nowak and Ivana Bozic for helpful comments and suggestions. Support from the John Templeton Foundation and the NSF Graduate Research Fellowship Program is also gratefully acknowledged.

REFERENCES

Almenberg, J., Dreber, A., Apicella, C. L., & Rand, D. G. (2011). Third Party Reward and Punishment: Group Size, Efficiency and Public Goods. In: N. M. Palmetti & J. P. Russo (Eds.), *Psychology and Punishment*. Hauppauge, NY: Nova Science Publishers. 73-92.

Andreoni, J., Harbaugh, W. T., & Vesterlund, L. (2003). The carrot or the stick: Rewards, punishments and cooperation. *American Economic Review, 93*, 893-902.

Axelrod, R. (1984). *The Evolution of Cooperation*. New York, NY: Basic Books.

Balliet, D., Parks, C., & Joireman, J. (2009). Social value orientation and cooperation in social dilemmas: A meta-analysis. *Group Processes and Intergroup Relations, 12*, 533-547.

Bateson, M., Nettle, D., & Roberts, G. (2006). Cues of being watched enhance cooperation in a real-world setting. *Biology Letters, 2*, 412-414.

Bolton, G. E., Katok, E., & Ockenfels, A. (2005). Cooperation among strangers with limited information about reputation. *Journal of Public Economics, 89*, 1457-1468.

Bowles, S. (2006). Group competition, reproductive leveling, and the evolution of human altruism. *Science, 314*, 1569-1572.

Bowles, S., & Gintis, H. (2003). Origins of Human Cooperation. In: P. Hammerstein (Ed.), *Genetic and Cultural Evolution of Cooperation*. Cambridge, MA: MIT Press. 429-443.

Boyd, R., Gintis, H., & Bowles, S. (2010). Coordinated punishment of defectors sustains cooperation and can proliferate when rare. *Science, 328*, 617-620.

Boyd, R., Gintis, H., Bowles, S., & Richerson, P. J. (2003). The evolution of altruistic punishment. *Proceedings of the National Academy of Sciences, 100*, 3531-3535.

Boyd, R., & Richerson, P. (1990). Group selection among alternative evolutionarily stable strategies. *Journal of Theoretical Biology, 145*, 331-342.

Boyd, R., & Richerson, P. (1992). Punishment allows the evolution of cooperation (or anything else) in sizable groups. *Ethology and Sociobiology, 13*, 171-195.

Brandt, H., Hauert, C., & Sigmund, K. (2003). Punishment and reputation in spatial Public Goods games. *Proceedings of the Royal Society B: Biological Sciences, 270*, 1099-1104.

Burnham, T., & Hare, B. (2007). Engineering human cooperation. *Human Nature, 18*, 88-108.

Capraro, V., Jordan, J. J., & Rand, D. G. (2014). Cooperation increases with the benefit-to-cost ratio in one-shot Prisoner's Dilemma experiments. *Available at SSRN: http://ssrn.com/abstract=2429862*.

Choi, J. K., & Bowles, S. (2007). The coevolution of parochial altruism and war. *Science, 318*, 636-640.

Cinyabuguma, M., Page, T., & Putterman, L. (2006). Can second-order punishment deter perverse punishment? *Experimental Economics, 9*, 265-279.

Condon, P., & DeSteno, D. (2011). Compassion for one reduces punishment for another. *Journal of Experimental Social Psychology, 47*, 698-701.

Cushman, F., Dreber, A., Wang, Y., & Costa, J. (2009). Accidental outcomes guide punishment in a "trembling hand" game. *PLoS ONE, 4*, e6699.

Cushman, F., & Macindoe, O. (2009). The coevolution of punishment and prosociality among learning agents. Paper presented at: *The Proceedings of the 31st Annual Conference of the Cognitive Science Society.*

Denant-Boemont, L., Masclet, D., & Noussair, C. (2007). Punishment, counterpunishment and sanction enforcement in a social dilemma experiment. *Economic Theory, 33*, 145-167.

Dreber, A., Ellingsen, T., Johannesson, M., & Rand, D. G. (2013). Do people care about social context? Framing effects in Dictator games. *Experimental Economics, 16*, 349-371.

Dreber, A., Rand, D. G., Fudenberg, D., & Nowak, M. A. (2008). Winners don't punish. *Nature, 452*, 348-351.

Egas, M., & Riedl, A. (2008). The economics of altruistic punishment and the maintenance of cooperation. *Proceedings of the Royal Society B: Biological Sciences, 275*, 871-878.

Ellingsen, T., Herrmann, B., Nowak, M. A., Rand, D. G., & Tarnita, C. E. (2012). Civic capital in two cultures: The nature of cooperation in Romania and USA. *Availabe at SSRN: http://ssrn.com/abstract=2179575.*

Engel, C., & Rand, D. G. (2014). What does "clean" really mean? The implicit framing of decontextualized experiments. *Economics Letters, 122*, 386-389.

Fehr, E., & Fischbacher, U. (2003). The nature of human altruism. *Nature, 425*, 785-791.

Fehr, E., & Fischbacher, U. (2004). Third-party punishment and social norms. *Evolution and Human Behavior, 25*, 63-87.

Fehr, E., & Gächter, S. (2000). Cooperation and punishment in Public Goods experiments. *American Economic Review, 90*, 980-994.

Fehr, E., & Gächter, S. (2002). Altruistic punishment in humans. *Nature, 415*, 137-140.

Forsythe, R., Horowitz, J. L., Savin, N. E., & Sefton, M. (1994). Fairness in simple bargaining games. *Games and Economic Behavior, 6*, 347-369.

Fowler, J. H. (2005). Altruistic punishment and the origin of cooperation. *Proceedings of the National Academy of Sciences, 102*, 7047-7049.

Fowler, J. H., Johnson, T., & Smirnov, O. (2005). Human behaviour: Egalitarian motive and altruistic punishment. *Nature, 433*, E1-E2.

Frank, R. H., Gilovich, T., & Regan, D. T. (1993a). Does studying economics inhibit cooperation? *The Journal of Economic Perspectives, 7*, 159-171.

Frank, R. H., Gilovich, T., & Regan, D. T. (1993b). The evolution of one-shot cooperation: An experiment. *Ethology and Sociobiology, 14*, 247-256.

Fu, F., Tarnita, C. E., Christakis, N. A., Wang, L., Rand, D. G., & Nowak, M. A. (2012). Evolution of in-group favoritism. *Scientific Reports, 2*, 460.

Fudenberg, D., & Maskin, E. S. (1990). Evolution and cooperation in noisy repeated games. *American Economic Review, 80*, 274–279.

Fudenberg, D., Rand, D. G., & Dreber, A. (2012). Slow to anger and fast to forgive: Cooperation in an uncertain world. *American Economic Review, 102*, 720-749.

Gächter, S., & Herrmann, B. (2009). Reciprocity, culture and human cooperation: Previous insights and a new cross-cultural experiment. *Philosophical Transactions of the Royal Society B: Biological Sciences, 364*, 791-806.

Gächter, S., & Herrmann, B. (2011). The limits of self-governance when cooperators get punished: Experimental evidence from urban and rural Russia. *European Economic Review, 55*, 193-210.

Gächter, S., Herrmann, B., & Thöni, C. (2010). Culture and cooperation. *Philosophical Transactions of the Royal Society B: Biological Sciences, 365*, 2651-2661.

Gächter, S., Renner, E., & Sefton, M. (2008). The long-run benefits of punishment. *Science, 322*, 1510.

García, J., & Traulsen, A. (2012). Leaving the loners alone: Evolution of cooperation in the presence of antisocial punishment. *Journal of Theoretical Biology, 307*, 168-173.

Goette, L., Huffman, D., & Meier, S. (2006). The impact of group membership on cooperation and norm enforcement: Evidence from random assignment to real social groups. *American Economic Review, 96*, 212-216.

Gray, K., Ward, A. F., & Norton, M. I. (2012). Paying it forward: Generalized reciprocity and the limits of generosity. *Journal of Experimental Psychology: General, 143*, 247-254.

Hallatschek, O., & Nelson, D. R. (2008). Gene surfing in expanding populations *Theoretical Population Biology, 73*, 158-170.

Hamilton, W. D. (1964). The genetical evolution of social behaviour. I. *Journal of Theoretical Biology, 7*, 1-16.

Hauert, C., & Doebeli, M. (2004). Spatial structure often inhibits the evolution of cooperation in the snowdrift game. *Nature, 428*, 643-646.

Hauert, C., Traulsen, A., Brandt, H., Nowak, M. A., & Sigmund, K. (2007). Via freedom to coercion: The emergence of costly punishment. *Science, 316*, 1905-1907.

Hauser, O. P., Nowak, M. A., & Rand, D. G. (2014). Punishment does not promote cooperation under exploration dynamics when anti-social punishment is possible. *Available at SSRN: http://ssrn.com/ abstract=2298851.*

Helbing, D., Szolnoki, A., Perc, M., & Szabó, G. (2010). Evolutionary establishment of moral and double moral standards through spatial interactions. *PLoS Computational Biology, 6*, e1000758.

Henrich, J. (2004). Cultural group selection, coevolutionary processes and large-scale cooperation. *Journal of Economic Behavior & Organization, 53*, 3-35.

Henrich, J., & Boyd, R. (2001). Why people punish defectors: Weak conformist transmission can stabilize costly enforcement of norms in cooperative dilemmas. *Journal of Theoretical Biology, 208*, 79-89.

Henrich, J., Ensminger, J., McElreath, R., Barr, A., Barrett, C., Bolyanatz, A., Camilo Cardenas, J., Gurven, M., Gwako, E., Henrich, N., Lesorogol, C., Marlowe, F., Tracer, D. & Ziker, J. (2010). Markets, religion, community size, and the evolution of fairness and punishment. *Science, 327*, 1480-1484.

Herrmann, B., Thoni, C., & Gächter, S. (2008). Antisocial punishment across societies. *Science, 319*, 1362-1367.

Hilbe, C., & Traulsen, A. (2012). Emergence of responsible sanctions without second order free riders, antisocial punishment or spite. *Scientific Reports, 2*, 458.

Holmes, W. G., & Sherman, P. W. (1983). Kin recognition in animals. *American Scientist, 71*, 46-55.

Houser, D., Xiao, E., McCabe, K., & Smith, V. (2008). When punishment fails: Research on sanctions, intentions and non-cooperation. *Games and Economic Behavior, 62*, 509-532.

Isakov, A., & Rand, D. G. (2011). The evolution of coercive institutional punishment. *Dynamic Games and Applications*, *2*, 97-109.

Jansen, V. A. A., & van Baalen, M. (2006). Altruism through beard chromodynamics. *Nature, 440*, 663-666.

Janssen, M. A., & Bushman, C. (2008). Evolution of cooperation and altruistic punishment when retaliation is possible. *Journal of Theoretical Biology, 254*, 541-545.

Jordan, J. J., McAuliffe, K., & Rand, D. G. (2014). Third-party punishment is motivated by anger and is not an artifact of self-focused envy or the strategy method. *Available at SSRN: http://ssrn.com/abstract=2427274.*

Jordan, J. J., Rand, D. G., & Peysakhovich, A. (In Press). Why We Cooperate. In: J. Decety & T. Wheatley (Eds.), *The Moral Brain: Multidisciplinary Perspectives*. Cambridge, MA: MIT Press.

Lieberman, D., Tooby, J., & Cosmides, L. (2007). The architecture of human kin detection. *Nature, 445*, 727-731.

Lindgren, K., & Nordahl, M. G. (1994). Evolutionary dynamics of spatial games. *Physica D, 75*, 292-309.

Milinski, M., Semmann, D., & Krambeck, H. J. (2002). Reputation helps solve the 'tragedy of the commons'. *Nature, 415*, 424-426.

Nakamaru, M., & Iwasa, Y. (2005). The evolution of altruism by costly punishment in lattice-structured populations: Score-dependent viability versus score-dependent fertility. *Evolutionary Ecology Research, 7*, 853-870.

Nakamaru, M., & Iwasa, Y. (2006). The coevolution of altruism and punishment: Role of the selfish punisher. *Journal of Theoretical Biology, 240*, 475-488.

Nakamura, M., & Masuda, N. (2011). Indirect Reciprocity under Incomplete Observation. *PLoS Computational Biology, 7*, e1002113.

Nikiforakis, N. (2008). Punishment and counter-punishment in Public Goods games: Can we still govern ourselves? *Journal of Public Economics, 92*, 91-112.

Nikiforakis, N., & Mitchell, H. (2013). Mixing the carrots with the sticks: Third party punishment and reward. *Experimental Economics*, *17*, 1-23.

Nowak, M. A. (2006). Five rules for the evolution of cooperation. *Science, 314*, 1560-1563.

Nowak, M. A., & May, R. M. (1992). Evolutionary games and spatial chaos. *Nature, 359*, 826-829.

Nowak, M. A., & Sigmund, K. (1992). Tit for tat in heterogeneous populations. *Nature, 355*, 250-253

Nowak, M. A., & Sigmund, K. (1993). A strategy of win-stay, lose-shift that outperforms tit-for-tat in the Prisoner's Dilemma game. *Nature, 364*, 56-58.

Nowak, M. A., & Sigmund, K. (1998). Evolution of indirect reciprocity by image scoring. *Nature, 393*, 573-577.

Nowak, M. A., & Sigmund, K. (2005). Evolution of indirect reciprocity. *Nature, 437*, 1291-1298.

Ohtsuki, H., Hauert, C., Lieberman, E., & Nowak, M. A. (2006). A simple rule for the evolution of cooperation on graphs and social networks. *Nature, 441*, 502-505.

Ohtsuki, H., & Iwasa, Y. (2006). The leading eight: Social norms that can maintain cooperation by indirect reciprocity. *Journal of Theoretical Biology, 239*, 435-444.

Ohtsuki, H., Iwasa, Y., & Nowak, M. A. (2009). Indirect reciprocity provides only a narrow margin of efficiency for costly punishment. *Nature, 457*, 79-82.

Ostrom, E., Walker, J., & Gardner, R. (1992). Covenants with and without a sword: Self-governance is possible. *The American Political Science Review, 86*, 404-417.

Ouss, A., & Peysakhovich, A. (2013). When punishment doesn't pay: 'Cold Glow' and decisions to punish. *Available at SSRN: http://ssrn.com/ abstract=2247446*.

Paulsson, J. (2002). Multileveled selection on plasmid replication. *Genetics, 161*, 1373-1384.

Peysakhovich, A., Nowak, M. A., & Rand, D. G. (2014). The cooperative phenotype. *Available at SSRN: http://ssrn.com/abstract=2426472*.

Peysakhovich, A., & Rand, D. G. (2013). Habits of virtue: Creating norms of cooperation and defection in the laboratory. *Available at SSRN: http://ssrn.com/abstract=2294242*.

Pfeiffer, T., Tran, L., Krumme, C., & Rand, D. G. (2012). The value of reputation. *Journal of the Royal Society Interface, 9*, 2791-2797.

Powers, S. T., Taylor, D. J., & Bryson, J. J. (2012). Punishment can promote defection in group-structured populations. *Journal of Theoretical Biology, 311*, 107-116.

Rand, D. G., Arbesman, S., & Christakis, N. A. (2011). Dynamic social networks promote cooperation in experiments with humans. *Proceedings of the National Academy of Sciences, 108*, 19193-19198.

Rand, D. G., Armao IV, J. J., Nakamaru, M., & Ohtsuki, H. (2010). Anti-social punishment can prevent the co-evolution of punishment and cooperation. *Journal of Theoretical Biology, 265*, 624-632.

Rand, D. G., Dreber, A., Ellingsen, T., Fudenberg, D., & Nowak, M. A. (2009). Positive interactions promote public cooperation. *Science, 325*, 1272-1275.

Rand, D. G., Greene, J. D., & Nowak, M. A. (2012). Spontaneous giving and calculated greed. *Nature, 489*, 427-430.

Rand, D. G., & Nowak, M. A. (2011). The evolution of antisocial punishment in optional Public Goods games. *Nature Communications, 2*, 434.

Rand, D. G., & Nowak, M. A. (2013). Human cooperation. *Trends in Cognitive Sciences, 17*, 413-425.

Rand, D. G., Ohtsuki, H., & Nowak, M. A. (2009). Direct reciprocity with costly punishment: Generous tit-for-tat prevails. *Journal of Theoretical Biology, 256*, 45-57.

Rand, D. G., Peysakhovich, A., Kraft-Todd, G. T., Newman, G. E., Wurzbacher, O., Nowak, M. A., & Green, J. D. (2014). Social heuristics shape intuitive cooperation. *Nature Communications, 5*, 3677.

Rapoport, A. (1965). *Prisoner's Dilemma: A Study in Conflict and Cooperation*. Ann Arbor, MI: University of Michigan Press.

Rockenbach, B., & Milinski, M. (2006). The efficient interaction of indirect reciprocity and costly punishment. *Nature, 444*, 718-723.

Sekiguchi, T., & Nakamaru, M. (2009). Effect of the presence of empty sites on the evolution of cooperation by costly punishment in spatial games. *Journal of Theoretical Biology, 256*, 297-304.

Sigmund, K., Hauert, C., & Nowak, M. A. (2001). Reward and punishment. *Proceedings of the National Academy of Sciences, 98*, 10757-10762.

Sommerfeld, R. D., Krambeck, H.-J., Semmann, D., & Milinski, M. (2007). Gossip as an alternative for direct observation in games of indirect reciprocity. *Proceedings of the National Academy of Sciences, 104*, 17435-17440.

Sylwester, K., Herrmann, B., & Bryson, J. J. (In press). Homo homini lupus? Explaining antisocial punishment. *Journal of Neuroscience Psychology and Economics.*

Traulsen, A., Hauert, C., De Silva, H., Nowak, M. A., & Sigmund, K. (2009). Exploration dynamics in evolutionary games. *Proceedings of the National Academy of Sciences, 106*, 709-712.

Traulsen, A., & Nowak, M. A. (2006). Evolution of cooperation by multilevel selection. *Proceedings of the National Academy of Sciences, 103*, 10952-10955.

Traulsen, A., Röhl, T., & Milinski, M. (2012). An economic experiment reveals that humans prefer pool punishment to maintain the commons. *Proceedings of the Royal Society B: Biological Sciences, 279*, 3716-3721.

Trivers, R. (1971). The evolution of reciprocal altruism. *Quarterly Review of Biology, 46*, 35–57.

Ule, A., Schram, A., Riedl, A., & Cason, T. N. (2009). Indirect punishment and generosity toward Ssrangers. *Science, 326*, 1701-1704.

van Veelen, M., García, J., Rand, D. G., & Nowak, M. A. (2012). Direct reciprocity in structured populations. *Proceedings of the National Academy of Sciences, 109*, 9929-9934.

Wedekind, C., & Milinski, M. (2000). Cooperation through image scoring in humans. *Science, 288*, 850-852.

Wilson, D. S. (1975). A theory of group selection. *Proceedings of the National Academy of Sciences, 72*, 143-146.

Wu, J.-J., Zhang, B.-Y., Zhou, Z.-X., He, Q.-Q., Zheng, X.-D., Cressman, R., & Tao, Y. (2009). Costly punishment does not always increase cooperation. *Proceedings of the National Academy of Sciences, 106*, 17448-17451.

Yoeli, E., Hoffman, M., Rand, D. G., & Nowak, M. A. (2013). Powering up with indirect reciprocity in a large-scale field experiment. *Proceedings of the National Academy of Sciences, 110*, 10424-10429.

In: Antisocial Behavior
Editor: Justine H. Gallo
ISBN: 978-1-63321-521-4

Chapter 2

NOVEL NEUROPSYCHOLOGICAL OPPORTUNITIES IN THE TREATMENT OF ANTISOCIAL BEHAVIOR

Ron van Outsem, Ph.D.*
Bouman GGZ, Rotterdam, the Netherlands

ABSTRACT

Attention Deficit Hyperactivity Disorder (ADHD) and Substance Use Disorders (SUDs) are known to be important contributing factors in the development and exacerbation of various types of antisocial behavior. The treatment of patients who exhibit frequent antisocial behavior and suffer from these conditions is often experienced as challenging by therapists and usually produce very modest effects, if any at all. Recent advances in neuropsychology, however, may offer new perspectives concerning the efficacy of offender treatment in these patients.

This chapter will focus on two interesting new developments in offender treatment with patients suffering from ADHD and SUDs: Neurofeedback and the Relapse Early Warning And Response System (REWARS). Neurofeedback is a method of influencing the brain's activity by way of operant conditioning. REWARS is a daily test and intervention protocol for patients suffering from SUDs. It makes use of the attentional bias concerning stimuli that are related to the substance the subject is addicted to. This attentional bias is typically shown by the subject twelve to twenty-four hours before the onset of craving for the substance and subsequent relapse.

Both treatment methods will be explained extensively. Their empirical bases and implementability will also be discussed.

INTRODUCTION

Substance Use Disorders (SUDs) and Attention Deficit /Hyperactivity Disorder (ADHD) are both important contributing factors in the development and exacerbation of many different kinds of antisocial and criminal behavior. They are also significant hampering factors in

* ronvanoutsem@casema.nl.

offender treatment, leading to a high rate of attrition, a low level of compliance to treatment, and a decreased ability in the patient to integrate new insights, new skills, and alternative behavior patterns ('t Hart- Kerkhoffs, 2010; Vermeiren, 2002; Wilson & Cumming, 2009). Treatment success in antisocial patients suffering from SUDs and/or ADHD is indeed a very rare phenomenon (Adshead & Brown, 2003; Van Outsem, 2009;Weijers, 2008;Wilson & Cumming, 2009). ADHD and SUDs are conditions that are often found among forensic patients, both juveniles and adults (Adshead & Brown, 2003; Van Wijk, 2005; Vermeiren, 2002; Welldon & Van Velsen, 1996; Wilson & Cumming, 2009).

Forensic psychotherapy as a whole faces many challenges. First of all, most treatment outcome studies in the forensic field reveal only limited sized effects, if any effects at all (Atkinson, 1999; Babcock & Steiner, 1999; Chambers et al., 2008; Craissati, et al., 2009; Gondolf, 1997; Gordon & Moriarty, 2003; Hanson et al., 2002; Hanson et al., 2003; Kohl & Macy, 2008; Lin et al., 2009; Loeber et al., 2001; Macy et al., 2010; Marshall et al., 1999; Peek & Nugter, 2009; Plichta & Falik, 2001; Seager et al., 2004; Van Wijk et al., 2007; Weijers, 2008). Consequently, the current forms of psychotherapy seem to be of only limited value in the efforts to prevent re-offense. Second, there is the problem of attrition and therapy compliance, not only in the patients suffering from SUDs and/or ADHD. In forensic psychotherapy, overall attrition rates tend to be very high and treatment compliance levels very low (Beech et al., 1998; Chambers et al., 2008; Lin et al., 2009; Loeber et al., 2001; Marshall et al., 1999; Miner, 2002; Peek & Nugter, 2009; Ryan & Lane, 1997; Seager et al., 2004; Van Outsem, 2009; Van Wijk et al., 2007; Weijers, 2008). In this respect, the problem of low compliance rates of medication intake, especially in patients with ADHD, should be noted. Third, many (forensic) patients have great difficulty in discussing their thoughts, feelings, and experiences adequately enough for psychotherapy to be fruitful. Among the main reasons for this are mistrust, shame, lack of introspective abilities, weakness of verbal expression, and cognitive disabilities (Van Outsem, 2009). Finally, especially in multicultural societies, there is the problem of language barriers. Insufficient mastering of the language in which the treatment is conducted can be a major problem in conducting the treatment successfully. It can be concluded that new approaches in forensic psychotherapy are needed to overcome these problems.

Recent advances in neuropsychology, however, offer new perspectives on the treatment of patients who frequently display antisocial and criminal behavior and who suffer from SUDs and/or ADHD. Two of these recent advances are those in the field of neurofeedback, and those in the field of attentional bias in SUDs.

What Is Neurofeedback?

Neurofeedback is a type of biofeedback that uses electroencephalography (EEG) to provide a signal that can be used by a person to receive feedback about his or her present cortical brain activity. It is also called neurotherapy, neurobiofeedback, or EEG biofeedback. The method makes use of real-time displays of EEG to illustrate cortical brain activity with the goal of controlling this activity, and thus reducing symptoms and/or enhancing mental capabilities. Sensors are placed on the scalp to measure activity. The measurements are displayed using video and/or sound. The process of neurofeedback is usually understood as being based on a form of operant and/or classical conditioning. When cortical brain activity changes in the direction desired by the therapist directing the treatment, a 'reward' feedback is given to the patient. When the change is in the opposite direction from what was intended, then either different feedback is given or the provision of otherwise attained 'reward' feedback is inhibited. Rewards, or reinforcements, can be as simple as a change in pitch of a tone or as complex as a certain type of movement of a character in a video game. EEG pattern targets are based on extrapolations from research describing normal and abnormal EEG patterns. Different structures within the cerebral cortex play crucial roles in the origin and/or manifestation of different kinds of behavior and of emotional responses (Demos, 2005; Evans & Arbarbanel, 1999). Various forms of psychopathology are closely associated with specific dysfunctions in these cortical structures (Demos, 2005; Evans & Arbarbanel, 1999). Neurofeedback aims at restoring the activity of these structures to the level and pattern that is present in the corresponding cortical structures of healthy individuals by way of the conditioning process described earlier. The beneficial effects of neurofeedback on behavior and emotion are understood to be a consequence of the fact that the patient's cerebral cortex is trained to function in ways that approximate those of symptom-free individuals.

Several types of neurofeedback, so-called training protocols, exist. Each training protocol has its own specific purpose, technique, and effect. Different protocols are used for the treatment of different conditions, or for the enhancement of different specific brain functions. Some protocols are aimed at the regulation of the activity of a specific region of the cerebral cortex, other protocols target multiple cortical regions simultaneously. There are protocols that focus on the regulation of a single type of brain rhythm (i.e. a brain rhythm that falls within a certain frequency range), while other protocols work with brain rhythms of multiple frequencies. While some protocols aim at stimulating certain activities of the brain, others aim at synchronizing these activities. Probably the most well-known neurofeedback protocol is the so-called Alpha training (or Deep State training) protocol. This protocol aims at attaining a state of profound relaxation by stimulating a specific type of (low frequency) brain activity that reads on the electroencephalogram as 'alpha waves' (7.5- 12.5 Hz waves). Demos (2005) provides an extensive overview of all of these protocols, their techniques, and their effects.

Neurofeedback is mostly a non-verbal method, making it adequate for patients who do not express themselves easily verbally or who do not master the country's language sufficiently. The latter is an important advantage in multi-cultural societies since it makes the method suitable for patients of different cultures and languages (Kelley, 1997; Othmer, Othmer, & Kaiser, 1999).

Neurofeedback is still a rarely used treatment method in forensic psychotherapy and offender rehabilitation programs all over the world. The method is all but ignored despite of its reported success rates (Kwan, 2002; Quinn, Bodenhamer-Davis, & Koch, 2004). An important reason for this could be that there is a widespread belief that neurofeedback is not an evidence based treatment method. Therefore, many practitioners are reluctant to adopt it and many insurance companies and mental health care subsidizers are equally reluctant to finance it. The sometimes fanatical and uncritical manner, in which some publicists have presented neurofeedback to their audiences and readerships, often referring to research of insufficient scientific rigor, may also have contributed considerably to the skepsis concerning this method. Another reason why neurofeedback is ignored in the field of forensic psychotherapy could be that most psychologists, psychiatrists and other mental health care workers are trained to perceive anti-social and criminal behavior mostly as a result of a problematic development and/or traumatic experiences. They usually have learned that the most effective way to treat these phenomena is to influence their patient's perceptions, thought patterns, and emotional reactions with the use of spoken (and written) word, role play, and medication. Neurofeedback's basic approach, i.e., healthier thinking, feeling and behaving by way of stimulating the brain to function in a healthier manner, is usually quite alien to them. The often perceived incompatibility of neurofeedback's basic approach and the basic approaches of traditional forms of psychotherapy may also account for some of the reluctance in the field to adopt this treatment method.

The Practice of Neurofeedback

First of all, neurofeedback, unfortunately, is not for everybody. Several exclusion criteria for the method are found in the literature. These exclusion criteria are related to the occurrence of adverse effects and/or symptom exacerbation in the patient when applying the treatment. General consensus exists on the following exclusion criteria:

- The diagnosis of schizophrenia and/or psychotic episodes in the patient's history.
- The diagnosis of borderline personality disorder.
- The diagnosis of bipolar disorder.
- The current daily use of significant quantities of alcohol and/or the frequent use of drugs. Patients suffering from SUDs need to be abstinent for at least one month before neurofeedback treatment can be administered. The detoxification phase of SUDs treatment needs to be completed before starting neurofeedback.

A neurofeedback treatment is usually completed after 30–60 sessions, depending on the severity of the symptoms that are treated and on the pace with which the patient's brain reacts to the treatment. Usually the treatment is discontinued if no change in the EEG readings is found after 10–15 sessions. The reason for this is that, in most cases, no further effects are to be expected if changes remain absent after 10–15 sessions (Demos, 2005). Neurofeedback can be incorporated in both inpatient and outpatient treatment programs. The frequency of the sessions can vary between once a week and four sessions a day. A typical neurofeedback session takes about thirty minutes to complete.

The application of neurofeedback protocols is relatively easy to be trained in for licensed psychotherapists and psychiatrists. Neurofeedback courses are available in a growing number of countries. There are also good quality neurofeedback courses to be found online.

High-quality neurofeedback equipment is easy to acquire and is quite affordable for most practitioners. A complete high-quality neurofeedback system should not cost more than three thousand U.S. dollars. Additional requirements include:

- A laptop computer.
- A comfortable chair, preferably a TV chair, for the patient to sit in.
- A second computer screen.
- A quiet room.

A typical neurofeedback session consists of the following elements:

1 The patient is welcomed.
2 The patient is briefly asked about his/her current emotional and physical state, about any recent consumption of alcohol or drugs, about any important recent events that may affect neurofeedback training, and about any positive or adverse effects the patient experiences during the neurofeedback treatment. The session will be cancelled if the patient is under the influence of alcohol and/or drugs, or if the patient is hung-over after consuming alcohol or drugs the previous day. The session will also be cancelled if the patient reports adverse effects of the treatment. In this case, it will be discussed with the patient whether the treatment will be continued using another protocol or whether the treatment will be discontinued altogether.
3 The patient is seated in the training chair and the electrodes are attached to the patient's head. This is done using a sticky paste that is a good conductor of electricity. Before attaching the electrodes, the specific locations on the scalp where the electrodes are placed are scrubbed gently using a special scrubbing gel. This is called a skin preparation gel.
4 The neurofeedback training is conducted, usually for a period of twenty minutes. With many patients, it is advisable to take a one-minute break halfway the training session. With some patients, a one-minute brake once every five minutes is necessary.
5 When the training is finished, the electrodes are removed from the patient's head and the remaining conductive paste is wiped off the patient's scalp and hair.
6 The course of thc training is discussed with the patient. The patient is asked about his/her emotional state and the session is concluded.

It is inadvisable to combine psychotherapy and neurofeedback in one session. Although neurofeedback and psychotherapy are a complementary combination, conducting both psychotherapy and neurofeedback within the same session is often experienced as too fatiguing by many patients. Therefore, neurofeedback and psychotherapy should be conducted in separate sessions.

Neurofeedback in the Literature That is Relevant to Forensic Psychotherapy

In a review of 31 research publications concerning the efficacy of neurofeedback in areas that are relevant to forensic psychotherapy (Van Outsem, 2011), beneficial effects of neurofeedback treatment were reported in all publications. In none of the studies that were reviewed, grounds were found to designate neurofeedback as a totally ineffective treatment method. Negative effects, or side effects, were found to be absent in 25 of the 31 publications. In the remaining six publications, the presence or absence of negative effects was not discussed.

The attrition rates of neurofeedback treatment that were reported in the reviewed publications were considerably lower than what is usual in most of the current forms of psychotherapy. While attrition rates of 30–50% are very common among current forms of forensic psychotherapy (Van Wijk et al., 2007; Wilson & Cumming, 2009), the average attrition rate for neurofeedback treatment is found to be only around 15%.

In the reviewed publications in which neurofeedback was compared to other treatment methods, the reported success rates of neurofeedback exceeded those of the other methods, including cognitive behavioral therapy and medication (Gruzelier & Egner, 2005; Hammond, 2003; McKnight & Fehmi, 2001; Vernon et al., 2004). This was also the case when the effects were evaluated again after a follow-up period of 1–5 years (Butnik, 2005; Evans & Arbarbanel, 1999; Gruzelier & Egner, 2005; McKnight & Fehmi, 2001; Scott et al., 2002; Quinn et al., 2004; Vernon et al., 2004). However, because of the relatively small number of comparative studies that are conducted to date, one should be careful to draw definitive conclusions as to the efficacy of neurofeedback in comparison to other treatment methods in a considerable number of areas.

When investigating the efficacy of any method of treatment, it is necessary to assess the role of factors that are not specific to the treatment method itself, but which nonetheless may influence the measurements of its effects. Three of such factors, which are very important are the placebo effect, the patient–therapist relationship, and the therapist's personal qualities. In the conducted review, two studies on the efficacy of neurofeedback were found which referred specifically to the role of these non-specific factors. Engelbrecht et al. (2010) concluded from their placebo controlled study that changes in EEG patterns after treatment were to be attributed to the neurofeedback program itself, and not to any extent to the placebo effect. In this study, no post treatment changes in EEG patterns were found in the placebo group. Conversely, the intended changes were found in the treatment group. The subjects in the placebo group had completed a sham neurofeedback program. According to the authors, all subjects were convinced that they had followed the real neurofeedback treatment. McKnight and Fehmi (2001) found in their evaluative study that the health benefits of neurofeedback that were reported by their subjects were independent of the skill or experience of the therapist who treated them. Also, no correlation was found between the treatment outcome and the reported quality of the relationship between therapist and patient. These findings are consistent with the premise that the effects of neurofeedback are not the result of non-specific factors. They rather constitute support for the efficacy of the treatment program itself.

To date, there is insufficient evidence to be found in the literature that neurofeedback could reduce aggressive and/or anti-social behavior in patients suffering from personality disorders. Personality disorders are regularly diagnosed among forensic patients (Nestor, 2002). The possibility exists, however, that this treatment method could alleviate some of the symptoms that are associated with the various types of personality disorders. Further research in this area is needed to determine whether, and if so to what extent, neurofeedback can be of value in the treatment of forensic patients suffering from personality disorders. Valid research on the effects of neurofeedback in patients suffering from psychotic disorders like schizophrenia is also still scarce. So far, it cannot be determined whether neurofeedback could be of any use in the treatment of psychotic forensic patients.

In most of the reviewed publications, it is not in any way advocated that neurofeedback should replace traditional forms of psychotherapy altogether in the areas of treatment for which evidence of neurofeedback's efficacy exists. While neurofeedback may create an ability in the patient to achieve behavioral and emotional change by optimizing certain brain functions, other forms of psychotherapy, e.g. cognitive behavioral therapy, can provide guidance as to the directions in which this change could take place. For instance, partial or total recovery from (long-term) addiction and/or psychopathology often places the patient in a situation in which a new personal life-style has to be developed. The patient may change his/her choice of friends, change his/her way of relating to other people, take up a new career, etc. Counseling is generally considered as being very useful when a patient stands before the challenge of designing and adopting a new personal life-style. Therefore, neurofeedback and traditional forms of psychotherapy should be seen as complementary partners rather than as competitors.

Possible Applications of Neurofeedback in Offender Treatment

According to the literature, neurofeedback could play a role in the following areas of offender treatment:

Aggression, Anti-Social, and Criminal Behavior Related to Substance Abuse

Substance abuse, especially the abuse of alcohol, opiates, cocaine, and amphetamines, is a well-known cause, catalyst, and perpetuator of aggressive, anti-social, and criminal behavior such as theft, burglary, street-robbery, physical and sexual violence, drug trafficking, etc. (Glass, 1991; Martin & Johnson, 2005; Nestor, 2002; Wekerle & Wall, 2002). In most of these cases, solving the substance dependency problem is tantamount to solving the total behavior problem (Glass, 1991; Wekerle & Wall, 2002). Since neurofeedback has shown good results in helping patients to recover from their addiction and to stay abstinent, it should be seriously considered when substance abuse is a pivotal factor in the patient's problem behavior.

Domestic Violence

In the field of domestic violence, there are several processes in which neurofeedback could prove helpful. First, there is again the problem of substance abuse. The abuse of alcohol is by far the most powerful predictor of re-offense after treatment in domestic violence offenders (Lin et al., 2009). Second, much of the violent behavior within intimate relationships is caused by conditioned emotional responses to cues, which are interpreted as a confirmation of certain aversive cognitions (Dutton, 2006; Hamel & Nicholls, 2007; Hampton et al., 2006; Jackson, 2007; McCue, 2008; Van Outsem, 2001). The most common of these responses are pathological jealousy (a strong emotional response to a perceived confirmation of the thought that the subject's partner is being unfaithful), fear of abandonment (which occurs strongly when the subject perceives any cue as a sign that his/her partner is planning to leave him/her), and sense of disqualification (a strong response of anger and humiliation when the subject perceives any cue as a confirmation of his/her conviction that his/her partner does not take the subject seriously, does not care for the subject, or puts the subject's abilities into question). Neurofeedback could be used here as a tool to enhance the subject's flexibility of thinking and of emotional response as is described by McKnight and Fehmi (2001). As a result, the patient may become more able to challenge and modulate his/her own negative cognitions and to generate more constructive behavioral responses to perceived negative cues. Third, again as described by McKnight and Fehmi (2001), neurofeedback could be effective in relieving stress, which results from the unconscious effort to maintain habitual forms of focused attention. This translates into the stress which is experienced in daily life and which is usually accompanied by the phenomena of rumination and 'gripping' (i.e. hyperfocusing on stress-provoking cues). These phenomena often play an important role in fuelling domestic violence (Dutton, 2006; Hamel & Nicholls, 2007; Hampton et al., 2006; Jackson, 2007; McCue, 2008; Van Outsem, 2001). The enhancement of flexibility of thinking and of emotional response is also here a key process of recovery.

Neurofeedback may also be a valuable tool in the treatment of other forms of violent and anti-social behavior, i.e., that takes place outside intimate relationships, in which an important role is played by the phenomena that are mentioned above.

Aggression Problems and Delinquency Caused by, or Catalyzed by, Attention Deficit Hyperactivity Disorder (ADHD)

Aggression problems and criminal behavior are often a part of the total problem behavior that is displayed by patients suffering from ADHD ('t Hart-Kerkhoffs, 2010; Peniston et al., 1993; Vermeiren, 2002; Wilson & Cumming, 2009). The efficacy of neurofeedback in treating ADHD, as is reported in the literature, may offer possibilities for the reduction of the impulsive aggressive behavior that is often associated with this condition. This may especially be the case in patients who do not react satisfactorily to medication or who fail to comply with the medication regime.

Aggression Problems and Delinquency Caused by, or Catalyzed by, Autism Spectrum Disorder (ASD) and Post Traumatic Stress Disorder (PTSD)

These disorders are also sometimes accompanied by aggressive outbursts and delinquent behavior ('t Hart-Kerkhoffs, 2010; Vermeiren, 2002; Wilson & Cumming, 2009). The efficacy of neurofeedback in treating these specific conditions is less empirically supported than that in treating ADHD and SUDs, although some evidence does exist (Kouijzer et al., 2008; Martin & Johnson, 2005; Peniston et al., 1991, 1993; Peterson, 2000; Smith & Sams, 2005; Van Outsem, 2011).

Prevention of Delinquent Behavior

Neurofeedback could also play a role in the *prevention* of criminal behavior. The early treatment of conditions such as ADHD, Post Traumatic Stress Disorder (PTSD), and SUDs could probably reduce the probability of development of criminal behavior in (young) patients who are treated successfully. Also, the treatment of learning difficulties with the use of neurofeedback may, at least to some extent, prevent drop-out from school. This may also have a preventive effect on delinquency. According to a growing body of research, neurofeedback offers good results in the treatment of various types of learning disabilities (Fenger, 1998; Fernández et al., 2003; Hammond, 2007; Tansey, 1991; Thompson & Thompson, 1998)

EMPIRICAL SUPPORT FOR THE EFFICACY OF NEUROFEEDBACK IN ADHD AND SUDS

The two areas of treatment in which neurofeedback's efficacy is most empirically supported, and which are relevant for offender treatment, are ADHD and SUDs.

ADHD

In this area, the efficacy of neurofeedback is well established and documented (Arns et al., 2009; Butnik, 2005; Carmody et al., 2001; Fuchs et al., 2003; Gruzelier & Egner, 2005; Heinrich et al., 2004; Kaiser & Othmer, 2000; Linden et al., 1996; Lubar & Lubar, 1999; Masterpasqual & Healey, 2003; Monastra et al., 2002; Monastra et al., 2005; Nash, 2000; Patrick, 1996; Robbins, 2000; Rossiter & La Vaque, 1995; Schulenburg, 1999; Thompson & Thompson, 1998; Tinius & Tinius, 2000; Vernon et al., 2004). In these publications, a total of 1232 subjects were studied. Randomized controlled trials are the most prevalent in this area of treatment (five studies). Heterogeneity was not significant ($I^2 = .22$, $p = .15$). No significant publication bias was found (Egger's $p = .9$). Symptom reduction was found in patients of all age groups. Around 80% of patients show measurable improvements, which, in most studies, are corroborated by parents, teachers, and/or spouses. These improvements consist of increases in concentration and self-control and of the amelioration of social behavior in general. The social behavior of the treated patients tends to become more empathic, while impulsive and aggressive behavior toward others significantly decreases. The magnitude of the desired effects of neurofeedback in patients with ADHD is at least comparable to that of stimulant medication therapy, and is in many cases greater (Arns et al., 2009; Fuchs et al., 2003; Gruzelier & Egner, 2005; Heinrich et al., 2004; Kaiser & Othmer, 2000; Linden et al., 1996; Monastra et al., 2002, 2005; Rossiter & La Vaque, 1995). Arns et al. (2009) concluded from their meta-analytic study that neurofeedback can be considered efficacious and specific as a treatment for ADHD since both prospective controlled studies and studies employing a pre- and post-design found large effect sizes for neurofeedback on impulsivity and inattention, for both Hedges' $\hat{g} = .8$, and medium effect sizes on hyperactivity, Hedges' $\hat{g} = .6$. Most authors name as an important advantage of neurofeedback over stimulant medication treatment for ADHD that the desired effects remain for a prolonged period of time after treatment, and that these effects are often permanent (Arns et al., 2009; Fuchs et al., 2003; Gruzelier& Egner, 2005; Heinrich et al., 2004; Kaiser & Othmer, 2000; Linden et al., 1996; Monastra et al., 2002, 2005; Rossiter & La Vaque, 1995; Schulenburg, 1999; Thompson & Thompson, 1998; Vernon et al., 2004). Conversely, the effects of stimulant medication end when the intake of these substances ends. Moreover, the often present side effects of stimulant medication, which have a strong negative effect on compliance with this type of treatment, are totally absent when neurofeedback is applied (Fuchs et al., 2003; Gruzelier & Egner, 2005; Kaiser & Othmer, 2000; Monastra et al., 2002, 2005; Rossiter & La Vaque, 1995; Vernon et al., 2004). The temporary worsening of symptoms of ADHD when medication is not taken on time, the so-called rebound effect, is also not a problem when neurofeedback treatment is chosen (Fuchs et al., 2003; Gruzelier & Egner, 2005; Heinrich et al., 2004; Kaiser & Othmer, 2000; Rossiter & La Vaque, 1995). The advantages of neurofeedback over stimulant medication therapy in patients with ADHD are especially eminent in the light of the fact that in stimulant medication therapy compliance is usually very low and attrition very high (Fuchs et al., 2003; Gruzelier & Egner, 2005; Linden et al., 1996; Monastra et al., 2002, 2005; Rossiter & La Vaque, 1995).

SUDs

Considerable documentation on neurofeedback's effectiveness in the area of alcohol and drug dependency can be found in the literature (Burkett et al., 2005; Kelley, 1997; Peniston & Kulkoski, 1999; Scott et al., 2002; Scott et al., 2005; Quinn et al., 2004; Trudeau, 2000). In the studies of abstinence (0–4 uses after completion of treatment) versus relapse (more than four uses after treatment completion) during a follow-up period of 1–5 years, the computed effect sizes (odds ratio) ranged between 4.1 (crack cocaine, 1-year follow-up) and 6.7 (alcohol, 5 years follow-up). Effect sizes in studies on the self-reported number of uses during 1–5 years after treatment completion ranged between Hedges' $\hat{g}$ = .6 (crack cocaine, 1-year follow-up) and .9 (alcohol, 5 years follow-up). According to four studies, the efficacy of neurofeedback exceeds that of current treatment methods in this area after a follow-up period of 1–5 years (Burkett et al., 2005; Callaway & Bodenhamer-Davis, E., 2008; Quinn et al., 2004; Trudeau, 2000). After completion of conventional forms of substance abuse treatment, 65–70% of patients take (any amount of) alcohol or drugs again within the first year (McKay et al., 1999). For neurofeedback treatment, this rate is 45–50% (Burkett et al., 2005; Quinn et al., 2004; Trudeau, 2000). Of the evaluative studies that were selected on neurofeedback as a treatment method for alcohol and drug dependency, three were randomized controlled studies. Significant heterogeneity (I^2 = .79, p = .002) was found. This was caused by the fact that patients with different types of addiction were studied. Relapse in crack cocaine addiction was considerably more prevalent than in addiction to alcohol or marijuana. No significant publication bias (Egger's p = .4) was found. A total of 511 subjects participated in these studies.

Two large studies in Texas (Callaway & Bodenhamer-Davis, 2008) showed quite remarkable results. One study was done within the state corrections system, the other with addicted homeless people (95% of whom were crack cocaine addicts). Three-year follow-up data was strongly indicative of success using the neurofeedback treatment. Sixty-nine patients completed treatment and have been followed for from six months to one and one-half years after treatment. Success was defined very stringently, through four criteria, all of which had to be met:

1 Not on drugs (verified though random urine analysis).
2 Not homeless.

3 Not unemployed (at work or in school).
4 Not arrested.

None of these patients were employed or had a home when they entered treatment, and all had lengthy police records. After one and one-half years 83% of patients were successful in meeting all four criteria.

Neurofeedback in ADHD

The neurofeedback protocols that are used in treating ADHD are all so-called qEEG-guided, or qEEG-informed, protocols. These are protocols that are based on the result of the patient's qEEG.

The qEEG (quantitative electroencephalogram) is also known in popular terms as a "brain map". An electroencephalogram is a report on electrical activity within the brain that provides detailed information about brain function. The report is produced by a biomedical device called an electroencephalograph. A quantitative EEG differs from a traditional EEG in that it performs an extensive set of computerized statistical analyses on the collected raw EEG data. The EEG patterns from an individual's brain are compared with a normative database containing data from a large number of other individual EEGs. The EEG data within this database are collected from a group of carefully-selected, symptom free, healthy people of different age groups. The individual's EEG is always compared to the EEG data in the normative database of other individuals in a similar age group. This statistically analyzed EEG, the qEEG, provides the clinician with a great deal more specific information about brain function than a traditional EEG.

Important kinds of information quantified by the qEEG include:

- A measure of the amount of electrical activity (in a range of different frequency bands) at many standardized scalp locations. This information is called a "power analysis".
- A measure of the nature of the connections, or communication pathways, between different locations on the brain's cortex. This information is called a "coherence analysis".

More in-depth information about the qEEG is found in the introductory book by John Demos (2005). Interpreting a qEEG is a complex matter with a steep learning curve. However, it is also possible for the clinician to only collect the raw EEG data and to have them analyzed by specialized professionals. These professionals will usually also provide the neurofeedback treatment protocol to be used based on the qEEG report.

In treating ADHD with neurofeedback, qEEG-guided protocols are preferred to standard protocols. The reason for this is that different variants of dysfunctional EEG patterns exist within the group of patients suffering from ADHD. The two most common EEG patterns found in ADHD patients are:

- Frontal slowing: This is an excess of slow synchronized activity in the range of 1 to 12 Hz located in the frontal areas of the cerebral cortex. Around 70% of patients suffering from ADHD show this EEG pattern (Thompson & Thompson, 2003).
- Diffuse Beta: This is an excess of fast desynchronized activity (usually above 20 Hz) that is found over the entire cerebral cortex. This pattern is found in about 20% of all ADHD patients (Thompson & Thompson 2003).

The remaining 10% of ADHD patients show various kinds of atypical EEG patterns.

In the case of frontal slowing, most qEEG-guided neurofeedback protocols that are used target frontal, prefrontal and central cortical areas and are designed to reduce slow frontal activity and to enhance faster desynchronized frontal activity. In the case of the diffuse Beta variant, the protocols that are most frequently used target central and parietal cortical areas. These protocols are designed to eliminate the excessive fast and desynchronized cortical activity. The general idea is to customize the neurofeedback protocol so that it stimulates every individual patient's brain to counteract its own specific dysfunctional cortical activity pattern.

NEUROFEEDBACK IN SUDs

Patients suffering from SUDs are eligible for neurofeedback treatment when they are abstinent for at least one month. The detoxification phase of SUDs treatment needs to be fully completed before starting neurofeedback.

The best empirically supported neurofeedback protocol is the Peniston protocol with the Scott and Kaiser modifications (Bodenhamer-Davis & Callaway, 2004; Callaway & Bodenhamer-Davis, 2008; Scott et al., 2005; Sokhadze et al., 2008). Several slightly different versions of this protocol exist.

A Neurofeedback Protocol for the Treatment of SUDs

This protocol is based on the Peniston protocol with the Scott and Kaiser modifications. It is one of the many variants of it that exist.

After the completion of detoxification (i.e. at least a month after attaining stable and complete abstinence), and when all diagnostic conclusions are reached, the patients have several (at least two) sessions with the neurofeedback therapist in which the following subjects are discussed:

- General information about neurofeedback.
- What the patient can and cannot expect from neurofeedback treatment.
- The necessity of psychotherapy next to neurofeedback (neurofeedback *is not an alternative for* psychotherapy. Neurofeedback and psychotherapy are complementary treatment modalities).
- What is expected from the patient (total abstinence during treatment, attending all sessions, reporting adverse effects, reporting relapse, etc.).

- What the neurofeedback training sessions are like.
- The expected number of sessions, the planning of the sessions during the week, and the time-span of the complete neurofeedback treatment.
- Any questions the patient may have.
- How to use the symptom and craving self report diary.

During neurofeedback treatment, the patients keep a self report diary in which subjective progress in terms of symptoms and craving is monitored. It is generally considered useful to employ rating scales to quantify subjective symptoms and craving.

Before starting the neurofeedback treatment, the therapist and the patient write three to five so-called vignettes. These vignettes are short patient-personalized stories about successfully rejecting alcohol and/or drugs.

When all preparations are completed, the neurofeedback sessions will start. The applied treatment protocol is a standard neurofeedback protocol, so no qEEG is required. The protocol comprises two phases:

Phase 1

In phase one, fifteen to twenty sessions of Sensory Motor Rhythm (SMR) and Theta training will take place. In these sessions, the augmentation of the production of SMR (12-15 Hz activity) on the Cz location (one channel) or C3 and C4 locations (two channels) is rewarded. Simultaneously, the decrease of the production of Theta (4-8 Hz activity) at Cz or C3 and C4 is also rewarded. The designated scalp locations are in accordance with the International 10-20 system of electrode application.

Phase 2

In phase two, twenty sessions of Alpha-Theta training is administered. The patient is rewarded when the power of Theta (4-8 Hz activity) exceeds that of Alpha (8-12 Hz activity) at the scalp locations Pz (one channel) or P3 and P4 (two channels). Immediately before starting the training, one of the vignettes is read to the patient by the therapist. The patient is instructed to imagine the vignette as vividly as possible.

VIGNETTES

Vignettes are written according to the following criteria:

- Vignettes are short. They take no longer than one minute to be read.
- The vignettes describe situations that are common risk situations in the patient's daily life.
- The vignettes are written in the patient's own words.

- The type of alcoholic beverage the patient typically drinks and/or drug the patient is addicted to is explicited. These substances are referred to using the names the patient uses for them.
- The vignettes have the following basic structure: 1: the description of the risk situation, 2: the description of the experience of temptation and craving, 3: the overcoming of the temptation and the craving, and 4: the experience of positive emotions as a result of overcoming the situation.

SOME EXAMPLES OF VIGNETTES

Vignette "Yesterday's Friends"

Imagine yourself walking down a street in your neighborhood. Suddenly you see a couple of old friends you used to drink/do drugs with (specify the drug the patient is addicted to). You have a very nice talk with them, reviving old memories of the good old "wild" times.

One of your old friends then says he knows about a great party taking place tonight. It's just the kind of party you used to go to and enjoy together with your old friends. The idea is born to meet up at this old friend's house, have a drink and a ....(specify drug) first, and then go to the party. Everybody is very enthusiastic about the idea. You know you do have the money to go to this party. You really feel the temptation to go.

Then suddenly you start getting second thoughts about going to the party. Of course you like seeing your old friends again. Of course you would like to party again. Of course you would like to have a drink/use some...............................(specify drug) again. You feel your heart is racing. You feel the craving again!

But then you start thinking about your addiction. You realize that going to this party is a very risky thing. This party could mean total relapse. You start thinking about your addiction and about all the problems it has brought you in your life. You start thinking about how unhappy your addiction has made you feel.

Then you hear the voice of your conscience. It sounds a lot louder and convincing than usual. It's a warm and friendly voice that tells you to imagine how happy you would be without the alcohol/..............................(specify drug). You start thinking about all the things you could do without the addiction holding you back. You feel that your craving for the alcohol/.................................(specify drug) is getting less and less, until it goes away completely. You start feeling calm, happy and confident!

You tell your old friends that you are not going to the party this evening and you explain to them why. You are not affected in any way by their protests and objections. You don't mind being called a party crasher or a wet blanket. You don't care if they say you will miss out on an awesome night. You don't care that they say that they won't have so much fun without you....you don't feel guilty about it.

You walk away feeling happy and proud of yourself. You feel like a winner!

Vignette "The Liquor Store"

On a Saturday afternoon you walk past a liquor store. You can't help noticing an advertisement-board in the window. Your favorite drink is on sale! This week only, you can buy two whole bottles of ………………………………………………(specify product, brand and type/variant) for the price of one. You look at the big full color picture of the …………………………………………………(specify). It looks tempting and delicious! You really feel like entering the liquor store and buy your ………………..…………..(specify).

Your heart is racing. You can taste the ………………………………(specify) in your mouth. You really feel the craving for the …………………………………(specify).

Then you hear the voice of your conscience. It sounds a lot louder and convincing than usual. It's a warm and friendly voice that tells you to imagine how happy you would be without the alcohol/…………………………(specify). You start thinking about all the things you could do without the addiction holding you back. You feel that your craving for the alcohol/……………………………(specify) is getting less and less, until it goes away completely. You start feeling calm, happy and confident!

You decide not to go in and by any alcohol. You feel strong and confident. You think of all the things you can do without your addiction to alcohol.

You walk away feeling happy and proud of yourself. You feel like a winner!

Vignette "In the Bar"

You know it probably wasn't a very good idea, but you agreed to go to a bar with some friends. You may even have thought that this was a good opportunity to prove to yourself and to your friends that you could stay off the booze even in very tempting situations.

You enter the bar and you see a lot of old friends you used to have good times with. You engage in very nice conversations with them and you drink only Coca Cola or mineral water. You feel proud that you haven't given in to the temptation to drink alcohol.

It's getting later and later, and you are getting a bit tired. Everybody else is clearly having a lot of fun. Everybody is drinking alcohol, some people obviously quite a lot! You are starting to feel a little lonesome. You are considering going home, but you feel bad to go home before your friends do. They are having a lot of fun. You feel you don't fit in the party.

Before you know it, you begin saying things to yourself like "Well, one drink won't hurt". Or "I have been sober for months, having one drink doesn't mean I'll relapse".

Then you hear the voice of your conscience. It sounds a lot louder and convincing than usual. It's a warm and friendly voice that tells you to imagine how happy you would be without the alcohol. You start thinking about all the things you could do without the addiction holding you back. You feel that your craving for the alcohol is getting less and less, until it goes away completely. You start feeling calm, happy and confident!

You decide to call it a night and to go home. You feel strong and confident. You think of all the things you can do without your addiction to alcohol.

You walk away feeling happy and proud of yourself. You feel like a winner!

Vignette "Home Alone"

You are home alone. You feel very bored, you have nothing to do. Actually, you don't really feel like doing anything. There is no one you can call or meet up with. You watch some television and make some coffee. You walk a bit about the house, you feel very, very bored. This feeling of emptiness is really getting to you.

Your old medicine for these kind of situations was having a ....(specify drink or drug). This really made you feel better, more relaxed, more energetic, more self-confident. That empty feeling used to go away after having a ....(specify). Life seemed a lot more fun when having a ....(specify) was still OK.

You can't get your mind off having a ....(specify). Your heart starts racing. You really feel the craving for a ....(specify).

Then you hear the voice of your conscience. It sounds a lot louder and convincing than usual. It's a warm and friendly voice that tells you to imagine how happy you would be without the ....(specify). You start thinking about all the things you could do without the addiction holding you back. You feel that your craving for the ....(specify) is getting less and less, until it goes away completely. You start feeling calm, happy and confident!

You decide not to have a ....(specify) but to call an old friend or family member instead. You feel strong and confident. You think of all the things you can do without your addiction to ....(specify).

You feel happy and proud of yourself. You feel like a winner!

Vignette "Quarrel with the Wife/Husband"

Again you had a fight with your wife/husband/boyfriend/girlfriend. The fights are always about the same problems that just seem unsolvable. These problems, and fights, just keep coming back.

You are very angry with your wife/husband/boyfriend/girlfriend. You feel that he/she isn't doing enough to make your relationship better. Sometimes you get the impression that he/she doesn't really care anymore. Maybe his/her love for you is ebbing away, maybe he/she doesn't love you anymore. You're feeling angry and sad at the same time. Sometimes you even feel desperate and powerless. You just don't know what to do anymore.

You feel consumed by all these bad feelings and want to get away from it all. You really want to have a ....(specify drink or drug). After all, who cares anymore? Having a ....(specify) now seems the only way out of all this. You may even feel you have the right to have a ....(specify) because of the way your wife/husband/boyfriend/girlfriend makes you feel.

Then you hear the voice of your conscience. It sounds a lot louder and convincing than usual. It's a warm and friendly voice that tells you to imagine how happy you would be without the ....(specify). You start thinking about all the things you could do without the addiction holding you back. You feel that your craving for the ....(specify) is getting less and less, until it goes away completely. You start feeling calm, happy and confident!

You decide not to have a …………………………(specify) but to call a good friend or a family member to talk about the problems in your relationship. Maybe you'll get some good advice about what to do. You feel strong and confident. You think of all the things you can do without your addiction to ………………………(specify). You feel happy and proud of yourself. You feel like a winner!

Completion of the Neurofeedback Treatment

When phases one and two are completed, the neurofeedback treatment is completed. The treatment is evaluated as to its results and further treatment is discussed with the patient.

Attentional Bias in SUDs

What is Attentional Bias in General?

Attentional bias is a phenomenon wherein an individual focuses more of his/her attention toward a specific stimulus or a sensory cue. Often, this leads to a poor sense of judgment or an incomplete recollection of a certain event or memory. Attentional biases can also lead to poor decision-making, as the individual already has a bias towards one stimulus and may more likely base his/her decision on that preference.

Various experts believe that humans already have a tendency to show attentional bias in some situations due to the evolution of human intelligence and the need to survive. For this reason, individuals usually give more of their attention to stimuli that pose a threat to them. This enhanced attention, or hyperattention, is usually associated with sensory responses such as a tunnel vision, in which the frightened person temporarily loses his peripheral vision and focuses on the threatening object. It frequently sets off a set of physiological responses such as an adrenaline rush and an increased heart rate, and also several neurological reactions that allows the person to respond more rapidly to whatever occurs as the situation evolves.

Certain forms of attentional bias in some situations may be innate in humans and may be appropriate for their survival and well-being. But several other types of attentional bias, the same types of it in other situations, or an exaggerated degree of it in the appropriate situations, may be symptoms or results of a psychological disorder. For instance, being focused constantly on signs of impending danger may be adequate while exploring deep into an unknown jungle, but is clearly dysfunctional when lying safely in bed at home.

When individuals make decisions, they sometimes become so focused on particular aspects of the situation they are in that they tend to ignore other relevant information. This type of attentional bias can have a major impact on the decision-making process, and strongly influence the choices that are ultimately made.

One approach to measuring attentional bias is the Stroop task. In this test, color-pertaining words are written out in different colors. For example, the word "red" is written out in the color green. The individual is then asked to say out loud the *color* of the word, not the word itself. In this example, the correct answer would be "green" and not "red". A person with a high level of attentional bias may take longer to answer correctly. In some case studies, it was shown that patients who had severe anxieties and phobias had a difficult time saying the color of some suggestive words such as "spider" or "blood," as their inclination to focus on the word itself gets in the way of getting the main task done. The Stroop task is considered to measure selective attention, cognitive flexibility and processing speed, and it is used as a tool in the evaluation of executive functions. An increased interference effect is found in disorders such as brain damage, dementias and other neurodegenerative diseases, ADHD, or a variety of mental disorders such as schizophrenia, addictions, and depression. There are different test variants commonly used in clinical settings, with differences between them in the number of subtasks, type and number of stimulus, times for the task, or scoring procedures.

What is Attentional Bias in SUDS?

Attentional bias has been studied not only in relation to phobias and other forms of psychopathology, but also in the context of alcoholism and substance abuse. In separate experiments, participants (drug users and alcoholics), exhibited more delayed responses in the Stroop task to words that implied drugs or alcohol (or the consumption of them) than members of control groups who were not addicted (Cane et al., 2009; Carpenter et al., 2006; Drobes et al., 2006; Field & Cos, 2008; Field et al., 2009; Hester et al., 2006; Marhe, 2013; Streeter et al., 2007; Waters et al., 2012).

Attentional bias often seen in eye tracking movements is thought to be an underlying issue of addiction. Smokers linger on smoking cues compared with neutral cues. Researchers found higher activation in the insular cortex, the orbitofrontal cortex and the amygdala when presented with smoking cues (Janes et al., 2012; Kang et al., 2012; Luijten et al., 2011; Stippekohl et al., 2012). Similar activation patterns are observed in subjects who are addicted to other substances (Euser, 2013). The orbitofrontal cortex is known to be associated with drug-seeking behavior and the insular cortex and amygdala are involved in the autonomic and emotional state of an individual. Neural activity is also shown to decrease upon the beginning of smoking, causing the smoker to focus his attention on his next cigarette. Therefore, when smoking cues are nearby it is harder for a smoker to concentrate on other tasks. This is seen in the activation of the dorsal anterior cingulate cortex, known for focusing attention on relevant stimuli (Janes et al., 2012; Kang et al., 2012; Luijten et al., 2011; Stippekohl et al., 2012). Again, similar activation patterns are observed in subjects who are addicted to other substances (Euser, 2013).

These studies not only illustrate the importance of attentional bias in addiction and cravings, they also influence the way we look at addiction from a scientific point of view. The behavioral and emotional aspects of addiction and craving are extensively covered. However, the perceptual and neurological aspects of attentional bias and the role they play in SUDs is supported by recent research to be significant.

The intervention method that is presented below makes use of the phenomenon of attentional bias in SUDs.

RELAPSE EARLY WARNING AND RESPONSE SYSTEM (REWARS)

The Relapse Early Warning And Response System (REWARS) is a set of relapse prevention techniques that is applied *immediately before* the risk of relapse is at its highest. It is an additional tool for (forensic) SUDs treatment. It is neither an alternative nor a substitute for other evidence based offender treatment or SUDs treatment methods. REWARS is suitable only for patients who are motivated to stay abstinent. It is not recommended to use REWARS with patients who are (still) ambivalent towards substance use and abstinence. In these cases, motivation techniques should be used first. REWARS can be used in both inpatient and outpatient treatment settings. It is typically used for the first six months of abstinence after the detoxification phase of treatment is fully completed.

The basic philosophy of REWARS is that relapse prevention techniques are the most powerful when applied shortly before acute cravings start. Therefore, it is of crucial importance to be able to identify these particular windows of time. Waters & Li (2008), Waters et al., (2012) and Marhe (2013) demonstrated that acute cravings and subsequent relapse are preceded by a relatively short period of time (twelve to twenty-four hours) in which the addicted subject exhibits strong substance related attentional bias. During this period of time, the subject is still able to think clearly and is not yet profoundly affected in his/her decision-making by the experience of craving for the substance. So, relapse prevention interventions can be expected to be the most effective during this "early warning phase" before actual relapse.

The Addiction Stroop Task (AST)

A key instrument for detecting these "early warning phases" of relapse is the *Addiction Stroop Task (AST)*. This is a variant of the standard Stroop task. The AST is a neuropsychological test used to measure a person's reaction time for recognizing the color of alcohol-related or drug-related words compared to neutral words that appear on a computer or PDA (Personal Digital Assistant) screen. A computerized response box with colored buttons is used to indicate the color of each word. Each individual word appears in the middle of the screen. The objective is to click the correct colored button without thinking about the word. The time is measured in milliseconds.

When at a certain point in time the patient's AST reaction times on alcohol-related or drug-related words are sufficiently elevated (above a preset cut off score) it is indicative for the fact that the patient is highly at risk of relapsing during the next twelve to twenty four hours.

The words to be used in the AST must be specific to the substance the patient is addicted to, and also to the country, the culture, the subculture, and the age of the patient. The alcohol or drug words should be as descriptive and concrete as possible. Equal numbers of neutral control words should be matched in as many ways as possible (complexity of words, including word length, number of syllables per word, and how common they are); words associated with colors should be avoided (e.g., sky, tomato). The neutral words and alcohol/drug-related words should be intermingled randomly.

Examples of neutral words: Was, Window, Invite, Lamp, Key, Shoe, House, Carpet, Floor, Boots, Bulb, Read, Table, Card, Building, Telephone, Cape, Box, Chain, Watch.

Examples of marijuana-related words: Baked, Bamboo, Bong, Bored, Bud, Burn, Chronic, Cough, Food, Herb, Hydro, Joint, Music, Papers, Pot, Rolling, Skunk, Trees, Weed, Blunt.

Examples of cocaine-related words: Stem, Pipe, Rock, Lighter, Crack, Coke, Blast, Baking Soda, Dime, Escape, Lonely, More, Numb, Paranoid, Screen, Crash, Glass, Razor, Ye-yo, Eightball.

Examples of heroin-related words: Dope, Sick, Needle, Nod, Cooker, Blood, Spoon, Works, Cotton, Sleep, Copping, Calm, Medicine, Ties, Bitter, Bundle, Dee, Energy, Jail, Sad.

Examples of mixed drugs-related words: Money, High, Sex, Relax, Bags, Straw, Pain, Smoke, Hit, Happy, Powder, Sniff, Snort, Pleasure, Nickle, Death, Hate, Fun, Rush, Anger, Pill.

Examples of alcohol-related words: Drink, Glass, Drunk, Bottle, Bar, Juiced, Tipsy, Liquor, Faced, Booze, Shot, Beer, Loaded, Thirst, Cheers, Sauced, Gin, Tanked.

The equipment that is needed for the AST is: a personal computer/laptop or a PDA (many modern telephones are also suitable), a response box that measures the patient's response to the computer program in milliseconds, and statistical software that can perform an Analysis of Variance (ANOVA) test on reaction time data.

Several companies have developed the measurement software needed to conduct the AST and other variants of the Stroop task. The AST can be website-based, for instance as a part of an e-health program, or it can be installed on the PDA or telephone.

More detailed information on the Stroop task and the AST is found in Carpenter et al. (2006), Cox et al. (2006), Golden (1976), Waters & Li (2008), and Waters et al. (2012).

The Basic Structure of REWARS

REWARS is a 24-hour relapse prevention program that has the following structure:

1. Fifteen to thirty minutes after waking up in the morning, the patient completes the AST.
2. If no elevated risk of relapse is indicated by the AST, the patient will carry on with his/her daily life without undertaking any special action.
3. If an elevated risk of relapse is indicated by the AST, a message (an e-mail or a text message) will be sent automatically to the patient's therapist and, if possible, to other people who can offer positive support to the patient. The therapist will then contact the patient and arrange for an extra appointment on that day. The therapist and the patient will also call each other several times during the day to further minimalize the risk of relapse. Relevant others will support the patient during that day in accordance to whatever is agreed upon with the patient and the therapist.
4. If an elevated risk of relapse is indicated by the AST, the patient will follow an "emergency protocol" during the next twenty-four hours. This protocol is a personalized set of rules about what to do and what not to do during high-risk days. It is designed by the patient and therapist together.

The "emergency protocol" will have (at least) the following elements:

1. *Today's no-go areas*: these are the places where the patient is not allowed to go to on high-risk days. These are the places where temptations are most present.
2. *Today's no-see persons*: these are the persons the patient is not allowed to have contact with on high-risk days. These are people that may tempt the patient to drink alcohol or use drugs.
3. *Today's safety areas*: these are the places where temptations are absent and where the patient is safe from relapse-provoking stimuli and people. These are the places where the patient is recommended to be for as long as possible during high-risk days.
4. *Today's safety people*: these are the people who can and will support the patient in his/her struggle against relapse. It is recommended that the patient will be in the company of these people for as long as possible during high-risk days.
5. *Today's safety actions*: this is a set of things the patient *must* do during high-risk days in order to reduce the probability of relapse. These actions can include taking medication, employing stress reduction and relaxation techniques, doing physical exercise, etc.

The patient will keep a diary in order to be able to evaluate the effectiveness of this protocol over time together with the therapist. The protocol should be adjusted until the best results are reached. The AST software will record relevant data of every completion of the AST in order to monitor treatment compliance.

REWARS is not suitable for the following categories of patients:

- Patients with an IQ lower than 80.
- Psychotic patients (with manifest symptoms of psychosis).
- Patients suffering from advanced Korsakoff's syndrome.
- Patients without stable housing conditions.
- Patients with seriously impaired eyesight (who are unable to complete the AST).
- Patients who are unable to use a computer or a PDA.
- Patients who have severe difficulties in adhering to a daily task (as is the case in patients with severe ADHD).

The availability of supportive persons (either professionals or non-professionals) is of the utmost importance for the success of the REWARS system. The recruitment of a social support network for the patient, therefore, should be an integral component of the total SUDs treatment program.

CONCLUSION

The two methods that are presented in this chapter are both new and require more empirical testing and further development. Presently, neurofeedback comes forward in the literature as a promising addition to various forms of offender treatment. It is stressed here that neurofeedback is still a relatively new subject of empirical research. Much more research, especially of the randomized controlled trial design, is needed to establish its value for the field of offender treatment more precisely. REWARS is also in its beginning stages of development. Recent discoveries and insights concerning attentional bias in SUDs may yield more practical applications that may prove valuable in the reduction of antisocial behavior in addicted patients. Audacity, inventiveness and creativity are needed for further progress in offender treatment.

REFERENCES

Adshead, G., & Brown, C. (2003). *Ethical issues in forensic mental health research.* London: Jessica Kingsley.

Arns, M., De Ridder, S., Strehl, U., Breteler, M., & Coenen, T. (2009). Efficacy of neurofeedback treatment in ADHD: The effects on inattention, impulsivity and hyperactivity. A meta-analysis. *EEG and Clinical Neuroscience, 40*, 180–189.

Atkinson, B. (1999). The emotional imperative psychotherapists cannot afford to ignore. *Family Therapy Networker, 23*, 22–33.

Babcock, J.C., & Steiner, R. (1999). The relationship between treatment, incarceration, and recidivism of battering: A program evaluation of Seattle's coordinated community response to domestic violence. *Journal of Family Psychology, 13*(1), 23–34.

Beech, A., Fisher, D., & Beckett, R. (1998). *STEP-3: An evaluation of the prison sex offender treatment programme.* Oxford: Oxford Regional Forensic Service.

Bodenhamer-Davis E., Callaway T., (2004). Extended follow-up of Peniston protocol results with chemical dependency. *Journal of Neurotherapy, 8* (2): 135.

Burkett, V.S., Cummins, J.M., Dickson, R.M., & Skolnick, M. (2005). An open clinical trial utilizing real-time EEG operant conditioning as an adjunctive therapy in the treatment of crack cocaine dependence. *Journal of Neurotherapy, 9*, 27–47.

Butnik, S.M. (2005). Neurofeedback in adolescents and adults with attention deficit hyperactivity disorder. *Journal of Clinical Psychology, 61*, 621–625.

Callaway, T.G., Bodenhamer-Davis, E., (2008). Long-term follow-up of a clinical replication of the Peniston Protocol for chemical dependency. *Journal of Neurotherapy, 12* (4), 243 – 259.

Cane, J. E., Sharma, D. D., & Albery, I. P. (2009). The addiction Stroop task: Examining the fast and slow effects of smoking and marijuana-related cues. *Journal Of Psychopharmacology, 23*(5), 510-519.

Carmody, D.P., Radvanski, D.C., Wadhwani, S., Sabo, M.J., & Vergara, L. (2001). EEG biofeedback training and attention deficit/hyperactivity disorder in an elementary school setting. *Journal of Neurotherapy, 4*, 5–27.

Carpenter, K. M., Schreiber, E., Church, S., & McDowell, D. (2006). Drug Stroop performance: Relationships with primary substance of use and treatment outcome in a drug-dependent outpatient sample. *Addictive Behaviors, 31*(1), 174–181.

Chambers, J.C., Eccleston, L., Day, A., Ward, A., & Howells, K. (2008). Treatment readiness in violent offenders: The influence of cognitive factors on engagement in violence programs. *Aggression and Violent Behavior, 13*, 276–284.

Cox, W. M., Fadardi, J. S., & Pothos, E. M. (2006). The addiction-Stroop test: Theoretical considerations and procedural recommendations. *Psychological Bulletin, 132*(3), 443–476.

Craissati, J., South, R., & Bierer, K. (2009). Exploring the effectiveness of community sex offender treatment in relation to risk and re-offending. *The Journal of Forensic Psychiatry & Psychology, 20*, 769–784.

Demos, J.N. (2005). *Getting started with neurofeedback*. New York: W.W. Norton & Company.

Drobes, D.J., Elibero, A., Evans, D.E. (2006). "Attentional bias for smoking and affective stimuli: A Stroop task study.". *Psychology of Addictive Behaviors 20* (4): 490–495.

Dutton, D.G. (2006). Rethinking domestic violence. Vancouver, BC: UBC Press.

Engelbrecht, H.J., Kok, G., Vis, R., Keeser, D., & Deijen, J.B. (2010). Instrumentele conditionering van frontaalkwabactiviteit bij gezonde jongvolwassenen: Een dubbelblind placebogecontroleerd onderzoek naar EEG-neurofeedback. *Tijdschrift voor Neuropsychologie, 1*, 16–26.

Euser, A.S. (2013). *Neurocognitive Endophenotypes of Substance Use Disorders. Evidence from high-risk adolescents*. Rottredam, Erasmus University,

Evans, J.R., & Arbarbanel, A. (Eds.). (1999). *Introduction to quantitative EEG and neurofeedback*. San Diego, CA: Academic Press.

Fenger, T.N. (1998). Visual-motor integration and its relation to EEG neurofeedback brain wave patterns, reading, spelling, and arithmetic achievement in attention deficit disordered and learning disabled students. *Journal of Neurotherapy, 2*, 9–18.

Fernández, T., Herrera, W., Harmony, T., Díaz-Comas, L., Santiago, E., Sánchez, L., Bosch, J., Fernández-Bouzas, A., Otero, G., Ricardo-Garcell, J., Barraza, C., Aubert, E., Galán, L., Valdés, R. (2003). EEG and behavioral changes following neurofeedback treatment in learning disabled children. *Clinical EEG, 34*, 3, 145-152.

Field, M., & Cos, W. M. (2008). Attentional bias in addictive behaviors: A review of its development, causes, and consequences. *Drug and Alcohol Dependence*, *97*(1-2), 1–20.

Field, M., Munafò, M. R., & Franken, I. A. (2009). A meta-analytic investigation of the relationship between attentional bias and subjective craving in substance abuse. *Psychological Bulletin, 135*(4), 589-607.

Fuchs, T., Birbaumer, N., Lutzenberger, W., Gruzelier, J.H., & Kaiser, J. (2003). Neurofeedback treatment for attention-deficit/hyperactivity disorder in children: A comparison with methylphenidate. *Applied Psychophysiology & Biofeedback, 28*, 1–12.

Glass, I.B. (1991). The international handbook of addiction behaviour. London: Routledge.

Golden, C. J. (1976). Identification of brain disorders by the Stroop color and word test. *Journal of Clinical Psychology, 32*(3), 654–658.

Gondolf, E. (1997). Patterns of reassault in batterer programs. *Violence and Victims, 12*, 338–349.

Gordon, J.A., & Moriarty, L.J. (2003). The effects of domestic violence batterer treatment on domestic violence recidivism. *Criminal Justice and Behavior, 30*, 103–110.

Gruzelier, J., & Egner, T. (2005). Critical validation studies of neurofeedback. *Child and Adolescent Psychiatric Clinics of North America, 14*, 83–104.

Hamel, J., & Nicholls, T.L. (2007). *Family interventions in domestic violence: A handbook of gender-inclusive theory and treatment*. New York, NY: Springer.

Hammond, D.C. (2003). QEEG-guided neurofeedback in the treatment of obsessive compulsive disorder. *The Journal of Neurotherapy, 7*, 25–52.

Hammond, D.C. (2007). What is Neurofeedback? *Journal of Neurotherapy, 10*, 4, 25-36.

Hampton, R.L., Gullotta, T.P., & Ramos, J.M. (2006). *Interpersonal violence in the African American community: Evidence-based prevention and treatment practices*. New York, NY: Springer.

Hanson, R.K., Gordon, A., Harris, A.J.R., Marques, J.K., Murphy, W., Quinsey, V.L., & Seto, M.C. (2002). First report of the collaborative outcome data project on the effectiveness of psychological treatment for sex offenders. *Sexual Abuse: A Journal of Research and Treatment, 14*, 169–194.

Hanson, R.K., Morton, K.E., & Harris, A.J.R. (2003). Sexual offender recidivism risk: What we know and what we need to know. *Annals of the New York Academy of Sciences, 989*, 154–166.

Heinrich, H., Gevensleben, H., Freisleder, F.J., Moll, G.H., & Rothenberger, A. (2004). Training of slow cortical potentials in attention-deficit/hyperactivity disorder: Evidence for positive behavioral and neurophysiological effects. *Biological Psychiatry, 55*, 772–775.

Hester, R., Dixon, V., & Garavan, H. (2006). A consistent attentional bias for drug-related material in active cocaine users across word and picture versions of the emotional Stroop task. *Drug and Alcohol Dependence, 81*(3), 251–257.

Jackson, N.A. (2007). *Encyclopedia of domestic violence*. New York, NY: Routledge.

Janes, A. C., Pizzagalli, D. A., Richardt, S., Frederick, B. D. B., Holmes, A. J., Sousa, J., Kaufman, M. J. (2012). Neural substrates of attentional bias for smoking-related cues: An fMRI study. *Neuropsychopharmacology, 35*, 2339-2345.

Kaiser, D.A., & Othmer, S. (2000). Effect of neurofeedback on variables of attention in a large multi-center trial. *Journal of Neurotherapy, 4*, 5–15.

Kang, O.S., Chang, D.S., Jahng, G.H., Kim, S.Y., Kim, H., Kim, J.W., Chung, S.Y., Yang, S.I., Park, H.J., Lee, H., Chae, Y. (2012). "Individual differences in smoking-related cue reactivity in smokers: An eye-tracking and fMRI study". *Progress in Neuro-Psychopharmacology and Biological Psychiatry 38* (2): 285–293.

Kelley, M.J. (1997). Native Americans, neurofeedback, and substance abuse theory: Three year outcome of alpha/theta neurofeedback training in the treatment of problem drinking among Dine' (Navajo) people. *Journal of Neurotherapy, 2*, 24–60.

Kohl, P.L., & Macy, R.J. (2008). Profiles of victimized women among the child welfare population: Implications for targeted child welfare policy and practices. *Journal of Family Violence, 23*, 57–68.

Kouijzer, M.E.J., De Moor, J.M.H., Gerrits, B.J.L., Buitelaar, J.K., & Van Schie, H.T. (2008). Long-term effects of neurofeedback treatment in autism. *Research in Autism Spectrum Disorders*. doi:1016/j.rasd.2008.10.003.

Kwan, G. (2002). Play attention! Can custom-made video games help kids with attention deficit disorder? *Berkeley Medical Journal Issues, 1*, 1–3.

Lin, S.C., Su, C.Y., Chou, F.H.C., Chen, S.P., Huang, J.J., Wu, G.T.E., Chen, C.C. (2009). Domestic violence recidivism in high-risk Taiwanese offenders after the completion of violence treatment programs. *The Journal of Forensic Psychiatry & Psychology, 20*, 458–472.

Linden, M., Habib, T., & Radojevic, V. (1996). A controlled study of the effects of EEG biofeedback on cognition and behaviour of children with attention deficit disorder and learning disabilities. *Biofeedback & Self Regulation, 21*, 35–51.

Loeber, R., Slot, N.W., & Sergeant, J.A. (2001). *Ernstige en Gewelddadige Jeugddelinquentie: Omvang, oorzaken en interventies.* Houten/Diegem: Bohn Stafleu Van Loghum.

Lubar, J.F., & Lubar, J.O. (1999). Neurofeedback assessment and treatment for attention deficit/hyperactivity disorders. In R. Evans & A. Arbarbanel (Eds.), *Introduction to quantitative EEG and neurofeedback* (pp. 103–143). San Diego, CA: Academic Press.

Luijten, M., Veltman, D., den Brink, W., Hester, R., Field, M., Smits, M., & Franken, I. (2011). Neurobiological substrate of smoking-related attentional bias. *Neuroimage, 54*(3), 2374-2381.

Macy, R.J., Giattina, M.C., Parish, S.L., & Crosby, C. (2010). Domestic violence and sexual assault services: Historical concerns and contemporary challenges. *Journal of Interpersonal Violence, 25*, 3–32.

Marhe, R. (2013). *Neurocognitive Predictors of Drug Relapse*. Rotterdam, Erasmus University.

Marshall, W.L., Anderson, D., & Fernandez, Y. (1999). *Cognitive behavioural treatment of sexual offenders*. Chichester: Wiley.

Martin, G., & Johnson, C.L. (2005). The boys Totem town neurofeedback project: A pilot study of EEG biofeedback with incarcerated juvenile felons. *Journal of Neurotherapy, 9*, 71–86.

Masterpasqual, F., & Healey, K.N. (2003). Neurofeedback in psychological practice. *Professional Psychology: Research & Practice, 34*, 625–656.

McCue, M.L. (2008). *Domestic violence: A reference handbook*. 2nd ed. Santa Barbara, CA: ABC-CLIO.

McKay, J., Atterman, A., Rutherford, M., Cacciola, J., & McLellan, A. (1999). The relationship of alcohol use to cocaine relapse in cocaine dependent patients in an aftercare study. *Journal of Studies in Alcoholism, 60*, 176–180.

McKnight, J.Y., & Fehmi, L.G. (2001). Attention and neurofeedback synchrony training: Clinical results and their significance. *Journal of Neurotherapy, 5*, 45–61.

Miner, M. (2002). Factors associated with recidivism in juveniles: An analysis of serious juvenile sex offenders. *Journal of Research in Crime and Delinquency, 39*, 677–689.

Monastra, V.J., Lynn, S., Linden, M., Lubar, J.F., Gruzelier, J., & La Vaque, T.J. (2005). Electroencephalographic biofeedback in the treatment of attention deficit/hyperactivity disorder. *Journal of Neurotherapy, 9*, 5–34.

Monastra, V.J., Monastra, D.M., & George, S. (2002). The effects of stimulant therapy, EEG biofeedback and parenting style on the primary symptoms of attention deficit/hyperactivity disorder. *Applied Psychophysiology & Biofeedback, 27*, 231–249.

Nash, J.J. (2000). Treatment of attention deficit/hyperactivity disorder with neurotherapy. *Clinical Electroencephalography, 31*, 30–37.

Nestor, P.G. (2002). Mental disorder and violence: Personality dimensions and clinical features. *American Journal of Psychiatry, 159*, 1973–1978.

Othmer, S., Othmer, S.F., & Kaiser, D.A. (1999). EEG biofeedback: An emerging model for its global efficacy. In R. Evans & A. Arbarbanel (Eds.), *Introduction to quantitative EEG and neurofeedback* (pp. 243–310). San Diego, CA: Academic Press.

Patrick, G.J. (1996). Improved neuronal regulation in ADHD: An application of fifteen sessions of photic-driven EEG neurotherapy. *Journal of Neurotherapy, 1*, 27–36.

Peek, W.H.M., & Nugter, M.A. (2009). Ik zit mijn tijd wel uit. . . Forensisch psychiatrische pilotstudie naar recidive bij patiënten met een strafrechtelijke plaatsing. (English summary: I'll serve my time . . . . A pilot study on recidivism in forensic patients forcibly hospitalized and treated for one year and on factors which affect recidivism). *Tijdschrift voor Psychiatrie, 51*, 715–725.

Peniston, E.G., & Kulkoski, P.J. (1991). Alpha-theta brainwave neurofeedback for Vietnam veterans with combat-related post-traumatic stress disorder. *Medical Psychotherapy, 4*, 1–14.

Peniston, E.G., & Kulkoski, P.J. (1999). Neurofeedback in the treatment of addictive disorders. In J.R. Evans & A. Arbarbanel (Eds.), *Introduction to quantitative EEG and neurofeedback* (pp. 157–179). San Diego, CA: Academic Press.

Peniston, E.G., Marrinan, D.A., Deming, W.A., & Kulcoski, P.J. (1993). EEG alpha-theta brainwave synchronization in Vietnam veterans with combat-related post traumatic stress disorder and alcohol abuse. *Advances in Medical Psychotherapy, 6*, 37-40.

Peterson, J.M. (2000). Notes on the role of neurotherapy in the treatment of posttraumatic stress disorder. *Biofeedback, 28*, 10–12.

Plichta, S.B., & Falik, M. (2001). Prevalence of violence and its implications for women's health. *Women's Health Issues, 11*, 244–258.

Quinn, J.F., Bodenhamer-Davis, E., & Koch, D.S. (2004). Ideology and the stagnation of AODA treatment modalities in America. *Deviant Behavior, 25*, 109–131.

Robbins, J. (2000). *A symphony in the brain*. New York: Atlantic Monthly Press.

Rossiter, T.R., & La Vaque, T.J. (1995). A comparison of EEG biofeedback and psychostimulants in treating attention deficit hyperactivity disorders. *Journal of Neurotherapy, 1*, 48–59.

Ryan, G., & Lane, S. (1997). *Juvenile sexual offending: Causes, consequences, and corrections.* San Francisco: Jossey-Bass Publishers.

Schulenburg, N.P. (1999). Neurofeedback therapy for ADHD and related neurological disorders. *Journal of Neurotherapy, 3*, 10–20.

Scott, W., Brod, T.M., Siderof, S., Kaiser, D., & Sagan, M. (2002). Type-specific EEG biofeedback improves residential substance abuse treatment. Poster presentation at the meeting of the American Psychiatric Association, Philadelphia. Retrieved from http.//members.aol.com/williamscott/research.htm

Scott, W., Kaiser, D., Othmer, S., Sideroff, S. (2005). Effects of an EEG Biofeedback Protocol on a Mixed Substance Abusing Population. *American Journal of Alcohol and Drug Abuse, 31*, 3, 455 – 469.

Seager, J., Jellicoe, D., & Dhaliwal, G. (2004). Refusers, dropouts, and completers: Measuring sex offender treatment efficacy. *International Journal of Offender Therapy and Comparative Criminology, 48*, 600–612.

Smith, P.N., & Sams, M.W. (2005). Neurofeedback with juvenile offenders: A pilot study in the use of QEEG-based and analog-based remedial neurofeedback training. *Journal of Neurotherapy, 9*, 87–99.

Sokhadze, E. M., Cannon R. L., & Trudeau D. L. (2008). EEG biofeedback as a treatment for Substance Use Disorders: review, rating of efficacy, and recommendations for further research. *Journal of Neurotherapy, 12*(1), 5- 43.

Stippekohl, B., Walter, B., Winkler, M. H., Mucha, R. F., Pauli, P., Vaitl, D., & Stark, R. (2012). An early attentional bias to BEGIN stimuli of the smoking ritual is accompanied with mesocorticolimbic deactivations in smokers. *Psychopharmacology, 222*, 593-607.

Streeter, C., Terhune, D., Whitfield, T., Gruber, S., Sarid-Segal, O., Silveri, M., Tzilos, G., Afshar, M., Rouse, E., Tian, H., Renshaw, P., Ciraulo, D., & Yurgelun-Todd, D. (2007). Performance on the Stroop Predicts Treatment Compliance in Cocaine-Dependent Individuals *Neuropsychopharmacology, 33* (4), 827-836.

Tansey, M.A. (1991). Wechsler (WISC-R) changes following treatment of learning disabilities via EEG biofeedback training in a private practice setting. *Australian Journal of Psychology, 43*, 147–153.

't Hart-Kerkhoffs, L.A. (2010). *Juvenile sex offenders: Mental health and reoffending*. Amsterdam: Department of Child and Adolescent Psychiatry, VU University Medical Center.

Thompson, L., & Thompson, M. (1998). Neurofeedback combined with training in metacognitive strategies: Effectiveness in students with ADD. *Applied Psychophysiology & Biofeedback, 23*, 243–263.

Tinius, T.P., & Tinius, K.A. (2000). Changes after EEG biofeedback and cognitive retraining in adults with mild traumatic brain injury and attention deficit hyperactivity disorder. *Journal of Neurotherapy, 4*, 27–44.

Trudeau, D.L. (2000). The treatment of addictive disorders by brain wave biofeedback: A review and suggestions for future research. *Clinical Electroencephalography, 31*, 13–22.

Van Outsem, R.E. (2001). *De Aanpak: Systeemgerichte Hulp bij geweld in relaties*. Utrecht: Transact.

Van Outsem, R.E. (2009). *Exploring psychological characteristics of sexually abusive juveniles*. Utrecht: Forum Educatief.

Van Outsem, R.E. (2011). The applicability of neurofeedback in forensic psychotherapy: a literature review. *Journal of Forensic Psychiatry and Psychology, 22*, 2, 223-242.

Van Wijk, A. Ph. (2005). *Juvenile sex offenders and non-sex offenders: A comparative study*. Amsterdam: VU University.

Van Wijk, A. Ph., Bullens, R.A.R., & Van den Eshof, P. (2007). *Facetten van Zedencriminaliteit.* s-Gravenhage: Elsevier.

Vermeiren, R. (2002). *Delinquents disordered? Psychopathology and neuropsychological deficits in delinquent adolescents*. Antwerp: Universiteit Antwerpen.

Vernon, D., Frick, A., & Gruzelier, J. (2004). Neurofeedback as a treatment for ADHD: A methodological review with implications for future research. *Journal of Neurotherapy, 8*, 53–82.

Waters, A.J., & Li, Y. (2008). Evaluating the utility of administering a reaction time task in an ecological momentary assessment study. *Psychopharmacology, 197*, 25-35.

Waters, A.J., Marhe, R., & Franken, I.H.A. (2012). Attentional bias to drug cues is elevated before and during temptations to use heroin and cocaine. *Psychopharmacology, 219*, 909-921.

Welldon, E.V., & Van Velsen, C. (1996). *A practical guide to forensic psychotherapy.* London: Jessica Kingsley.

Wekerle, C., & Wall, A.M. (2002). *The violence and addiction equation: Theoretical and clinical issues in substance abuse and relationship violence*. New York, NY: Taylor & Francis.

Wijers, I. (2008). *Justitiële interventies voor jeugdige daders en risicojongeren. (Mandatory interventions for juvenile delinquents and for juveniles who are at risk of becoming delinquent)*. Den Haag: Boom Juridische Uitgevers.

Wilson, S., & Cumming, I. (2009). *Psychiatry in prisons*. Philadelphia, PA: Jessica Kingsleys.

In: Antisocial Behavior
Editor: Justine H. Gallo

ISBN: 978-1-63321-521-4

Chapter 3

ANTISOCIAL AND DELINQUENT BEHAVIOR IN ADOLESCENCE: PREVALENCE AND RISK FACTORS

David Moreno[1], Estefanía Estévez[2], Cándido J. Inglés[2] and Juan Carlos Marzo[2]

[1]Universidad Pablo de Olavide de Sevilla, Spain
[2]Universidad Miguel Hernández de Elche, Alicante, Spain

ABSTRACT

This chapter describes and analyzes delinquent and antisocial behavior in adolescence. The first section highlights the importance of defining the concept of delinquency when talking about minors. Data from both recent social research and government sources from different countries are presented. In the second section, the evolution of adolescent delinquent and antisocial behavior over the last few years is discussed and examined in both sexes and for different ages during the adolescent period. A third section includes the most relevant social and psychological explanatory models of adolescent delinquency provided by research in social sciences. The main important individual, family, school, and community risk factors studied in scientific literature are analyzed in depth in order to understand the origin, development and continuity of this kind of behavior in young people.

1. WHAT IS ADOLESCENT DELINQUENCY?

A revision of the main studies and statistics on criminal behavior in adolescents makes it possible to observe a decrease in crimes committed by juveniles. However, certain peculiarities with respect to the nature of this type of behavior are also made evident. One of the most unusual characteristics to stand out is the low decrease in crimes committed by young women in comparison with men.

In short, it is possible to talk of a qualitative and quantitative change in criminal and vandalistic behavior patterns in adolescents, as well as a decrease in criminality, which is significantly reflected in the crimes perpetrated against people and property. Furthermore, it is necessary to situate criminal behavior and the main expressions of adolescent violence in the context of our sociocultural environment. To do so, it is necessary to define exactly what adolescent delinquency is.

Table 1. Diagnostic criteria for anti-social personality disorder

The person presents: A. A general pattern of disregard and violation of the rights of others, which appear from the age of 15, as indicated by three (or more) of the following items: 1. Failure to conform to social norms with respect to lawful behaviors as indicated by repeatedly performing acts that are grounds for arrest. 2. Deceitfulness, as indicated by repeated lying, use of aliases, or conning others for personal profit or pleasure. 3. Impulsivity or failure to plan ahead. 4. Irritability and aggressiveness, as indicated by repeated physical fights or assaults. 5. Reckless disregard for safety of self or others. 6. Consistent irresponsibility, as indicated by repeated failure to sustain consistent work behavior or honor financial obligations. 7. Lack of remorse, as indicated by being indifferent to or rationalizing having hurt, mistreated, or stolen from another. B. The individual is at least 18 years old. C. There is evidence of anti-social disorder, which has its onset before the age of 15. D. Anti-social conduct does not occur exclusively during the course of schizophrenia or manic episodes.

According to Cohen, one of the most eminent researchers on criminal behavior, delinquency can be defined as “behavior which violates institutionalized expectations, that is, expectations which are shared and recognized as legitimate within a social system”. If we take this conceptualization into account, then adolescent criminal behavior refers to all violations of legitimate expectations or offenses committed by adolescent citizens.

It is important to point out that the significance of offense implies a relationship with the justice system, and is closely linked to the norms in force within the social context an adolescent lives in. These offenses, apart from being qualified as inadmissible behaviors by society, put the person who commits them and other people at physical and psychological risk. In this sense, the unusual nature of this behavior is related to a violation of social norms, besides being a risk for the people involved.

Adolescents who violate social norms usually start out by taking part in less serious acts which later become more serious. Indeed, delinquent behavior covers a wide repertoire of behaviors, from vandalistic acts to aggressions against other people, robbery or even some violent behaviors expressed at school.

In fact, criminal behavior is often related to aggression and violence, and is an indicator of *anti-social personality disorder*, which can be found in diagnostic manuals in the area of psychology and psychiatry, such as DSM-IV-TR (Diagnostic and Statistical Manual of

Mental Disorders 4th edition, revised text) and the ICD.10 (International Classification of Diseases 10th Edition). The following table presents some of the diagnostic criteria for the anti-social personality disorder.

In this sense, violent behavior can be said to be the best means of predicting delinquency in both boys and girls, since violence implies a violation of formal and informal norms. Nevertheless, not all crimes are violent, that is to say, not all criminal behavior involves aggression and violence.

1.1. Data and Legal Reports

Criminal behavior and violation of social norms are the essence of the concept of delinquency, and a large number of studies make use of legal and police data as indicators of the evolution of these behaviors. However, due to the official nature of the data itself, if only this type of data is considered, calculations errors are likely. Such a limited explanation of delinquency does not include all those actions that are not officially reported, the majority of which are offenses that are dealt with informally or by the social services if they are discovered. In fact, official data only usually register more serious offenses, whereas a large number of "minor" criminal behaviors committed by adolescents are not officially known. As Aebi and Linde (2010) point out, the official figures about crimes committed do not provide a measure of juvenile delinquency, but are rather interventions from different institutions which, as indicated above, usually restrict themselves to the number of complaints filed and judicial interventions that do not contemplate, for example, the large number of offenses committed by adolescents. For these reasons, it is essential to consider the different factors involved in delinquency in the adolescent context that go beyond legal and institutional aspects.

In the latter case, besides the evident interest that public and legal administrations have in adolescent and juvenile delinquency, there is also concern about this issue from other scientific areas. For example, in social sciences analyses have been made about the possible factors that lead to understanding and explaining this behavior in youngsters, which go beyond the purely legal aspects. In social sciences, data are gathered primarily through questionnaires and interviews. However, the data compiled in this way are not free of errors, for example: biases from adolescents who want to give the researcher a socially acceptable and correct image, the behavior assessed becomes distorted due to a poor memory, and errors are made by researchers in structuring the questions and administering the questionnaire to the people selected as a source of information. Even so, considering the errors outlined above, the results from the application of questionnaires are considered reliable and meet scientific criteria for gaining more knowledge about this issue.

2. How Has Adolescent Delinquency Evolved over the Last Few Years?

The statistics presented in this section have been taken from the bulletin published by Office of Juvenile Justice and Delinquency Prevention in December 2013 about juvenile arrests in 2011. In this sense, the data presented represent one of the most prestigious and trustworthy sources in the USA, as they come from information that local law enforcement agencies send to the Federal Bureau of Investigation's (FBI's) Uniform Crime Reporting (UCR) Program.

These statistics report the number of arrests that law enforcement agencies make in each of the years referred to. The number of arrests, as key statistical data, is different from the number of people arrested and the number of crimes committed. For example, the number of people arrested does not include information about individuals who are arrested more than once in a year. Neither do the statistics for arrests represent the number of crimes a person commits; several crimes committed by a single person can culminate in one arrest. On the other hand, a single crime can result in the arrest of more than one person. The latter example, where several arrests are a consequence of a single crime is more characteristic of criminal conduct by minors who are more liable than adults to commit crimes as a group. Consequently, the use of statistics is not suitable as a measure of crimes committed by people, but as a set of data related to entry in the justice system. The data about the number of arrests also have limitations for detecting the volume of arrests per specific crime. These restrictions arise because in the framework of the UCR program, the FBI requires organizations responsible for enforcing the law to register each arrest by the most serious crime committed, although the arrest may involve several crimes.

Arrest statistics also differ from the data that report solved cases. For example, a single arrest can solve 10 crimes if the person was accused of committing all of them, and multiple arrests can also solve a single crime if it was committed by a group of delinquents. The FBI requires solved cases, where both adults and minors are involved, to be counted as crimes committed by adults. In this sense, juvenile delinquency cases that are solved underestimate the participation of minors in committing crimes because they only include crimes which adult delinquents were not involved in.

Therefore, although these data do not constitute a definitive description of the participation of minors in delinquency, they present the available measure which is closest to the volume of crimes known by law enforcement agencies.

As table 2 illustrates, in 2011, law enforcement made almost 1.5 million arrests of people under 18. Moreover, the four crimes that comprise the *Violent Crime Index* decreased notably between 2007 and 2011: murder (-37%), rape (-22%), robbery (-31%) and aggravated assault (-29%). Noteworthy events are the 190,000 arrests of minors for simple assault which were registered in 2011, 36% of which were committed by women. Girls also constituted 9% of the arrests of minors for murder and 25% for aggravated assault. 59% of these arrests involved people of white ethnicity. With respect to age, 39% of these simple assaults were committed by minors of 15. It is interesting to note that minors under 15 represent more than half (57%) of all the arrests of minors for arson in 2011, and almost 40% of the arrests for vandalism (39%) and disorderly conduct (38%). In this context, it is necessary to highlight the enormous relevance of the age of onset in conjunction with the type of offense or crime, since it has been confirmed that both data are fundamental indicators for determining the possible persistence of criminal conduct. Therefore, the lower the age at first arrest, the more likely it is that a juvenile will reoffend in persistent criminal activity, and this probability is also greater if they start with violent crimes instead of crimes that do not involve violent aggressions.

Table 2. Estimated number of juvenile arrests, 2011

Most serious offense	2011 estimated number of juvenile arrests	Percent of total juvenile arrests: Female	Younger than 15	White	Percent change: 2002–2011	2007–2011	2010–2011
Total	1,470,000	29%	27%	66%	–31%	–29%	–11%
Violent Crime Index	68,150	18	27	47	–27	–29	–10
Murder and nonnegligent manslaughter	840	9	11	45	–36	–37	–17
Forcible rape	2,800	2	35	64	–40	–22	–2
Robbery	23,800	9	19	30	–3	–31	–13
Aggravated assault	40,700	25	32	56	–34	–29	–9
Property Crime Index	334,700	36	28	62	–30	–20	–9
Burglary	62,000	12	27	60	–28	–24	–5
Larceny-theft	253,800	44	28	63	–25	–15	–10
Motor vehicle theft	14,000	16	20	55	–69	–52	–11
Arson	4,900	15	57	72	–40	–31	8
Nonindex							
Other (simple) assaults	190,900	36	39	59	–19	–21	–9
Forgery and counterfeiting	1,600	29	13	66	–69	–49	–7
Fraud	5,200	35	16	60	–39	–27	–9
Embezzlement	400	39	10	66	–70	–75	–6
Stolen property (buying, receiving, possessing)	13,300	17	22	57	–48	–40	–9
Vandalism	67,900	15	39	76	–35	–39	–12
Weapons (carrying, possessing, etc.)	28,200	10	33	61	–20	–35	–10
Prostitution and commercialized vice	1,000	76	9	35	–32	–34	–7
Sex offense (except forcible rape and prostitution)	12,600	11	49	70	–35	–19	–3
Drug abuse violations	148,700	17	17	74	–20	–24	–13
Gambling	1,000	6	11	12	–35	–52	–28
Offenses against the family and children	3,600	39	31	70	–62	–39	–6
Driving under the influence	10,100	25	2	91	–53	–44	–16
Liquor laws	88,300	40	9	89	–39	–37	–7
Drunkenness	11,400	26	12	87	–39	–32	–10
Disorderly conduct	130,200	35	38	57	–28	–31	–11
Vagrancy	1,800	23	29	73	–10	–53	–15
All other offenses (except traffic)	264,900	26	23	69	–33	–29	–11
Suspicion (not included in totals)	100	28	31	51	–90	–65	8
Curfew and loitering	76,900	30	25	61	–46	–46	–19

*As of 2010, the FBI no longer reports arrests for running away.
Source: Puzzanchera (2013).

Between 1994 and 2004, there was a drop in the arrests of minors for the crimes considered in the *Violent Crime Index*. However, these types of arrests increased between 2004 and 2006 to then decrease every year until 2011. Consequently, the number of arrests for violent crimes by minors in 2011 was lower than in any of the previous 32 years, and 15% lower than the previous lowest point in 1984, reaching historically low levels in 2011, with the exception of aggravated assault.

After a decrease of 33% since 2008, arrests of minors for robbery in 2011 were at their lowest level since 1980. Likewise, the number of arrests of minors for forcible rape fell by 33% from 2004 reaching the lowest percentage for the period 1980-2011. Also, arrests of minors for homicide decreased in 2004, increased until 2007 and then fell by 37% in 2011 reaching the lowest level in three decades. Arrests of minors for aggravated assault decreased by half between 1994 and 2011, in this year they were 8% above the lowest point in 1983. Between 2002 and 2011, the number of arrests in all the categories of crimes committed by minors decreased sharply.

Table 3. Juvenile Arrest Rates for Violent Crime Index Offenses, 1980-2011

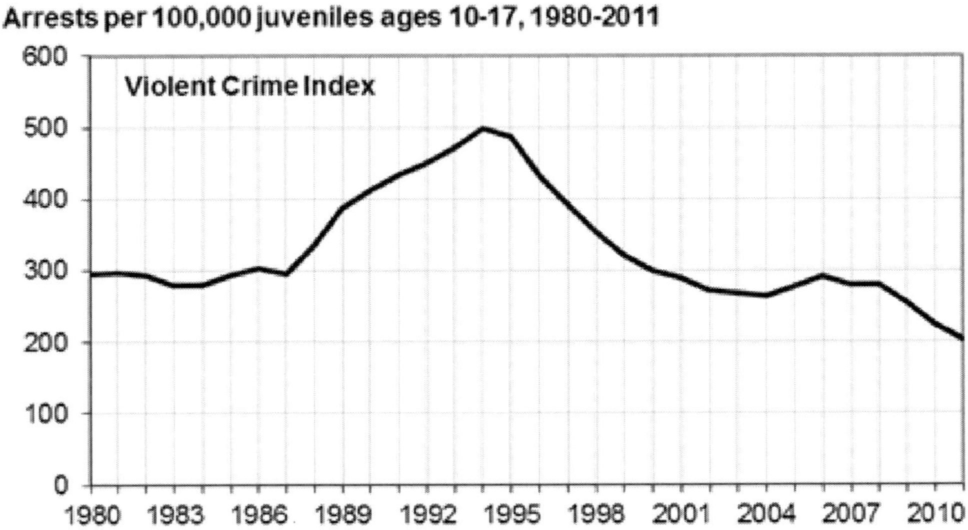

Note: Rates are arrests of persons ages 10-17 per 100,000 persons ages 10-17 in the resident population. The Violent Crime Index includes the offenses of murder and non-negligent manslaughter, forcible rape, robbery, and aggravated assault.

Source: OJJDP Statistical Briefing Book (2014).

With respect to the arrests of minors for crimes against property, they decreased for the third consecutive year. As with violent crime, the FBI evaluates the volume of crimes against property through the *Property Crime Index* which comprises four crimes that law enforcement agencies report consistently. These crimes are: burglary, larceny-theft, motor vehicle theft and arson.

Between1980 and1994, arrests of minors for crimes against property remained relatively stable. Later, between 1994 and 2006, the *Property Crime Index* fell until it decreased by half, reaching its lowest level since 1980, and 54% lower since its maximum level in 1988. This decrease was interrupted by an increase in arrests for crimes against property in 2007 and 2008. Later, between 2008 and 2011 there was a decrease of 22%. As a result, in 2011, it was less likely for minors to be arrested for crimes against property than at any other time in the last 30 years.

Furthermore, between 2008 and 2011, arrests of minors for each of the crimes included in the *Property Crime Index* decreased by the following rates: burglary (26%), larceny-theft (21%), motor vehicle theft (44%) and arson (24%). In this sense, the arrests of minors for burglary, larceny-theft and vehicle theft in 2011 were at their lowest level since 1980, whereas arrests for arson were 8% higher than in 2010, when committing this crime was at its lowest point. In 2011, larceny-theft represents 76% of all the arrests of the *Property Crime Index*. Thus, tendencies on the basis of this index largely reflect arrests for larceny-theft.

Table 4. Juvenile Arrest Rates for Property Crime Index Offenses, 1980-2011

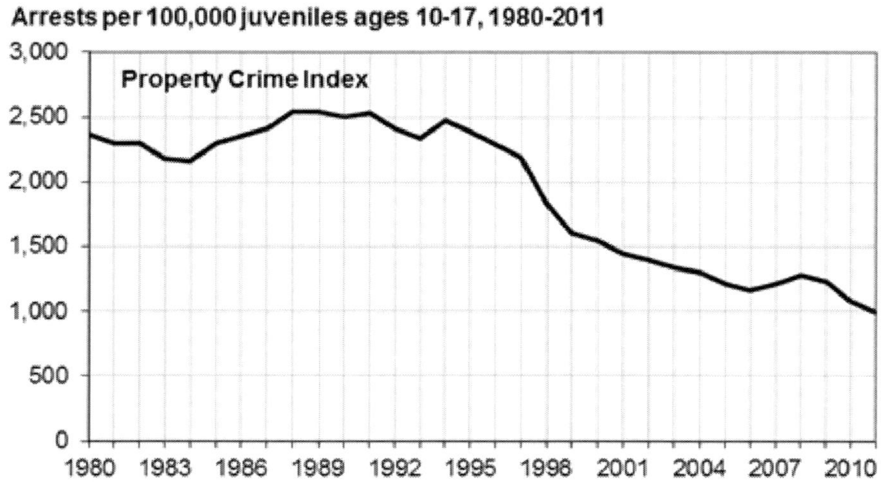

Note: Rates are arrests of persons ages 10-17 per 100,000 persons ages 10-17 in the resident population. The Property Crime Index includes the offenses of burglary, larceny-theft, motor vehicle theft, and arson.

Source: OJJDP Statistical Briefing Book (2014).

2.1. Gender Differences

With respect to the differences between men and women, the statistics report that the number of women arrested is much lower than that of men. Violent crimes in particular are fundamentally related to males. Likewise, research which has studied criminal conduct in adolescence constantly indicates differences between girls and boys. Nevertheless, there has also been mention of the so-called gender paradox which consists of the fact that, although girls participate in antisocial behaviors less than boys, young girls that do so present a worse long-term prognosis and consequences. That is to say, girls participate in violent behaviors at a lower rate than boys, but those that do are usually more violent and have difficulties in overcoming these problems.

It is increasingly more frequent for public opinion to generate the debate about the increase of feminine delinquency. However, according to statistics from different studies about the evolution of criminal conduct in adolescent women, a stable disposition can be observed in the results from questionnaires and a slight rise in trends in governmental data. In 2011, 1 out of every 5 arrests of minors for violent crimes involved women. In this year, women represented 29% of the arrests of minors. To be exact, 429.000 arrests of women under 18 years of age were made.

From 2002 to 2011, arrests of female minors decreased less than the arrests of boys in several crime categories (for example, simple and aggravated assault, larceny-theft, violation of liquor laws, and disorderly conduct). This result can be explained by a change in the juvenile justice system. In this sense, official documents show that criminal acts perpetrated by girls were declared before the competent institutions at a higher rate than in previous years.

Table 5. Juvenile Arrest Rates for Violent Crime Index Offenses by Sex, 1980-2011

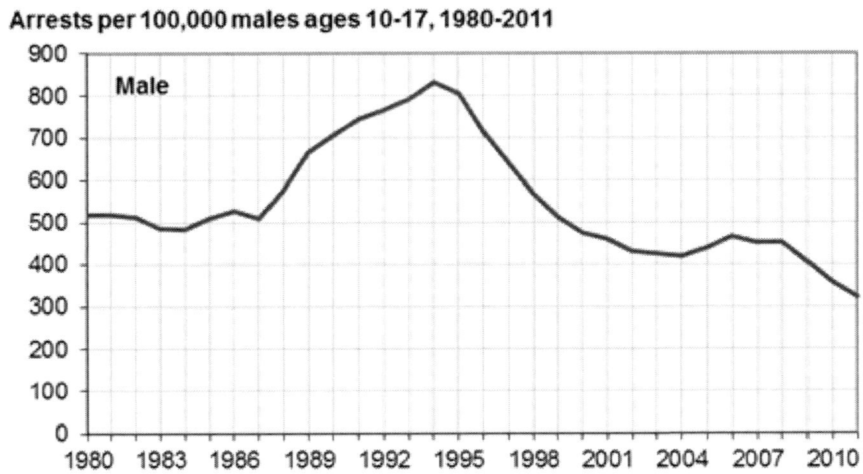

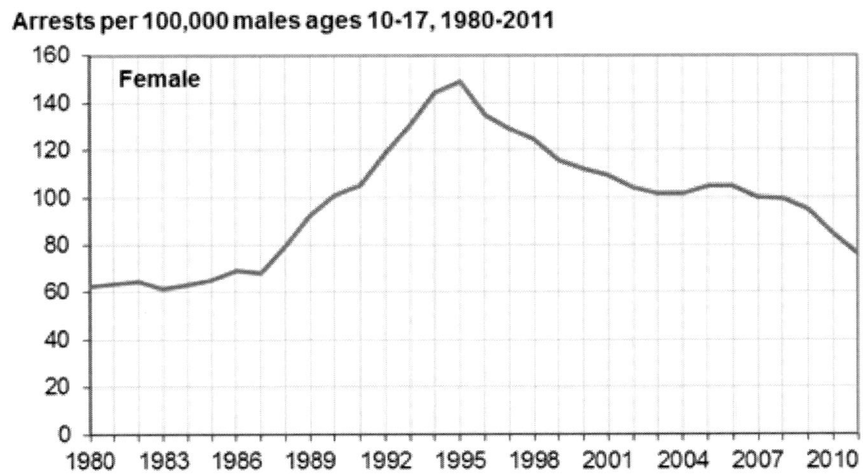

Note: Rates are arrests of persons ages 10-17 per 100,000 persons ages 10-17 in the resident population. The Violent Crime Index includes the offenses of murder and non-negligent manslaughter, forcible rape, robbery, and aggravated assault.

Fuente: OJJDP Statistical Briefing Book (2014).

For example, during the 1980s, the number of arrests of men for violent crimes was almost 8 times higher than it was for women. However, in 2011, the percentage of men arrested for these types of crimes was only 4 times higher. This progressive convergence in the number of arrests of men and women is due to a high increase in relation to female arrests. Between 1980 and 1994, the rate of men arrested for violent crimes increased 60%, while for women it increased by more than double.

Table 6. Juvenile Arrest Rates for Property Crime Index Offenses by Sex, 1980-2011

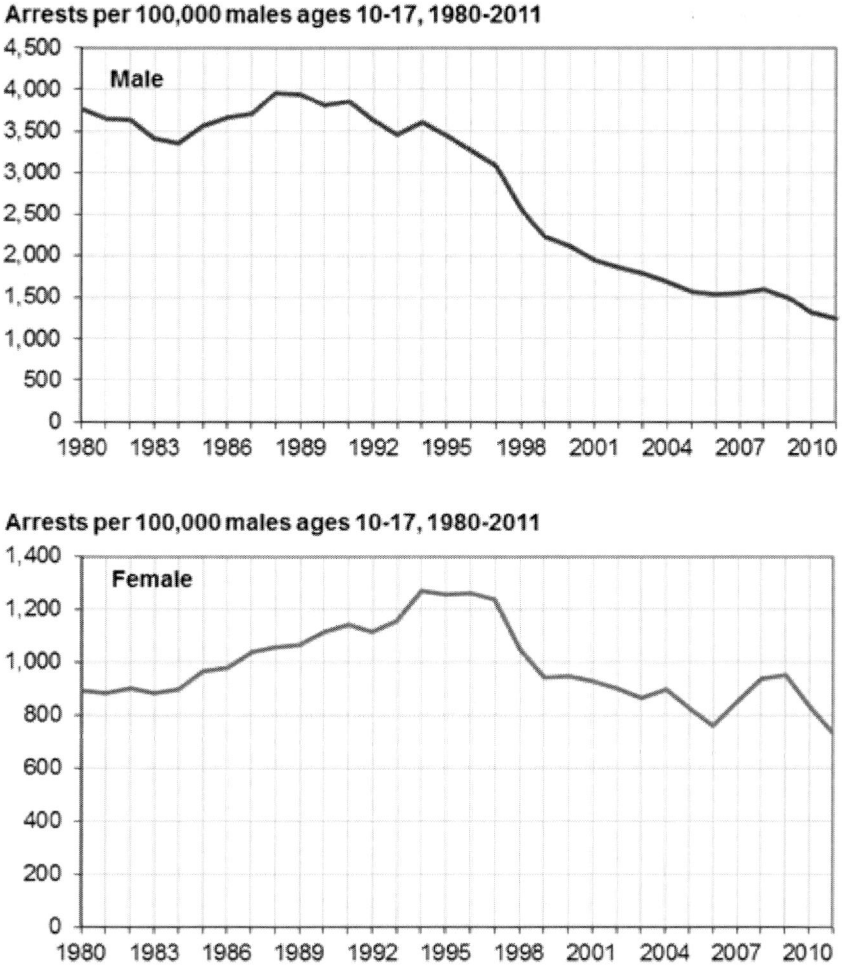

Note: Rates are arrests of persons ages 10-17 per 100,000 persons ages 10-17 in the resident population. The Property Crime Index includes the offenses of burglary, larceny-theft, motor vehicle theft, and arson.

Fuente: OJJDP Statistical Briefing Book (2014).

In 2011, the rate of male arrests decreased by 61% in comparison with its maximum peak in1994, thereby reaching its lowest level in at least three decades. Although the rate of arrests of women has also decreased since the middle of the1990s (47% less), the number of arrests related to the *Violent Crime Index* in 2011 was 23 % higher than in 1983, when it was at its lowest point. In 2011, the decrease in the volume of arrests for violent crimes was evident in both genders.

The volume of arrests of juveniles for crimes against property decreased more among men than among women. To be more exact, the arrests of men for crimes against property have decreased every year since the end of 1980. In the 10 years following 2002, arrests of males for this type of crime fell by 33%, reaching the lowest level in at least three decades. In contrast, the reduction in the arrests of women for crimes against property began almost 10 years later, and this decline was much slower for women (19% fewer arrests since 2002). After 3 consecutive years of decline, in 2011, the volume of this type of crime committed by women reached its lowest point since 1980. Also, between 2002 and 2011, the number of arrests for larceny-theft by juvenile women decreased by 16%, while for men it decreased by 30%. In short, in this period of time, arrests of minors in relation to crimes from the *Property Crime Index* decreased more for men than for women.

Table 7. Juvenile Arrest Rates for Violent Crime Index offenses by Ethnicity, 1980-2011

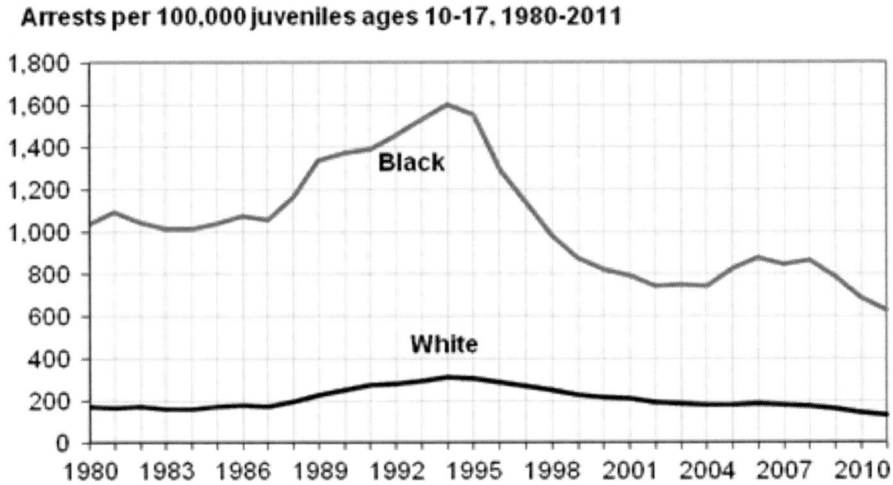

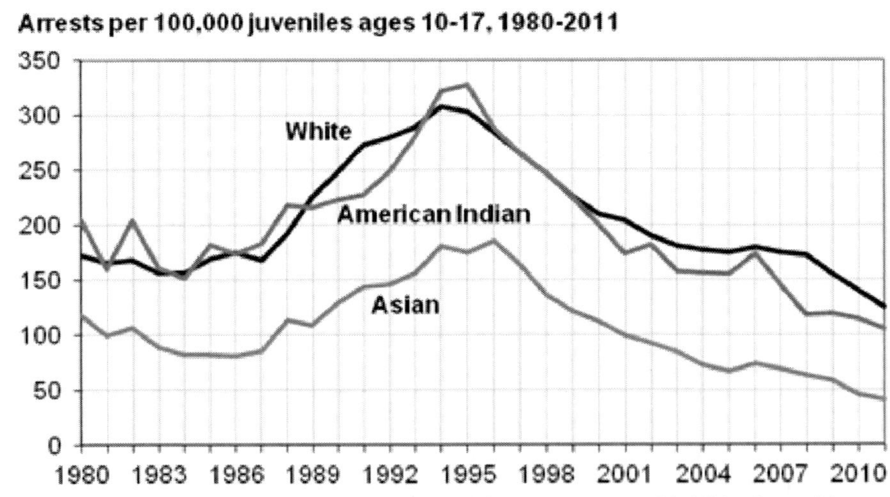

Note: Rates are arrests of persons ages 10-17 per 100,000 persons ages 10-17 in the resident population. Persons of Hispanic ethnicity may be of any ethnicity, i.e., white, black, American Indian, or Asian. Arrests of Hispanics are not reported separately.

The Violent Crime Index includes the offenses of murder and non-negligent manslaughter, forcible rape, robbery, and aggravated assault.

Fuente: OJJDP Statistical Briefing Book (2014).

2.2. Differences by Ethnic Group

In the USA, ethnic distribution of the juvenile population aged between 10 and 17 in 2011 was 76% white, 17% black, 5% Asian / Pacific Islanders and 2% American Indians. The majority of minors of Hispanic ethnicity are included in the white ethnic category. More than half (51%) of all the arrests of minors for violent crimes in 2011, involved young blacks, 47% were young whites, 1% were 1% young Asians and the remaining 1% were young American Indians.

The number of arrests related to the Violent Crime Index for all the ethnic groups decreased significantly between 2002 and 2011. To be exact, the decrease was greater for young Asians (56%), followed by American Indians (42%), whites (35%) and young blacks (15%). The volume of arrests for violent crimes has decreased in all racial groups in almost two decades with few exceptions. As a result of this decrease, the rates of arrests in 2011 for each racial group were at their lowest level of 59% or more since the middle of the 1990s.

Table 8. Juvenile Arrest Rates for Property Crime Index Offenses by Ethnicity, 1980-2011

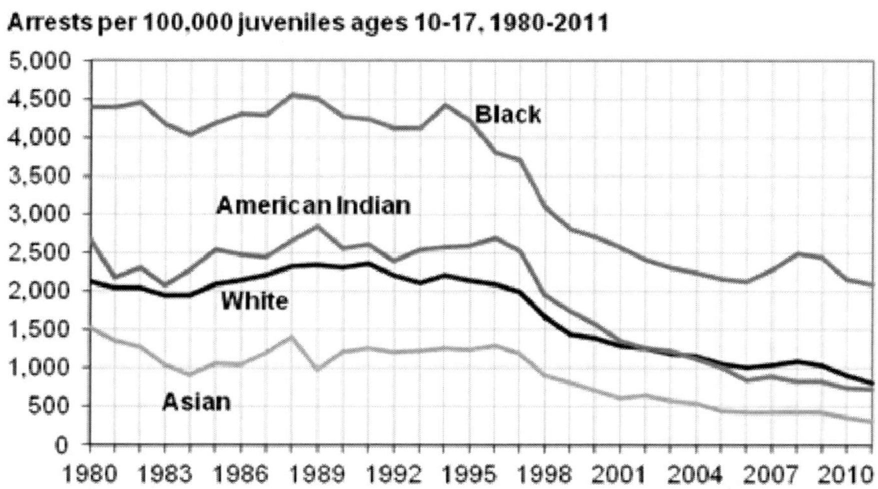

Note: Rates are arrests of persons ages 10-17 per 100,000 persons ages 10-17 in the resident population. Persons of Hispanic ethnicity may be of any ethnicity, i.e., white, black, American Indian, or Asian. Arrests of Hispanics are not reported separately.

The Property Crime Index includes the offenses of burglary, larceny-theft, motor vehicle theft, and arson.

Fuente: OJJDP Statistical Briefing Book (2014).

In 2011 the volume of arrests of minors for crimes against property is distributed as follows: 62% whites, 35% young blacks, 2% Asians and 1% American Indians. The rate of arrests of young blacks was overrepresented. The number of crimes against property decreased in all ethnic groups as did the number of violent crimes. In 2011, the percentage of crimes against property was at its lowest level for the last 10 years. This reduction was higher for young Asians (51%), followed by American Indians (43%), whites (35%) and young blacks (13%). As a result, in 2011 the volume of this type of crime reached its lowest point since at least 1980.

With respect to the criteria chosen, the sources consulted make a broad analysis which considers the ethnic group of the minors involved in arrests as reported by the local law enforcement agencies. The information related to ethnicity reflects that minority groups are disproportionately involved in criminal arrests. In this context, it is important to point out that several studies in the USA have shown the disparity of the criteria that law enforcement agencies use to exercise control over citizens according to their ethnic group. Therefore, in disadvantaged neighborhoods, people belonging to ethnic minorities are closely watched, arrested, condemned and imprisoned at a higher rate than the white majority (Kennedy, 2001; Rocque, 2011; Sánchez &Adams, 2011; Solis, Portillos & Brunson, 2009). In fact, after making a series of observations about arrests and police records, Weitzer & Tuch (2005) found evidence that police tended to consider ethnic minorities as highly suspicious and characterized by their criminal tendencies. Furthermore, it has also been found that the members of ethnic minorities are arrested more often and treated more harshly (Terrill & Reisig, 2003).

As reflected in other studies, it is logical, therefore, to assert that on the whole the white majority maintain a more positive attitude and perception towards authorities and legal procedures. In contrast, ethnic minorities, both adults and minors, present a widespread negative attitude towards the justice system (Estévez, Rachitskiy & Rodríguez, 2013; Tyler & Huo, 2002; Woodlard, Harvell & Graham, 2008).

For a socially cohesive multicultural society, it is of paramount importance to improve beliefs in the legitimacy of the justice institutions. A fundamental measure should be to focus on improving the perception of justice procedures and promoting a just and impartial behavior by the legal authorities (Estévez et al., 2013). In this sense, the competent institutions presenting data about juvenile delinquency should include psychosocial variables related to the risk of becoming involved in criminal behaviors among their analysis criteria, and not only ethnicity. Considering ethnicity in isolation in the analyses about arrest nurtures and perpetuates the negative stereotype that some sectors of society have about ethnic minorities.

These assertions and the data presented so far lead to the following question: What causes an adolescent to continue to commit a crime in later years or to abandon this behavior? The research carried out by Moffitt (1993) permits an explanation of criminal behavior in adolescence on the basis of two possible trajectories or "paths" that a young person's life can take towards adulthood: a transitory event or an event which persists over time. The next section gives an in-depth review of this contribution and others about adolescent delinquency.

3. Why Do Some Adolescents Become Involved in Criminal Behavior?

In the last few decades, adolescent delinquency has been studied intensively in sociology and psychology, which has favored the development of different theories about its onset and development. In this section, some of the important theories for explaining criminal behavior in youngsters and adolescents are described: the Moffitt model, Jessor's problem behavior theory, the social development model by Hawkins, Catalano and Miller, the interactional theory by Thornberry. In the following table there is a summary of these theories and the main contributions of each one.

Table 9. Principle explanatory hypotheses on adolescent and juvenile delinquency

- *Moffitt Model.* Criminal conduct is considered a *transitory behavior* for the majority of adolescents and is typical of this stage of experience. However, a minority, who has shown previous anti-social behavior, will follow a *persistent trajectory* in adulthood too, with behaviors which become increasingly more serious.
- *Jessor's problem behavior theory.* Criminal behavior is explained by *accumulative effects* derived from the presence of numerous *risk factors* in combination with the absence of protection factors.
- *Social Development Model by Hawkins, Catalano and Miller.* Criminal and pro social behaviors follow the same development process. Carrying out one type of action or the other will depend on risk and protection factors, on the social learning that adolescents acquire from the most important people in their environment, and on the success and gratification obtained from the consequences of their own behavior. Criminal behavior depends fundamentally on an adolescent's social context.
- *Thornberry's Interactional Theory:* Criminal behavior is the result of the interaction between a person's traits and a weak connection with the socially established values in the context of their development. The influence between a person and their context is bidirectional, so it also influences this environment with concrete results.

3.1. Criminal Trajectories Model

According to Moffitt (1993), delinquency can be divided into two different levels which are based on the personal history of the individual concerned. On the one hand, a vast majority of people only participate in anti-social behaviors during adolescence, and on the other, there is a group of people are involved in anti-social behaviors throughout all the stages of their lives.

In the first approach, these conducts are explained as forming part of a *transitory trajectory*, that is to say, they are largely adolescent experimental behaviors. In this stage of the life cycle, when adolescents experience scenarios and relations which have so far been unprecedented, such as having a partner, sexuality and search for independence, it is usual for them to want to try new experiences. Some of these experimental behaviors can be a risk for a person's integrity, but in many cases form part of a process of searching for and asserting personal autonomy and can, therefore, even be considered "habitual behaviors" in this evaluative period.

Adolescence also represents a period that tests the ability of the family system to adjust to the changes that adolescent children demand. In this situation, deviant behavior can have its origins in the family's failure, the school's failure, or both, to accept and satisfy an adolescent's growing need for independence, control and participation. For adolescents, risk behaviors and activities represent a type of social behavior which facilitates access to certain contexts which make them feel important and related to an adult status (smoking, drinking alcohol, driving vehicles without a license, risky sexual conduct, etc.).

In fact, it is possible to observe adolescents from both sexes and well-adjusted in childhood who begin to deviate in this period of their life cycle to the point that this problematic behavior becomes common and frequent. In this sense, criminal conduct would rather be a typical adolescent characteristic than a pathological behavior. Some adolescents have committed one or more offenses of different seriousness without being labeled delinquents, since they have neither been found out nor have they reoffended; that is to say, the most notable characteristic of these acts in adolescence is their transitory nature.

From this point of view, for the majority of adolescents the increase in committing anti-social and criminal behaviors during this stage declines at the end of adolescence, once they have overcome the phases of personal assertiveness and identity configuration. In fact, a decrease in these behaviors is noticeable in adulthood, reaching levels similar to those in periods prior to adolescence. Moffitt suggests that for many adolescents, disruption is not only common, but it is also "adaptive" in the sense that it is useful as a learning base which permits the expression and consolidation of an adolescent's independence. However, the frequency and apparent normality of these behaviors can be serious and entail negative results for adolescents themselves, their environment and society, and should, therefore, be studied in depth in order to prevent them.

The second approach is based on the situation that the expression of criminal and violent behaviors in adolescence is the result of a previous process and part of a *persistent trajectory*. There are adolescents who already present criminal behaviors at an earlier time in life, exacerbating these conducts in adolescence and adulthood. According to Moffitt, the precociousness of criminal behavior characterized by committing serious offenses is the best indicator of chronic delinquency. A situation of these characteristics would show a possible persistent trajectory of criminal behavior. That is to say, criminal behavior is the consequence of an accumulation of problems that are present in an adolescent's life at previous stages of development like infancy and childhood. These problems are influenced by a series of risk factors of a biological, psychological and social nature. The variables that most stand out are, for example: an authoritarian or negligent education in the family, school failure from the early educational stages, family problems, cognitive deficits, etc., which can have an early influence on the development of an aggressive and anti-social personality or behavioral style in adolescence.

Figure 1 presents the difference between the two trajectories according to age: the dotted line represents the persistent trajectory of criminal behavior and the continuous line represents the transitory trajectory.

It is important to once again highlight that the persistent pattern of violence is conceived as a constant and chronic characteristic of certain individuals in all stages. Once this criminal path begins and develops, people continue choosing environments that favor and sustain violent acts, like a gang of adolescent delinquents, thereby creating a long-lasting disposition for anti-social behavior. In this way, these behaviors become recidivist with the consequent deterioration of the personal and social adjustment of the individual. Moreover, there is a consensus among social researchers interested in juvenile delinquency that the root to criminal behaviors can be found fundamentally in the closest environments of a person: family, friends, school and neighborhood.

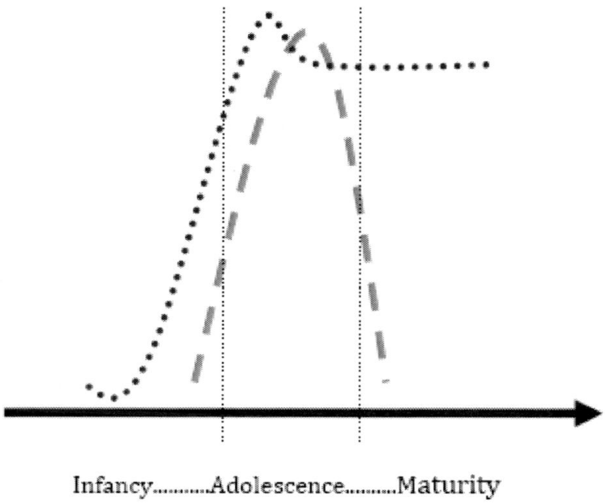

Figure 1.Criminal behavior trajectories.

If these explanations are taken into account, it can be concluded that risk behaviors in adolescence are either an integral part of an adolescent's search for consolidating their identity and autonomy, or the result of a previous process fundamentally focused on negative relations with important figures like parents or educators. Nevertheless, these two focuses suggest common points in the explanation of criminal behavior in adolescence (for example, the importance of family, school, community and peer environment)Consequently, they should not be considered as opposing but rather as complementary in the area of research into explanatory factors, and obviously in the prevention and intervention of these behaviors. In fact, in scientific literature related to the study of delinquency these two trajectories, transitory and persistent, are both considered significant interpretative and explanatory frameworks of adolescent delinquency.

3.2. Accumulation of Risks Model

This model is based on Jessor's problem theory (1993). This theory tries to explain why adolescents decide to violate the established norms in their context or community and end up becoming involved in crime. It is based on the idea that there are different risk factors, that is to say, different elements surrounding an adolescent which increase the probability that this boy or girl may commit a crime. Furthermore, the higher the number of risk elements or factors which form a part of their life, the greater likelihood there is of this happening. Let us think about the simile of the person who buys many lottery tickets and is clearly at an advantage for winning the prize. Well, this is what can happen with the final result of an unhealthy behavior in adolescence. The principal risk factors that influence the behavior of an adolescent, according to this proposal, are summarized in the table below:

Following on from the points outlined in the table, if an adolescent lives in a family where the father suffers from alcoholism and where there are economic difficulties, it is more likely for them to become involved in criminal activities. These risk factors are not presented separately, but are related, and it would be logical that in an environment of these characteristics (father's illness and poverty) an adolescent's personality and emotional life could be disrupted. This affective instability can, for example, have consequences like feelings of sadness and depression which negatively affect self-esteem and personal hopes and achievements, discouraging the adolescent from attending school. All these risk factors foster the conditions which are ideal for the onset of anti-social behaviors.

At the same time, the accumulation of *protector factors* decreases the probability of an adolescent becoming involved in criminal behaviors. Thus, although an adolescent may be surrounded by a host of risk factors from among those described above, aspects like good relations with parents, good integration at school and a high self-esteem can act as a buffer in the face of disadvantageous factors like living in a problematic neighborhood with negative behavior models.

Table 10. Risk factors of adolescent delinquent behavior

(1) Biological and genetic factors, as for example family history of alcoholism; (2) Social environment factors, which include, for example, poverty or quality of schools; (3) Perceived environment factors, like support from parents and friends. (4) Personality variables, like self-esteem, future expectations, the tendency to take risks and values related to achievement and health; (5) Behavioral factors which include variables like school attendance and involvement in violent behaviors.

Therefore, a risk situation will not have the same effect on all youngsters because each one has his "own defense profile", that is to say, a personal system of protection against risks. According to Jessor, a true understanding of criminal behavior requires taking into account the balance between risk factors and protection factors in all the contexts that are important to a person.

3.3. The Social Development Model

The social development model was developed by Hawkins, Catalano and Miller (1992) and follows the same hypotheses as the theory described in the synopsis above. That is to say, it considers the influence of different risk and protection factors that are related and frequently appear together, thereby influencing an adolescent's behavior in different environments. The interesting point of the model by Hawkins and his colleagues lies in that it is a general theory of human behavior. That is to say, it not only aims to explain antisocial behavior (like delinquency or illegal drug use) but also prosocial behavior. Pro social or altruistic conduct is one which is carried out in benefit of another, with freedom of choice and without apparent rewards for doing so. The authors of this model think that in this way, the process that involves the development of both types of behaviors, criminal and prosocial, is similar.

In the process that leads to one of these behaviors, Hawkins and his Colleagues highlight the repercussion that actions have on personal satisfaction and on the rewards that an adolescent hopes to obtain. It is in this point that family environment is of special importance. The rewards and the pleasure which an adolescent obtains from doing one or the other of the behaviors are largely determined by parents and through education. For example, it is more likely that in a family where parents encourage the expression of feelings and behaviors of support, children will imitate this behavior or even enjoy offering support and help to others, persisting in this pattern of action and integrating it within their own identity. However, in broken families the message that parents transmit to their children is to worry about themselves and their personal satisfaction, even though they perform actions that generate discomfort in other people. Besides, if antisocial behaviors, like a crime, have a "successful" result for adolescents, they gain practical experiential learning which reinforces this type of behavior and contributes to sustaining this model of rewarding behaviors. Finally, both types of behavioral patterns, prosocial and antisocial, which are influenced by the values, attitudes and norms of the people who are important to an adolescent, will determine either a delinquent or altruistic personality.

Once the theoretical foundations of this model have been studied, it is easy to be aware of the high importance that the socialization process acquires in different areas off adolescent development (fundamentally family, then school and neighborhood). The adolescents who are most vulnerable to becoming involved in high risk behaviors are, therefore, understood to have problems in multiple areas and tend to belong to social networks which maximize the development of these models of behavior. So, just as in the *theory of problem behavior*, it is established that the higher the number of risk factors adolescents are exposed to in the most important development contexts, the higher the likelihood is that they will commit criminal acts or will become chronic juvenile delinquents.

3.4. The Interaction Model

This model is based on the *interactional model* developed by Thornberry (1996), according to which, delinquent behavior is the result of a weak connection a person has with society and with the established norms that determine the behaviors which are socially acceptable and those that are not. Citizens learn to relate to each other and to participate in society through socialization. In this learning process, the most important people in an adolescent's life, parents, friends etc., are crucial, since in certain cases they can transmit inappropriate behaviors, like for example solving conflicts through violence. This negative learning is reinforced in conflictive social environments, like a family where there are patterns of abuse, or peer groups where violence is seen as a legitimate conduct to obtain what one wants. In this context, delinquency is initiated and develops through complex processes in which the individual and society mutually influence each other.

For Thornberry, conflicts in the family and at school are extremely important factors as the source of criminal behavior in adolescents. Furthermore, a learning context that reinforces the onset, development, maintenance and internalization of criminal behaviors and attitudes is basic. It is during the adolescent stage when peers play a very important role in this delinquent type of socialization. In this way, an adolescent's relation with deviant classmates and friends increases the possibility of the onset of delinquency. At the same time, this process favors the fact that by becoming involved in criminal acts youngsters could relate more easily to other delinquent adolescents.

Thornberry also gives special attention to studying the age at onset of antisocial behavior, and considers that the sooner criminal behavior starts, there is a greater likelihood that it will persist, since a spiral of behaviors will be created in which the criminal lifestyle will become a constant in the person's life.

4. What Aspects Have Been Observed in Risk Situations?

As illustrated in the previous section about the theories and explanatory hypotheses, delinquency in adolescence has been historically associated with a wide number of factors related to different areas of a young person's development. Nowadays, researchers still assume that there is no *single cause*, but advocate an interactive perspective between the typical characteristics typical of adolescents (their genetic inheritance and personality) and the characteristics of the environments that influence a person. Due to the great variety of causes and events involved in and related to the development of delinquency problems, this section discusses the most important and specific aspects in greater detail.

4.1. Education within the Family

There is a great deal of research about how the family's characteristics, and especially parents' educational styles influence the development of children's behavioral problems. Patterns of children's upbringing and education that are either too authoritarian or too permissive are among the family aspects most likely related to children developing behaviors of abuse and bullying at school, and this is also the case for delinquent behavior. The excessive use of punishment, and especially physical punishment, is narrowly related to this, and in different studies it is a strategy which has been verified as favoring criminal behavior in adolescents. This relation between physical punishment and involvement in antisocial behaviors is largely explained because adolescents who are mistreated physically by their parents can identify and learn to use violence as a resource or strategy for rapidly reaching the goals they propose or for solving their problems with other classmates. In fact, as García and Gracia (2010) point out, adolescents who are either educated by authoritative parents or by parents who are excessively lax and little involved in the education of their children, show more behavioral problems than adolescents educated by parents who are more understanding, involved and affectionate.

In this sense, adolescents who show fewer problems of behavior usually perceive their parents as caring, respectful and in short *democratic*. A democratic educational style, based on support, sensitiveness towards children, involvement in their upbringing and consistency in decisions, is related to a lower presence of behavioral and emotional problems in children, and contributes to strengthening their self-esteem and academic performance. The last two aspects are, at the same time, important protection factors regarding the development of psychological and social adjustment problems like delinquency.

In studies about family and criminal behavior, the poor quality of relations between parents and children has also proven to be one of the most significant indicators of deviant behavior in adolescent children. Some of the circumstances that most relate to the involvement of criminal actions are low family unity, that is to say a poor emotional connection between family members as well as a bad relation between parents and children. In contrast, the presence of close affective ties between parents and children constitutes an excellent barrier against the development of criminal behaviors.

Family conflict, as well as the use of inappropriate ways of coping with family problems, or the use of tools which are not very constructive to solving them (like physical punishment or constant avoidance of problems) have also been associated to the onset or increase in problems like children's antisocial behavior, both within and outside the home. Children from a family context with such troublesome characteristics feel poorly valued, and their dissatisfaction can be released by using violence against friends. At the same time, as they are educated in a violent environment, they do not have a good guide or behavioral model which will enable them to solve their problems pacifically. This situation can lead adolescents to seek refuge in friends more than in the family, and it is precisely their family dissatisfaction which is one of the main reasons for seeking their friends out. The danger comes if the friends that like and support an adolescent are also youngsters with difficulties who are involved in the world of delinquency. This is one of the most important factors that can favor an adolescent's onset into this way of life.

On the other hand, the use of positive and efficacious ways of solving family conflicts, such as dialogue and negotiation are related to adolescents being less involved in criminal behaviors. This is because these conflict management strategies provide the adolescent with efficacious resources for coping with and solving the problems that can occur in their interpersonal relations. Adolescents learn that it is more effective to deal with problematic situations calmly, using consensus and negotiation, thereby avoiding violent actions which aggravate the situation and cause more problems.

Generally, adolescents who show antisocial and criminal behaviors describe their family environment as negative, lacking opportunities for expressing their opinions and feelings freely; or, to the contrary, full of communication problems and negative, harmful or challenging interactions. A family climate where there is an open and fluid communication between parents and children, characterized by empathy (where everyone puts themselves in the other's position to try and understand it), affection and respect for others' points of view, promotes a positive attitude in adolescents towards the social norms of coexistence, thereby reducing the risk of becoming involved in criminal behaviors.

Finally, some studies have pointed out that family composition is an aspect associated to criminal behavior in children. In this research, the families that stand out are two-parent families, single parent families and blended families (consisting of a person who, after a separation, divorce or the death of their partner, rebuilds their sentimental life with another person and live with the children of both partners).

Generally, it has been pointed out that adolescents from single-parent and blended families have a greater risk of developing problems of emotional and behavioral adjustment, such as antisocial and criminal behavior. This risk is associated with the greater difficulties that these types of families usually have. For example, economic problems in the case of a single-parent family, and which in many cases forces the parent to spend a lot of time away from home working, so contact and time that parents and children have together is less, and the supervision of adolescents decreases. In these circumstances, the father or mother's socialization role is also obstructed by the lack of time shared, and adolescents are more likely to spend this time with, for example, other violent or antisocial friends from a near by environment, like the neighborhood, which provides a socialization based on violating the norms. In the case of blended families, the great challenge is based on the readjustment of the members from each family unit to the new members (stepfather, step mother, step brothers and sisters), which can sometimes entail a temporary emotional separation of an adolescent from his own parents, which is not exempt from possible adjustment problems.

4.2. Reputation among Friends

The cause of behavioral problems is not just limited to the family education context. Recent studies by Moreno and his colleagues (2012) highlight the importance of the type of relations adolescents have with the social network of friends, and the social image that they want to transmit to them (that is to say, the reputation they want to have). These aspects have been related to the involvement in antisocial and criminal behaviors. *Social reputation* refers more specifically to the image drawn from the opinions, in this case, that the group of friends have about an adolescent's personal and social qualities. In this sense, friends are continually valuing the image of group members, and this judgment determines the level of acceptance or rejection of an adolescent in the group, and also regulates their behavior. For example, "to always look fashionable" is an aspect which is appreciated among adolescents and can ensure more or less success when relating to others and being considered as important within the group.

Some adolescents become involved in illegal and criminal behaviors because they have become associated with friends who also participate in criminal behaviors. They define and create their own codes and norms among themselves and reinforce their own behaviors. Criminal actions are approved of by the group, so there is an increased likelihood that deviant behavior becomes worse. In this sense, several research papers have observed that many adolescents become involved in antisocial behaviors to, in fact, achieve social recognition and to improve their reputation among friends. This implies that the high importance that an adolescent gives to his *social image*, at the same time, makes him more vulnerable to the pressure of the group. For example, if all the friends insist on stealing a bottle of liquor from a supermarket and one of them offers very convincingly to take on the feat, it is likely that this event will favor this person's acceptance and improve their social *status* in a group of deviant friends.

In this regard, Carroll and her colleagues (2001) have formulated the *theory of reputation enhancement by goal setting* for analyzing and checking how to initiate the process in which an adolescent achieves a social reputation based on the goal of achieving respect, leadership and power in the group he wants. According to this theory, some adolescents can feel poorly committed to the objectives which are typical of their development like academic performance, and they start to commit to other types of goals which require a violent and disruptive conduct, for example, being accepted in a group of friends who develop criminal behaviors as mentioned above. This new behavior appears more attractive and brings them greater benefits within the group, like being more admired and valued and, therefore, having a better reputation among friends.

4.3. The Importance of School

School together with the family is the main socialization context throughout our lives and is obviously fundamental in the adolescent stage. In fact, it has been shown on several occasions that the predisposition to learn and a good school trajectory act as protector aspects in the face of school violence, while academic failure, laziness and negative climate in the classroom are characteristics which contribute to explaining certain antisocial behaviors at school. Therefore, because of its importance in the education of adolescents, school is a decisive environment in the development of maladjustment and marginalization, aspects which can lead to violent and criminal behavior. Some negative characteristics from the school as an institution can be added to the family problems as an influence on children's education, contributing to their involvement in criminal type behaviors.

Also, not attending classes is a risk indicator that contributes to facilitating the path to delinquency, since it represents an opportunity for exercising antisocial behaviors outside the school but in a period and timetable that should be occupied by school activities and coexistence.

At the same time, suspending students with behavior problems from school temporarily or permanently has proven to be an inefficacious disciplinary measure. In fact, the statistics indicate that the peak for violations committed by adolescents is during school hours. This reality is not a coincidence, but is linked to the fact that problem students who are suspended from the center, far from gaining beneficial effects, for the pupil it is a positive reinforcement, a reward a deferment and a worsening of the problem. This circumstance of aggravating antisocial conduct is produced because during suspension from the center the adolescent, on numerous occasions, does not have the supervision of other adults like parents who are at work during that time of the day. In cases of more serious behavior, disciplinary measures should be accompanied by other reductive interventions which involve other professionals who support and complement the center's decisions.

Different intervention programs have demonstrated that improvement of school climate and a positive attitude towards school can prevent violent and maladjusted behaviors in interpersonal relations within the center. In order to favor school coexistence, innovating activities for the classroom which promote cooperative learning should be designed, which are complementary to traditional school activities and far from a model of activities focused on competitiveness, which basically stress the success of a few. The effects of cooperative and competitive game programs show an increase in positive helping behaviors and a decrease in aggressive behaviors. Furthermore, studies on the effects of cooperative interaction confirm that it stimulates group cohesion, develops pro social behavior, favors acceptance of among group members, contributes to reducing conflicts between groups and negative social behaviors, and decreases physical aggression and negative verbal interactions, like insults between students.

4.4. The Importance of the Neighborhood

It is also extremely important that adolescents have resources available which are different from those of the family, and can count on members of the neighborhood who contribute positively to their development. In this sense, the lack of support and attention from other adults in the neighborhood at the onset of problems, like involvement in criminal type behaviors in adolescence, is of great importance. Relying on little support from adults makes the adolescent feel ignored and undervalued, and is a circumstance that can cause a separation or alienation between adults and young members of the neighborhood. Neighborhood community life, especially if it is characterized by marginalization and poverty, becomes much harder without support and education from adults. This is the moment when adolescents decide to become involved in antisocial types of behaviors that are neither regulated nor sanctioned in the neighborhood, and because they are to a certain extent adaptive to a reality of deprivation and marginalization, they can perpetuate in adolescent life.

Some researchers, like Jiménez and her colleagues (2009), consider community involvement, defined on the basis of the integration and participation of adolescents in their neighborhood community (for example, becoming involved in voluntary organizations and in the social life of the neighborhood), is a key aspect in their education. This is so, because parents and adults from the neighborhood act as social models and have the function of supervising and guiding the behavior of the youngest. This "attention" to the youngsters makes them feel valued and important in the community, which in turn becomes a feeling of worth and well-being, a feeling based on relations of friendship with other peers and adults in the neighborhood, which leads to a broadening and strengthening of an adolescent's support network.

Relations which are established in the neighborhood community, therefore, favor adolescent adjustment, and positively influence the concept that they have of themselves, their feelings, personal control and acceptance of established social norms. All this finally leads to a prevention process of the development of violent and criminal behaviors. This effect is largely produced in neighborhoods where there is a strong union among the members.

ACKNOWLEDGMENTS

This study was performed within the framework of the research PSI2012-33464 "*School violence, dating violence, and parent-child violence in adolescence from the ecological perspective*", subsidized by the Spanish Ministry of Economy and Competitiveness.

REFERENCES

Aebi, M., & Linde, A. (2010). El misterioso caso de la desaparición de las estadísticas policiales españolas [Themisterious case of the disappearance of Spanish pólice statistics]. *Revista Electrónica de Ciencia penal y Criminología,* 12-07. Retrived 26 November 2012 http://criminet.ugr.es/recpc/12/recpc12-07.pdf

APA (2002). *Manual Diagnóstico y Estadístico de los trastornos mentales, DSM-IV-TR [Diagnostic and Statistical Manual of Mental Disorders].* Barcelona: Masson.

Carroll, A., Houghton, S., Hattie, J., & Durkin, K. (2001). Reputation Enhancing Goals: Integrating reputation enhancement and goal setting theory as an explanation of delinquent involvement. In Columbus, F. H. (Ed.),*Advances in Psychology Research* (pp. 101-129). New York: Nova Science Publishers.

Estévez, E. Rachitskiy, M., & Rodríguez, C. (2013). Is perception of the mainstream legal system homogeneous across ethnic groups? *The European Journal of Psychology Applied to Legal Context,* 5, 33-38.

García, F., & Gracia, E. (2010).¿Qué estilo de socialización parental es el idóneo en España? Unestudio con niños y adolescentes de 10 a 14 años [What parental socialization style is the ideal in Spain? An study with children an adolescents from 10 to 14 years old]. *Infancia y Aprendizaje, 33*, 365-384.

Hawkins, J. D., Catalano, R. F., & Miller, J. Y. (1992). Risk and protective factors for alcohol and other drug problems in adolescence and early adulthood: Implications for substance abuse prevention. *Psychological Bulletin, 112*, 64-105.

Jessor, R. (1993). Succesful adolescent development among youth in high-risk settings. *American Psychology, 48*, 117-126.

Jiménez, T. I., Musitu, G., Ramos, M. J., & Murgui, S. (2009). Community involvement and victimization at school: an analysis through family, personal and social adjustment. *The Journal of Community Psychology, 37*, 959-974.

Kennedy, R. (2001). Racial trends in the administration of criminal justice. In N. J. Smelsen, W. J. Wilson, & F. Mitchell (Eds.), *America becoming: Racial trends and their consequences* (Vol. II, pp. 21-31). Washington, DC: National Academy Press.

Moffitt, T. E. (1993). Adolescence-limited and life-course-persistent antisocial behavior: a developmental taxonomy. *Psychological Review, 100*, 674-701.

Moreno, D., Jesus, S. N., Murgui, S., & Martínez, B. (2012). Un estudio longitudinal de la reputación social no conformista y la violencia en adolescentes desde la perspectiva de género [A longitudinal studyon non-conformist social reputation and violence in adolescents from a gende perspective]. *Psychosocial Intervention,21*, 67-75.

Puzzanchera, C. (2013). *Juvenile Arrests 2011.* Washington, D.C.: Office of Juvenile Justice and Delinquency Prevention.

Rocque, M. (2011). Racial disparities in the criminal justice system and perceptions of legitimacy: A theoretical linkage. *Race and Justice, 1*, 292-315.

Sanchez, C. G. V., & Adams, E. B. (2011). Sacrificed on the altar of public safety: The policing of Latino and African American youth. Journal of Contemporary Criminal Justice, 27, 322-341.

Solis, C., Portillos, E. L., & Brunson, R. K. (2009).Latino Youths' Experiences with and Perceptions of Involuntary Police Encounters. *The Annals of the American Academy of Political and Social Science, 623*, 39-51.

Terrill, W., &Reisig, M. D. (2003). Neighborhood context and police use of force. *Journal of Research in Crime and Delinquency, 40*, 291-321.

Thornberry, T. P. (1996). Empirican support for interactional theory: A review of the literature. In Hawkins, J. D. (Ed.), *Delinquency and crime: current theories* (pp. 198-235). Nueva York: Cambridge University Press.

Tyler, T. R. (2001). Public trust and confidence in legal authorities: What do majority and minority group members want from the law and legal institutions? *Behavioral Sciences & the Law, 19*, 215-235.

Weitzer, R., & Tuch, S. A. (2005). Racially biased policing: Determinants of citizen perceptions. *Social Forces, 83*, 1009-1030.

Woodlard, J. L., Harvell, S., & Graham, S. (2008). Anticipatory injustice among adolescents: Age and racial/ethnic differences in perceived unfairness of the justice system. *Behavioral Sciences & the Law, 26*, 207-226.

In: Antisocial Behavior
Editor: Justine H. Gallo

ISBN: 978-1-63321-521-4

Chapter 4

UNDERSTANDING AGGRESSION: WHY VIOLENT SENTIMENTS AND AGGRESSIVE PROBLEM-SOLVING STRATEGIES SHOULD BE A CLEAR FOCUS IN VIOLENT INTERVENTION PROGRAMS

Sally Fiona Kelty, Ph.D. [•]
School of Social Sciences, University of Tasmania,
Hobart, Tasmania, Australia

ABSTRACT

Is it what adult perpetrators of violence think or how they think that discriminates them most from non-violent members of the community? The research presented in this chapter investigated whether violent and criminal sentiments, attribution biases and/or violent grievance resolution strategies represented risk factors for aggressive behaviour. The participants were 546 adults comprising 105 violent offenders, 238 university students and 203 men and women from a community sample. The differences between offenders and non-offenders in violent attitudes was measured by the Violent and Criminal Sentiments Scale. The differences in attributional biases and problem solving was assessed by a set of measure designed for this study. The results showed that offenders were clearly different from non-offenders with the offenders endorsing significantly higher criminal and violent sentiments with an effect size of η^2 =.46. The offenders also reported a significantly higher level of violence-based resolution strategies to end grievances than non-offenders. However, the surprising finding was that the adult male high-risk offenders did not demonstrate more pronounced hostile attributional biases than either adult men and women students or men and women from the community. The results imply that believing violence is acceptable and being prepared to use violence is more explanatory than how a person interprets the social behaviour of others. These findings have important implications for our understanding of why people behave aggressively and for the development of more effective intervention programs.

[•] Phone:+061 450230115. E-mail: Sally.kelty@utas.edu.au or sally.fiona.kelty@gmail.com.

INTRODUCTION

Violent crime has far reaching social and economic effects on both a macro level, for society as a whole, and on a micro level for the persons directly affected by this form of crime. Although the true social cost cannot be quantified it has been estimated that the cost to run the criminal justice system alone exceeds $1 billion per annum. The cost to adjudicate (policing, trial and imprisonment) each murder case exceeds $1 million. Of the approximate 150,000 non-sexual assault victims per annum in Australia, around 30% (57,000 victims) require medical attention, in many cases surgery or prolonged physical rehabilitation (Mukherjee and Graycar, 1997).

There are also numerous economic and social costs for the persons directly affected. For the victim there is the potential for long periods of physical rehabilitation and medical treatment, the temporary or permanent loss of employment through injury, and the potential for sustained emotional trauma. These effects may carry over to the victims' immediate and extended family, friends and work colleagues. For the offender there is the loss of liberty, sometimes for a substantial period of their lives. There is the potential for disruption of, and dislocation from, the immediate and extended family unit. Disruption of the family unit and the separation of and reuniting with children upon release is especially problematic for female offenders and their families. There is also a potential for the loss of employment skills that may become redundant while imprisoned. This in turn can then provide for long-term unemployment upon release. The effect of having the label "violent offender" on criminal history can have profound implications such as the restriction to travel to certain countries and loss of employment opportunities because employers prefer not to employ ex-offenders (Graffam, Shinfield, Lavelle and Hardcastle, 2005). For example, in Australia it is common practice to request that new employees produce a criminal history. The sheet, obtained from Police stations, details both State offences (e.g. violent offences) and Federal (e.g.: social security fraud). Records of index violent offences (assault, robbery) remain on criminal history for 10 years, murder convictions remain for life.

Rehabilitation Programs for Violent Offenders

With the social and economic implications of violent crime for society in mind, public policy has turned its focus to the implementation of violence prevention initiatives (such as domestic violence help lines) and intervention programs for violent offenders aiming to reduce recidivism (Howells and Day, 1999). This interest in the rehabilitation of violent offenders is not unique to Australia but is an issue that has emerged worldwide. Howells, Watt, Hall and Baldwin (1997) noted that the rehabilitation of violent offenders is an important issue because violent offenders represent over 50% of the prison population in many countries and cause considerable social concern due to the perceived or real "risk" of their re-offending when released.

Rehabilitation of offenders can take different forms. Currently there are three categories: vocational training (such as carpentry apprenticeships); educational (basic literacy/numeracy to university degrees); and offending behaviour programs (drug use, violent and sex offending). It is often the case that completion of an offender behaviour program is a requirement passed down during judgement as a necessary condition for parole consideration or has been requested by the Parole Board.

The question of whether violent offending treatment programs or offender behaviour programs in general have been effective in reducing recidivism rates has been a contentious issue for the past 35 years. This issue is not just a philosophical debate (should offenders be rehabilitated?) or empirical (does rehabilitation reduce recidivism?), it is also underpinned by the economic factor of whether the benefit (reduction in recidivism) equals or exceeds the cost (all economic units in terms of resources required for the intervention) (South, 1998). With respect to the empirical question, one of the most controversial papers written on the topic was by Martinson who concluded that from the evidence it appeared that very little worked to reduce recidivism. As for the economic question, South's (1998) conclusion was equally as negative as Martinson's when he concluded that overall the cost of rehabilitation was probably too high, and for programs that were effective the cost-benefit ratio of carrying out an intervention was usually too low.

In contrast to the more negative position, there has been a growing number of extensive meta-analyses and empirical reviews using pooled samples in excess of 10,000 offenders from Canada, the U.S., England and Australasia which found that rehabilitation programs can significantly reduce recidivism rates by 5 to 20% (refer especially Andrews and Bonta, 2010; Gendreau, Little and Goggin, 1996; Polaschek and Collie, 2004). Bourgon and Armstrong (2005) reported that a 10% reduction in recidivism following program completion can equate to an average cost benefit to the community of between U.S. $4,653 to $80,000 per offender. Of the rehabilitation programs that were found to be successful, it appeared that the majority of these programs are underpinned by Andrews and Bonta's risk-needs-responsivity principles. These principles are outlined below.

The Risk Principle

The risk principle refers to the matching of an offender's recidivism risk to the level of intervention required. Assessing risk requires the identification of criminogenic variables, which are comprised of two distinct types. The first are static criminogenic variables, for example: criminal history; environmental factors during childhood; intellectual disability; and age at first offending. Although static variables correlate with offending behaviour they primarily represent historical factors that cannot be changed through intervention. The second criminogenic factors are the dynamic variables, which include: illicit drug use; criminal attitudes; criminal affiliations; problem solving skills; education; and employment skills. Dynamic variables correlate with criminal behaviour and as such are able to be addressed during rehabilitation programs. Both the static and dynamic variables predict recidivism risk (Ogloff and Davis, 2004).

This principle is underpinned by the rationale that level of risk is matched to level of intervention. It follows that only offenders at high risk of recidivism are provided with high intensity interventions (Ogloff and Davis, 2004). Bourgon and Armstrong (2005) recently assessed how the criminogenic needs of 482 male adult offenders were matched to interventions with regard to the length of the rehabilitation program in time and whether this impacted on recidivism rates. To assess recidivism risk Bourgon and Armstrong used "The Level of Service Inventory- Ontario Revised". They found that each week of treatment predicted 1.7% reduction in risk. For offenders at low-risk who had few needs, programs could reduce recidivism rates significantly after only after 100 hours (5 weeks) of intervention. For high risk offenders with multiple needs, recidivism rates could reduce by 20% but only after 300 hours of intervention was completed (15 weeks).

The Needs Principle

The needs principle holds that although all human beings have needs (such as accommodation) but not all needs are criminogenic in nature. Therefore, it is only criminogenic needs that should be targeted during rehabilitation. For example, most people like to have and need friends. Having friends per se should not be the focus of rehabilitation unless the friends are pro-criminal and act as a source of reinforcement for an individual's offending behaviour.

Ogloff and Davis (2004) argue that the needs identified for intervention may not be the same needs that an offender identifies. As such, there should be a distinction made between the identification of general needs and "treatment needs". The needs principle when applied correctly provides that although offenders may have a wide range of needs, to reduce recidivism risk one must concentrate on the variables directly related to why they offend.

The Responsivity Principle

The final principle is responsivity which relates to the identification of potential sources, be they internal or external, which impact upon the effectiveness of the program. Internal sources refer to individual difference factors, such as offenders' motivation to fully participate in a program, or the intelligence level of the offender. For example, if an offender has literacy problems and treatment staff are not fully aware of this, unfinished homework may be construed as poor motivation rather than what it actually represents. External sources refer to factors not directly related to an offender that can have a negative or positive impact on program effectiveness. For example, does the institution support and consider the program worthwhile; are treatment staff competent, trained, and supervised; and can the treatment staff employed develop a therapeutic relationship with the offenders in the program (Ogloff and Davis, 2004). Finally, of importance is the method of delivery. Empirical evaluations of programs have found that cognitive-behavioural approaches work better than other therapeutic methods (Andrews and Bonta, 2010).

Dynamic Criminogenic Needs of Violent Offenders

As discussed above, of vital importance to effective offending behaviour rehabilitation is the identification of dynamic criminogenic variables (treatment needs). The findings from extensive reviews and meta-analyses suggested that some of the important variables are antisocial attitudes, anti-social peers, poor problem solving skills, high impulsivity and low self-management, cognitive processing deficits (especially the appraisal and interpretation of social situations), lack of empathy and high hostility and anger (Howells and Day,1999).

In a review of rehabilitation programs for violent offenders, Polaschek and Collie (2004) argued there appears to be very little empirical understanding of which dynamic needs actually underpin violent behaviour. The Polaschek and Collie (2004) review found that anger management programs did not always have a significant effect in reducing violent recidivism and they argue that at present there is little empirical support to suggest that anger should be considered a special criminogenic need underpinning violent offending. They suggest that anger is neither necessary nor sufficient for violence to occur. Polaschek and Collie also found that cognitive processing deficits and problem solving skills could not yet be confirmed as important criminogenic variables because the empirical literature is too limited. This was also the case for beliefs that endorse violence.

Based on the seminal literature above, it appears that although the method for effective rehabilitation has been examined in detail it is reasonable to suggest that there is an urgent requirement to empirically establish what dynamic criminogenic needs underpin violent offending. This is especially so for countries with high rates of physical assault and violent crime to develop a richer understanding of what variables underpin aggressive behaviour of citizens. In many countries around the world, it is apparent that approximately 60% of violent incidents occur between people in a known relationship, either a close relationship or acquaintances. Although approximately 40% of violent incidents occur between strangers, especially for young males, many of these assaults occur in specific urban locations and under certain environmental conditions. For example, assaults are more common between young men at the weekends and in public places such as recreational venues or non-residential areas, primarily city centres. Ross and Polk (2005) considered that too much emphasis is placed on "violence between strangers" and that violent acts are not usually random or senseless, at least from the perspective of the offender. For instance, although the parties to a violent incident may state they did not know each other prior to the incident, the social interaction occurring between them, such as honour contests and reputation maintenance, is in essence not that different to the social interaction between the parties in a known relationship which escalate into serious or lethal acts of violence (Ross and Polk, 2005).

Grievance Escalation Theories and Criminognic Factors Underpinning Aggression

The Escalation of Grievances: Luckenbill and Doyle's Model

To explain how disagreements escalate into grievances which end in violence, Lukenbill and Doyle (1989) devised a grievance escalation model comprised of three interrelated successive stages. The first stage is "naming". Naming occurs when a negative outcome is transformed into a grievance. Grievances develop when one party (the victim) perceives/recognises that another party (victimiser) has caused harm. Furthermore, it is necessary that the victim holds the victimiser accountable for their "bad behaviour". The second stage of the model is "claiming". Claiming refers to the transformation of the grievance into a demand for reparation. Luckenbill and Doyle noted there were several outcomes that could occur during the claiming stage. The victimiser can apologise and make reparation thus bringing the grievance to an end. However, if the victimiser rejects the claim in whole or part, the grievance can escalate into the third stage, "aggression".

Luckenbill and Doyle's (1989) model does not imply that all problematic social encounters end in violence. What this model provides is an understanding of the stages of a conflict and how a grievance can escalate into violence. For escalation to occur, the model hypothesises that several factors are present. First, the injured party will not only have taken the position of a "victim" but is willing to demand that the harm be rectified. This willingness is referred to as disputationess. Disputationess is suggested to discriminate between people.

For example, not all people who experience injustice or are harmed by another will make a claim or persevere with a grievance. Therefore, their level of "disputationess" is considered low when they would rather let some incidents slide rather than persevere with all the grievances they encounter in their personal lives. The second factor is whether a person is willing to engage in coercive action or violence to end a grievance. This factor is called "aggressiveness". However, this factor is as much about a "victim" using violence to settle the grievance as it is about the social interaction between the parties. For example, after the "victim" makes a claim the manner in which the "victimiser" responds to the claim can have a significant impact on the likelihood of the grievance ending in coercion or violence. Escalation thus occurs through the interaction between the parties to the grievance in terms of their combined personal levels of disputationess and aggressiveness.

In this model disputationess and aggressiveness are suggested to relate to beliefs and values that state when and what type of harm cannot be ignored and when and where violence is not just warranted but required. These values and beliefs are considered to be subcultural and relate to certain groups in society. The suggestion that disputationess and aggressiveness are a manifestation of subcultural values was based upon the official criminal justice statistics which show an unequal distribution of violent behaviour occurring in most Western societies where it is specific demographic groups that engage in a disproportionate number of conflicts and amount of violence. For example, in the U.S. (where Lukenbill and Doyle's (1989) model was devised) a higher proportion of violence occurs: in the Southern States compared with the Northern States; between persons of low socio-economic status (SES) relative to higher SES peers; between African Americans than any other ethnic group; and violence occurs more often in urban than rural locations. Furthermore, young males have more interpersonal conflicts and engage in a far higher proportion of violence than older men or women of any age (Luckenbill and Doyle, 1989).

The values and beliefs that endorse high levels of disputationess and aggressiveness are not suggested to be strict codes of behaviour specifically related to places but rather to a group of people who share and understand these values. For example, some young males believe that derogatory remarks made about themselves, their mothers or girlfriends cannot be ignored because to do so is considered a display of weakness which would undermine their beliefs about honour and masculinity. The subculture (or group of associates) a person identifies can also be influence if they expect one of their peers / members to respond to an insult rather than let it slide. For the other party to the interaction (the insulter) the corresponding beliefs would be that to apologise is also a sign of weakness and "a real man doesn't back down". In this scenario, escalation would also be more likely given certain environmental conditions, such as in a recreational venue with significant peers present.

Support for the three stages of Luckenbill and Doyle's (1989) model was found by Kennedy and Forde (1996) and Bell and Forde (1999). Both studies tested the model using scenarios detailing interactions between a harm-doer and a victim. In the scenarios the level of harm was presented in a range from a minor conflict (name calling) to a severe high-intensity grievance (actual physical attack). Each participant was asked to take the role of the victim. Kennedy and Forde used a community sample of 2052 Canadian men and women with a mean age of 39 years. They found that the more intense and more severe the harm, the higher the levels of upset respondents reported. Regardless of a participant's SES level, or the amount of harm caused, approximately 65% of the sample stated they would make a claim and demand the harm-doer give an explanation or repair the damage. Kennedy and Forde also found that roughly 15% of this general community sample said they would resort to aggression to solve the grievance. Finally, the men in this sample were not only more likely to report they would make a claim, the men were also more likely to report they would resort to aggression to deal with the matter than women. Later research by Bell and Forde (1999) supported these findings.

This research is not just in line with U.S. criminal statistics, but mirrors the justice statistics found in the U.K. and Australia. This implies that Luckenbill and Doyle's (1989) model may be a reasonable basis to describe the process and stages of how grievances escalate in Western nations. However, the model only provides one reason for the escalation of grievances, namely that some people believe using force to settle some grievances is reasonable and legitimate and the discussion of violent beliefs is not comprehensive. Although attitudes and beliefs have been found to be a reasonable predictor of a range of behaviours (Ajzen and Fishbein, 1986) they alone do not account for 100% of the variance in thinking and behaviour (Ajzen and Madden, 1986). Therefore an extension of Luckenbill and Doyle's work could potentially provide a more comprehensive and useful working model of the factors that produce higher levels of disputationess and aggressiveness. There are three potential areas that could enhance the model. First, to explain the type of harm that can upset people enough to make them proceed into the second escalation stage and make a "claim". Second, to examine the psychological processes that people use to consider their harmdoer responsible and guilty for their injury. In other words, the transformation of harmdoer to victimiser. Finally, the model would benefit from a more in-depth discussion of how attitudes and beliefs influence the decision to engage in criminal and violent behaviour. Each of these areas will be discussed in more detail below. Included in the discussion will be the identification of several variables that could enhance the theoretical underpinning of this model.

Grievance Escalation and the Types of Harm that Underpin Aggressive Behavior

Tedeschi and Felson (1994) proposed four main types of harm that can underpin grievances: physical harm (injury, pain, or the threat of injury or pain); material damage (loss of goods or services); psychological harm (lack of respect, fairness or equality); political harm (violation of rights and freedoms by the state or organisations). The recent work of interactional justice theorists in Europe found that psychological harm (such as broken promises, selfish behaviour or lack of respect and loyalty) upsets people more than physical, material or political harm (Mikula, Perti and Tanzer, 1990). These researchers found that although physical, political and material harm are judged as wrongful acts, it is the effects of psychological harm(especially when the harm is carried out by significant others) that has more impact on the development of negative emotions and the desire for revenge. They found that people are more likely to experience a wider range of emotions (anger, despair, sadness, anxiety) when lied to, insulted by, unfairly accused or let down by a family member or friend rather than by their boss or an organisation (Mikula, Scherer and Athenstaedt, 1998). Bies and Tripp (1996) had found similar results in that people overwhelmingly experienced only anger and resentment when they believed their employer had acted unjustly towards them or their work colleagues. Miller (2001) suggested this occurs because people expect organisations to be less than honourable, so therefore when an organisation or representative thereof acts unjustly, although it is perceived as unpleasant and anger provoking, it is not totally unexpected. In contrast, a different and stricter set of standards is usually set for significant others and people we encounter in daily life (e.g., friends, co-workers, neighbours, even strangers) and when these people behave "badly" we are more affected because we expect to receive "better" behaviour from them. In other words we do not expect or consider it right that ordinary people lie, accuse, dishonour, cheat or insult us.

The standards of behaviour and expectations Miller (2001) referred to are the standards of interpersonal sensitivity continued in the psychological contract we have with others. These abstract contracts represent our idiosyncratic norms of behaviour that we not only expect but believe we are entitled to receive from others. Although most people report wanting similar behaviour from others (such as respect, fairness, equality; Mikula et al., 1990) the actual amount of that behaviour (e.g., how much respect or equality) required to satisfy idiosyncratic norms varies between persons. For example, one person can believe they deserve complete respect and fairness from all people all the time, while another person may not set such a strict standard and only expect respect and fairness from certain people. Hojjat (1997) refers to Miller's standards of behaviours as "ought" philosophies. "Oughts" are moral based values and beliefs which state what we believe ought to be. For example, marriage partners ought to be honourable, faithful, respectful and obey their partners (Hojjat, 1997).

Miller (2001) explained that one problem with holding "ought" beliefs is that when fundamental "oughts" are breached it can be upsetting, anger provoking and can also lead to resentment. One reason why people become upset and angry, according to Ferguson and Rule (1983), is that a wide discrepancy is created between the "is" and the "ought". "Is" beliefs are subjective evaluations of what we think happened. "Is" beliefs are then balanced against the "oughts"; beliefs about what ought or should have happened. The wider the discrepancy the more likely we are to feel negative emotions (whether it be disappointment, anger, sadness, humiliation) which in turn fuels the desire to get even (Miller, 2001).

Hogan and Emler (1981) stressed that when we think that another person has broken one of our "oughts", the other person has done more than just violate our expectations. The breach can be seen as a sign that the harmdoer does not care to play the social game with us and ignores the "rules" of reciprocity in respectful dealings between people. They also argued that the natural response to "ought" breaches is moralistic and righteous rage. The emotional and cognitive state of righteous rage can then flow naturally into the desire for revenge, justice and retribution. Miller (2001) argues that because righteous rage occurs out of a belief that another has immorally violated our "oughts", it is more likely that people will feel justified and right about seeking revenge. Getting even or an act of revenge can be seen as the means to restore justice. Bies and Tripp (1996) when examining grievances in workplaces found that the more a wronged employee considered their boss's behaviour to be "morally bad", the more likely they were to be morally outraged at their treatment. Many of these employees sought to get even through less personal work motivation or even acts of theft or industrial sabotage. Importantly, the employees reported that due to the "bad behaviour" to which they been subjected they felt that the psychological contract between them and the firm had been so fundamentally breached that decent behaviour toward the firm was no longer required. The findings of Bies and Tripp underpin the essence of Bandura's (1990) theory that once we believe another person has acted "immorally" toward us we feel justified in disengaging from the moral codes of behaviour we usually set for ourselves.

Applying Strict and Rigid "Oughts" to Others

In summary, the research to date has found that it is primarily psychological harm that upsets people the most. This is due to perceived breaches of the standards of behaviour people expect from others with regard to being treated fairly, equitably and respectfully (Mikula et al., 1990). It appears that for most people being treated fairly, respectfully and equitably represents fundamental "oughts" (Miller, 2001). One way that people perceive a harm is by benchmarking what they think the other person did and their responsibility for what they did ("is") against what they think other person should have done ("ought") (Ferguson and Rule, 1983). The wider the discrepancy between the "is" and the "ought" the more likely people are to experience anger, disappointment, resentment, frustration, anxiety and/or sadness (Mikula et al., 1998). When it is a fundamental "ought" that has been (or perceived to have been) breached this can not only lead to the development of negative emotions but also the desire to get even. The act of revenge, due to the very nature of the perceived breach, can be viewed by the victim (who becomes the retaliator) as a righteous act necessary to get justice (Aronson, 2004). In essence a wide "is/ought" discrepancy occurs due to a moral judgement about other's "bad behaviour".

Both Howells (1988) and Tedeschi and Felson (1994) suggested that the "is/ought" discrepancy represents a cognitive component in the initial development of grievances. The work of Felson (1982, 2000) has consistently shown that offenders appear to be highly sensitive to one form of psychological harm, namely insults and accusations, and that this type of harm creates a high desire to retaliate as a means of restoring personal honour and to maintain a favourable impression. As non-offenders also engage in this cognitive evaluation of the behaviour of others it cannot be implied that this discrepancy represents a dynamic criminogenic variable per se, although there are two ways that the process could potentially be problematic. The first is where people consistently encounter wide discrepancies due to the strict application of "ought" philosophies. Ellis (2002) noted that some people encounter difficulties in the relationships with others because "ought" philosophies become extreme and are manifested as "must haves" and "should haves". The problem that arises from strict and rigid "ought" application is that other people cannot usually live up to such rigid and high standards even if they wanted to. At the extreme such high "oughts" do not even leave room for non-intentional errors such as forgetting. This can lead a person who applies "oughts" too strictly to believe that their "oughts" are always being breached and can lead to the development of what Ellis (2002) calls irrational beliefs, such as "people always let me down, people cannot be trusted, loved ones hurt and humiliate me all the time".

The essence of what Ellis observed with non-offender clinical cases appears to underpin what Toch (1969) and Bush (1995) have found with offenders. Toch noted from his research that offenders appeared to find it acceptable to breach other people's "oughts" but found it intolerable when others broke their own "oughts" and caused them harm, be it psychological or physical.

Bush (1995) in his clinical work with violent offenders also noted similar aspects, in that offenders disliked having their autonomy threatened. This Bush suggested was based on the philosophy that they believe they have the right to set the rules for how they live their life. However, when others break their "oughts" and make them feel unpleasant, humiliated or guilty, they see the actions of others as an affront which turns from "how could they" to "how dare they make me feel bad".

Although the rigid stance that offenders take toward how other people should behave has been suggested by Bush (1995) it appears that the "is/ought" discrepancy has not been examined as a potential criminogenic variable.

After an extensive search of the literature and numerous databases no published work could be located examining the circumstances creating the "is/ought" discrepancy and the differences between an offender and non-offender sample. To see if this variable distinguishes offenders from non-offenders became one aim of this study.

Applying strict and rigid "oughts" to others is not the only manner in which a wide "is/ought" discrepancy could be problematic. Howells (1988) suggested that another way was when the discrepancy itself occurred due to biased cognitive attributions of intention, specifically the attribution of hostile intent.

When the discrepancy occurs in this manner it is possible that another person who breaches an "ought" is viewed as deliberately and maliciously causing harm, when in reality although harm occurred it occurred through an unintentional thoughtless error. The theory and research on the attribution of hostile intent is discussed below.

Attributions of Hostile and Malevolent Intent

Attributions of hostile intent are suggested to be influential in aggressive behaviour. Both Dodge (2006) and Krahe (2001) argue that the reason some people use violence is because they interpret the behaviour of others, especially in ambiguous situations, as motivated by hostility. Knowledge in this area originated in studies comparing aggressive children, violent juvenile offenders and older aggressive adolescences with their non-aggressive peers (Bailey and Ostrov, 2008; Dodge, 2006; Huesman, 1998; Slaby and Guerra, 1988). This literature has consistently found that violent children and adolescents, especially males, demonstrate a significantly higher level of Hostile Attributional Biases (HABs) than non-violent peers (de Castro, Veerman, Koops et al., 2002).

The link between HABs and violent behaviour in adults features heavily in the forensic theoretical literature. Despite this emphasis in the literature, the empirical research using adult samples (aged 18 years and over) appears to be less abundant than studies which uses children and adolescents. After an extensive search, using numerous electronic databases and literature reviews, only a few studies linking HABs and violent behaviour in adults could be located. In 1995, Epps and Kendall examined the HABs and violent behaviour link in an adult sample of 120 male and female psychology undergraduates divided into four groups: men and women who were high or low on trait anger and aggression. Each participant interpreted 22 social scenarios, such as "being jostled in the hallway". The scenarios were written to reflect three types of intent underpinning the harmdoer's behaviour in each scenario, either explicitly hostile or benign or where the intent was ambiguous. Epps and Kendall found that participants high on self-reported trait anger and aggression demonstrated significantly higher HABs than their less trait angry and aggressive peers in both the hostile and ambiguous scenarios, and also to a lesser extent in the benign scenarios. Further, participants high on trait anger/aggression were found to be much more accurate at seeing the hostile cues in the hostile situations than their peers. In the benign scenarios, the students high on anger/aggression were significantly more likely to hone in on the minority of hostile cues while passing over the majority benign cues. Sex differences were also found with males in the high anger/aggression group demonstrating higher HABs than any other group, especially for benign statements. Epps and Kendall hypothesised that aggressive people learn to expect aggression and therefore believe they see hostility and malice in the behaviour of others when no hostility was intended. They also suggested that as aggressive people store in memory new hostile social scripts they simultaneously reinforce old hostile scripts. This means that over time aggressive people expect aggression and hostility from others and therefore respond disproportionately to a minimum number of hostile cues while unconsciously ignoring non-hostile cues.

In 2002, Simourd and Mamuza reported the mean differences in HABs between two samples: 146 high-risk violent Canadian male prisoners and 104 male and 33 female low-risk U.S. offenders serving community probation sentences. HABs were measured using the "Hostile Interpretations Questionnaire" (HIQ: Simourd and Mamuza, 2002). The HIQ presents participants with a series of seven statements and asks them to interpret the motive of each harmdoer. Each situation in the HIQ was based on clinical experience of common social situations that Canadian offenders have found problematic, such as interactions with family members, police and parole officers. Although the HIQ manual did not provide any results on the statistical differences between the prisoner sample and community sample, the means presented in the manual showed that the community probationers had higher total HIQ mean scores (M = 69.9) than prisoners (M = 58.6), suggesting that the lower recidivism risk offenders demonstrated higher HABs than the higher risk violent prison sample. As Simourd and Mamuza said, the higher HABs demonstrated by the lower-risk non-violent offender sample was surprising.

In a recent study Seager (2005) examined hostile cognitive schemas as manifested through HABs, impulsivity and psychopathy. His sample were 50 male violent Canadian prisoners. Seager hypothesised that persistently violent men have greater expectations of a hostile social world (hostile schemata) which would be manifested through high impulsivity scores, high scores on the Psychopathy Check List -Revised (PCL-R) and high HABs to socially ambiguous written vignettes. The results supported this chain of reasoning. Higher psychopathy scores on the PCL-R were significantly and positively related with: higher impulsivity scores; higher number of assaults; prison violence rating; and high levels of HABs. Based on these results Seager suggested that written vignettes were a satisfactory measure to tap into the underlying construct of hostile social world schemas. He also hypothesised that violent men who expect the social world to be hostile impulsively confirm their HABs and react accordingly. However, as Seager pointed out, these results were speculative only and need replication primarily due to the small and "extreme" sample of prisoners used (violent offenders classified as high on psychopathy).

Although HABs have been shown to be a discriminant variable in adolescents, due to the lack of adult empirical findings and conflictory findings, it is difficult to determine whether HABs represent an adolescent limited risk factor or one that extends to adults past adolescence. Hence the criminogenic nature of HABs has yet to be fully demonstrated in adults. At present it appears that there is no published and peer-reviewed literature on the differences between mainstream (e.g., not high on psychopathy) adult violent offenders and non-offenders, especially a random sample of non-offenders from the general population. This gap in the literature is of concern because we cannot say with confidence whether HABs are an important criminogenic risk factor that discriminates offenders from non-offenders. This means we cannot assume that HABs should be targeted in violent offender rehabilitation.

Also of concern are the two discrepancies between study findings and some counterintuitive findings which deviate from what the hypothesis relating high HABs to violent behaviour would predict.

The first discrepancy is the conditions under which HABs operate most strongly. Unlike the child and adolescent empirical literature which found that HABs are primarily problematic under ambiguous social situations, the adult literature provides conflicting results. For example, Epps and Kendall (1995) found that aggressive university students demonstrated higher HABs in a wide range of both hostile and ambiguous, and to a lesser degree in benign social situations relative to their less aggressive student peers. However, Copello and Tata (1990), Matthews and Norris (2002), and Holtzworth-Munroe and Hutchinson (1993) found that HABs appeared problematic only in ambiguous situations.

The second discrepancy is whether HABs are associated with a range of violent behaviour by adults, especially interpersonally violent acts like assault, or only problematic for specific acts of violence like road rage and spousal abuse. If HABs are problematic for violent adults in a range of social situations then it is reasonable to suggest that people known to engage in high levels of interpersonal violence should demonstrate higher HABs than their less aggressive peers. The findings by Copello and Tata (1990), Simourd and Mamuza (2002), and now Vitale et al., (2005) appear counterintuitive to what would be expected.

Although the adult research reviewed above provides tentative support for the hypothesis that HABs represent a risk factor for adults who engage in violent behaviour, there is one question that the current literature cannot answer: do adult violent offenders engage in a higher level of HABs than non-offending adults from the general community? This question is of vital importance because due to the lack of empirical findings using adult samples, it is unclear whether HABs represent a dynamic criminogenic variable for adults or is primarily an adolescent limited cognitive process. Answering this question became one of the aims of the current project where HABs will be compared in three distinct samples: violent offenders; non-offender university students; and non-offender men from the community.

In order to carry out this aim it was necessary to consider how to compare HABs in violent offenders and non-offenders. As discussed above in the child and adolescent review, de Castro et al., (2002) found that the stimulus method used to measure HABs had a significant impact on the effect size obtained for assessing between group differences, the highest effect size being for actual staged social interactions between participants and research confederates. Despite this method being the most optimal from a research perspective, it would be highly unethical to stage a mock social interaction with adults who have a known history of engaging in serious acts of violence. Assessing HABs via written vignettes or scenarios was found to produce a medium effect size (de Castro et al., 2002). Six of the seven adult studies reviewed above had used this method and had reported good reliability and validity for the scenarios.

In Epps and Kendall's (1995) study vignettes were specially written to describe typical situations that students attending a university could relate to and would commonly find themselves in. Although Epps and Kendall reported good reliability, their scenarios were so specific to being a student (e.g., interactions between students and lecturers) they may not necessarily be relevant to offenders or adults who had not attended university or college. Simourd and Mamuza (2002), Seager (2005) and Vitale et al., (2005) presented their offender participants with scenarios detailing different kinds of situations that clinicians had noted offenders found problematic, such as interactions with prison inmates, police and parole officers. Again, although overall good validity and reliability were reported for each of these scales, the situations assessed were relevant for offenders and may not necessarily be relevant to non-offenders (for instance, interactions with parole officers). After assessing the content of the scenarios from the reviewed studies and after an extensive search of peer-reviewed published sources, a suitable scale to measure the differences between offenders and non-offenders could not be located. Therefore, an additional aim was to develop a psychometric scale that would be useful in multiple settings. To achieve this aim the scenarios contained in the scale would need to be applicable and relevant to prisoners, offenders on community orders, university undergraduates, and non-offenders in the community. As Aronson (2004) noted, if researchers want valid information about what or how people think, it is essential that people are asked to discuss issues they can understand and relate to. The aim here was that the scale once developed would be useful for both research purposes and for clinical applications.

Violent and Criminal Sentiments

Criminal beliefs and antisocial sentiments hold a prominent place in many influential sociology, criminology and psychology theories of criminal behaviour, such as seminal social learning theory (Akers, 1997). Within Andrews and Bonta's (2010) general personality and social psychological theory of criminal behaviour, pro-criminal attitudes and pro-criminal peer affiliations, along with criminal history and selected personality factors (such as impulsivity and antisocial personality) comprise the 'big four' risk factors for criminal behaviour.

Empirical research has found a series of highly significant relationships with high-risk offender samples reporting a higher negativity toward the criminal justice system, endorsing a higher level of attitudes supportive of law violation and higher identification with criminal peers compared with lower-risk offenders, and non-offenders (Andrews and Bonta, 2010; Stevenson, Hall, and Inness, 2004). Large meta-analytical studies (using pooled samples of up to 11,962 offenders), have found that endorsement of pro-criminal sentiments represents the highest risk factor for recidivism for both men and women (Gendreau, Little, and Goggin, 1996). High endorsement of these sentiments is one of the strongest predictors of violent recidivism and non-sexual recidivism for convicted sex offenders (Andrews and Bonta, 2010).

Over the past twenty years a large body of literature has detailed the role that criminal sentiments play in recidivism (Andrews and Bonta, 2010). In contrast, empirical knowledge of violent sentiments is limited (Kelty, Hall, and O'Brien-Malone, 2011). In Thomson's (1997) situational analysis of drinking and violent encounters in pubs located in Sydney, Australia, he found that participants did not specifically seek a "brawl", but rather they engaged in violent acts (often fights in the car park) following hostile altercations with other patrons. Common reasons for fights were explicit allegations of cheating at pool, approaches to girlfriends, and drink spills followed by verbal insults. Thomson suggested that most violence was related to "face-saving" rather than the pursuit of violence for the sake of it.

Kelty et al. (2011) in their study with 18 violent men obtained comparable results to Thomson and Indermaur. In the Kelty et al study, the men said their use of violence was to them acceptable and understandable given the "bad behaviour" they had been experienced from the other party to the grievance. Kelty et al. found that grievances developed after people believed they were insulted, lied to, or deceived and that violence was acceptable given that the other person did very little (i.e., apologise) to correct the harm. These findings suggest that people who use violence do not always approve of violence per se, but given some circumstances violence is justifiable or necessary. In this respect, violent acts are goal directed and underpinned by whether a person supports the use of violence to resolve certain situations in which they find themselves. As Polaschek and Reynolds (2001) argued, if attitudes supportive of violence are a risk factor for recidivism, it is desirable these beliefs be addressed in rehabilitation programs and that program outcomes are objectively assessed using a valid violent attitude scales both pre-and post intervention. Polaschek and Reynolds considered that our limited empirical knowledge of the endorsement of violent sentiments by offenders was primarily due to the lack of valid psychometric scales.

VIOLENCE BASED SOCIAL PROBLEM SOLVING STRATEGIES

In Luckenbill and Doyle's (1989) grievance escalation model it was proposed that a key factor influencing whether a grievance escalates aggressively is the concept of 'disputationess', or the willingness to end a dispute with the use/threat of physical force. This willingness is suggested to be underpinned by beliefs which view violence as an acceptable way to end disputes in order to maintain reputation, to enhance self image and/or to teach the harmdoer a lesson (Tedeschi, and Felson, 1994). Disputationess in Willingness in Luckenbill and Doyle's model is akin to Ajzen and Fishbein's (1980) psychological theory of reasoned action where the more positive your attitude towards a certain behaviour, (i.e. pro-violent beliefs) the more likely you will engage in that behaviour (i.e. violence). In this study 'disputationess' will be explored empirically through problem solving solutions to a range of social situations generated by violent offenders compared with non-offenders.

In a study by Slaby and Guerra (1988) they found that violent juvenile male and females were more likely to demonstrate aggression-based solutions to social problems than their non-offender peers. Moreover, the delinquent group were also more likely to come up with single solutions while their non-violent peers were more likely to come up with a number of alternative solutions to fix social problems. Slaby and Guerra argued that offenders have an inability to generate alternative solutions and this difficulty related to their reliance on aggression. The final aim of this study was to assess whether the Slaby and Guerra findings applied to adults; in essence to see whether their findings are adolescent limited or represent a risk factor for adults offenders as well.

AIMS AND HYPOTHESES OF THE CURRENT RESEARCH

This program of research comprises of two studies.

Study 1

The objective of study 1 is to explore the criminogenic nature of attributional biases and aggressive and non aggressive problem solving to a range of social situations. Three hypotheses are set for this study. Although pronounced HABs have been observed in violent adolescent samples, the adult literature has not yet fully demonstrated whether adult violent offenders are different to adult non-offenders.

If HABs are a criminogenic variable for adult offenders then for Hypothesis 1 it is predicted that: *male offenders will demonstrate significantly higher HABs, especially in ambiguous situations compared with non-offenders.* An additional aim is to investigate whether there were any differences between adult violent offenders and non-offenders on the two forms of HABs: hostile and malevolent intent.

The willingness to solve social problems with violence is tested in Hypothesis 2. If offenders have difficulty generating non-aggressive based solutions to everyday social problems they encounter, then the following patterns will be observed in the data: *male offenders will report more violence based solutions than male students. Younger male students in turn will report more violence based strategies than female students and men and women from the community.*

Finally, can the highly significant findings of Slaby and Guerra (1988), using an adolescent sample, generalise to adults. In Hypothesis 3 it is predicted that if a risk factor for violent behaviour is the generation of fewer alternative problem solving strategies then: *male offenders will report a lower number of problem solving solutions than non-offenders.*

Of note, although the optimal way to measure hostile intent would be to experimentally stage a socially problematic situation and observe how participants will respond, then ask them what they were thinking as close to the end of the staged event as possible. When measuring hostile situations that could escalate into violence this is not an ethically sound way to research the phenomenon. In this study the author used the method of presenting participants with scenarios, similar methods were developed in earlier studies on HABs.

Study 2

The objective of Study 2 was to explore further the criminogenic nature of violent sentiments. Two hypotheses are explored in Study 2. Hypothesis 1 explored whether violent sentiments represented a valid and related fourth construct to the current criminal sentiments framework. *It was predicted that if violent sentiments are related to criminal sentiments then highly significant relationships will exist where higher justifications for violence relate to a higher disrespect for the law and justice system, a greater willingness to neutralise criminal behaviour, and a higher identification with criminal others.*

The second hypothesis explored whether violent sentiments represent an important criminogenic risk factor that can discriminate offenders from non-offenders. *It was predicted that people with a low risk of actual violent behaviour will endorse a very low level of violent sentiments.*

As women represent a group in society with the lowest probability of behaving violently, women will endorse far lower violent sentiments than men.

In addition, as violence is primarily a young male phenomenon, with young Australian males three times more likely to be involved in violent altercations than older men, younger men in this study will endorse more pro-violent sentiments than older males. It was predicted in hypothesis two that: men offenders will endorse a higher level of violent and criminal sentiments than men or women non-offenders. Younger men will endorse more pro-violent sentiments than older men. Men will endorse more pro-violent sentiments than women.

STUDY 1: THE CRIMINOGENIC NATURE OF HABS AND AGGRESSIVE PROBLEM SOLVING

The objective of Study 1 was to explore further the potentially criminogenic nature of different types of social attributional biases and aggressive and non-aggressive problem solving strategies to social situations where the motives of the protagonists ranged from accidental to confrontational. Three hypotheses were set for Study 1.

Method

Participants and procedures. The Participants were 530 adult men and women recruited from three populations: offenders; students; and the general population. All procedures used complied with the NHMRC research guidelines. Consent was freely obtained and no rewards were provided to participants.

The Offender group were 87 men serving prison sentences for non-sexual violent index offences (firearms offences, armed robbery, assault); their mean age was 31.7 years (SD = 8.45, range = 18 to 54). Their effective sentence length (sentence to first eligible parole date) ranged from 2 to 30 years, with a mean of 8.1 years (SD = 7.64). None of the participants had participated in prior intensive intervention for criminal attitudes thus avoiding the possible confound of treatment effects. One hundred and one offenders were invited to participate and 87 consented (response rate 86.13%). Sixty-four percent of the sample was general offenders, having criminal histories covering both violent and non-violent offences (e.g. assault, armed robbery, drink driving, receiving stolen goods), while 36% had been convicted of violent offences only (primarily murder or assault). All offenders were classified as being at high-risk of recidivism.

All offender participants were seen individually. Consent to participate was fully discussed before completing the questionnaire pack. To address the potential for poor literacy, each participant was offered two administration options, either self-completion or oral where the author read out the questions and wrote down the responses. Twenty-three participants chose the oral method and 64 participants chose to complete the pack themselves. Upon completion of the questionnaire, participants were given an overview of the study and the aims. Several participants informed the author they enjoyed doing the pack as it gave them an opportunity to think about the law and social behaviour in a manner not normally discussed in prison.

The student group were 235 first year undergraduates from Murdoch University, Perth, Western Australia. The 96 student men had a mean age of 25.30 years (SD = 7.93, range = 18

- 51). The 139 student women had a mean age of 27.59 years (SD = 10.07, range = 18 - 61). Four hundred and eighty students were asked to participate, 257 consented (54% response rate). Nineteen students were excluded from the study as they were aged 17, making them comparable to juvenile offenders rather than adults. In order to obtain a sample of participants that was wider than simply psychology students, the sample was recruited from all of the University's main schools. Ninety-one participants were from Psychology, 50 from Humanities, 22 from Business, 31 from Law, and 44 from Science and Engineering.

Two procedures were used. For psychology students it is a course requirement to participate in a research project. All projects are advertised on the School of Psychology web page and students select the project of their choice. In this study, students signed up on-line, collected the questionnaire pack from the author and returned the questionnaire anonymously to a sealed box. For non-psychology students they were recruited by the author after a brief study presentation at the start of various first year lectures. Questionnaire packs were then given to student volunteers who returned them anonymously two weeks later.

The community group were 108 men with a mean age of 48.20 years (SD = 13.99, range = 19 - 81) and 100 women with a mean age of 45.70 years (SD = 13.72, range = 19 - 84). I used a stratified cluster sampling method to collect this random sample of adults residing in Perth, Western Australian was used.

The sample frame developed used the 2001 Census of Population and Housing (ABS, 2002) to create four socio-economic suburb clusters based on median weekly income, average monthly rent/mortgage repayments per household. The four clusters were: High SES suburbs; Medium to High; Medium to Low; and Low SES. The second stage in the cluster sampling was the random selection (using Microsoft Excel to generate random numbers) of two suburbs from each of the SES clusters. Finally the streets within each suburb were selected by computer generated random street directory map references. The final sampling list was a total of 80 streets randomly drawn from eight suburbs within metropolitan Perth. Eight hundred questionnaire packs were hand-delivered (100 to each) to the eight metropolitan suburbs. The packs were addressed "to the resident" and delivered to every second letter box in selected streets. Half the packs were intended for men, the other half for women. On page 2 of the pack was a request that where possible the pack should be completed by either an adult female or adult male. A reply paid envelope was provided for respondents to return the pack once complete. Two weeks after the packs had been delivered; reminder letters were hand delivered to the original letterboxes.

Of the 800 residences invited to participate, 218 completed the survey pack and returned it by post. Of these, 11 packs were unusable, leaving a sample size of 208. Only 1 respondent was an Indigenous Australian with the remaining respondents being non-Indigenous Australian citizens or permanent residents. Finally, on page 2 there was a request informing respondents that as data had been collected from Western Australian prisoners, if they had been to prison or had/were on a community sentence, (e.g. Community Supervision Order), they were asked not to complete and return the pack. However, such requests leave it to the respondents to act accordingly and we cannot categorically confirm that all respondents in this community sample were non-offenders.

The community sampling procedure was carried out according to the Dillman, Smyth and Christian (2008) guidelines.

Measures (questionnaire pack). All participants completed a questionnaire pack. Section 1 and 2 were the instructions, consent details and demographic questions asking participants their age, gender and education. Section 3 contained a number of measures including the Measure of Attributions and Problem solving (The MAPS: reported here) and the measures of pro-violent and criminal sentiments.

The 'Measure of Attributions and Problem solving' (MAPS) was a paper and pencil scale presenting five hypothetical scenarios each describing a social situation. As each scenario has a differing hostility level, the interest in the MAPS is to assess participants' responses scenario-by-scenario, rather than on the scenarios combined. Scenario 5 is clearly antagonistic. In Scenario 2, the harmdoer's behaviour was thoughtless, with no hostility intended and with an apology given for the harm caused. The remaining scenarios (1, 3 and 4) were specifically written in a way where the intent of each harmdoer is not clear; hence the intent is ambiguous. Participants were asked to read each scenario and to consider what they would think about the behaviour of the harmdoer's (social attributions). Part 1 (questions 1 to 4 on each scenario) asks participants whether they find the behaviour of each harmdoer acceptable or not and to consider the likelihood that the actions of the harmdoer were accidental or not (attribution of intent), and finally whether they agree or disagree with six specific social attributional biases for why the harmdoer may have behaved as they did. Part 1 items are scored using a 5-point Likert scale, (1) 'strongly agree' to (5) 'strongly disagree', and scaled in positive and negative directions. After reversal, the higher the attribution scores the more likely the harmdoer's behaviour is judged purposeful, and carried out with intent. The specific attributions are coded into three different types: malevolent intent; hostile intent; and negation of hostile intent. Part 1 is used to test Hypothesis 1. Part 2 of the MAPS were open-ended question asking participants to write the different types of dispute resolution strategies (problem solving) they would use to solve each scenario. Part 2 is used to test Hypotheses 2 and 3.

The Criminal Sentiments Scale (CSS) (Andrews and Wormith, 1984) is a 41-item measure divided into three subscales. Subscale 1 measures attitudes towards the Law, Courts and Police (ALCP); for example, "The law does not benefit the common person." Subscale 2, Tolerance for Law Violation (TLV) measures the degree to which a person tolerates offending behaviour; for example, "A hungry person has the right to steal." Subscale 3, Identification with Criminal Others (ICO); for example, "I would rather associate with people that obey the law than those that don't". Items are scored using a 5-point Likert scale: (1) "strongly agree" to (5) "strongly disagree." Each subscale contains positively and negatively worded items. After reversal, lower ALCP scores reflect higher negativity towards the justice system and higher TLV and ICO scores reflect a greater willingness to endorse neutralisations and positive identification with criminal others. Evaluation of the CSS using 200 Australian offenders and non-offenders, reported the reliability (Cronbach's alpha) for the ALCP, TLV and ICO respectively as .91, .81, .65 (Stevenson et al., 2004). The measure was also found to discriminate Canadian offenders from Canadian non-offenders (Andrews and Wormith, 1990), and Australian offenders from non-offenders (Stevenson et al., 2004).

The Justification for Violence (JFV) was devised by this author to be used as both a single measure or inserted into the Criminal Sentiments Scale as a complementary fourth subscale (CSS: Andrews and Wormith, 1984). The CSS was chosen as the optimal scale to insert the JFV items into because it is a theoretically based scale underpinned by Differential-Association, neutralisation and social learning theory. The JFV items are underpinned by neutralisation and social-learning theory hence they share the same theoretical basis. The CSS is also a widely used measure in both research and clinical settings and has high criterion-related validity differentiating between offenders and non-offenders and good reliability (Andrews and Wormith, 1990). Validation of the JFV has been published previously (Kelty, Hall and Watt, 2010).

Results

Prior to analyses, Parts 1 and 2 of the MAPS were scored in accordance with the scoring guide (please contact the author for the scoring guide). All missing items on Part 1 were replaced with an 'undecided' score. All qualitative responses were coded in accordance with the MAPS guide. As not all participants completed all questions within parts 1 and 2 of the MAPS, only the completed data was used for analysis and the reduced number of cases is within the results.

The internal reliability of the scenarios was then assessed using Cronbach's alpha. All alphas, with the exception of scenario 2 for the offender sample, were within Devillis' (1991) range of 'very good' indicating the MAPS, overall has good internal reliability. The alphas by group can be seen in Table 1.

Testing Hypothesis 1. As the objective was to determine whether HABs represented criminogenic variables, rather than present the results comparing all five groups, it was more optimal to present differences between the two most diverse groups only for 2 reasons. The analyses required to test differences between five groups across the scenarios would produce a large amount of output. Instead of inundating the manuscript, the analyses presented will be the difference between the two most diverse groups: male violent offenders and non-offender women from the general population. The rationale is that if attributional biases represent clear criminogenic variables (able to differentiate violent from non-violent people) then it can be argued that highly significant differences would be observed between violent offenders and non-offender women. The offender participants in the present study all have a known history of using violence. In contrast, although it cannot be confirmed that the community women in this study were non-offenders, it is reasonable to assume that most women living in the community are not high risk violent offenders. This can be inferred because it is known that women are the least violent members of most western societies and are less likely to engage in violence than men (Mukherjee and Graycar, 1997). The first prediction of Hypothesis 1 was that: male offenders would be more likely to see the acts of others as deliberately intended rather than accidental compared with non-offenders.

To test this, the score from the attribution of intent (item 3) was used for each of the scenarios. Item 3 asked whether the harmdoer carried out the act on purpose (i.e., deliberately) or whether it was more likely to be a thoughtless act. Five independent samples t-tests were performed to see whether male offenders assigned a different level of intent than the community women. The results together with the observed means and standard deviations can be seen in Table 2.

As can be seen above, no significant differences were observed showing that offenders assigned the same level of intentionality to each of the five situations as non-offenders. These results suggest that violent offenders are no more likely to see the actions of others as deliberate as non-offenders.

Table 1. Cronbach's Alpha Calculated by scenario by offender, student and community group

Scenarios by group	N [a]	Items [b]	α [c]
Sample: Students			
1. – Comments made by new cleaner	232	8	.82
2. – The neighbours' car	231	8	.70
3. – The unpaid debt owed by friend	230	8	.77
4.– Conditions and tasks assigned at work	232	8	.78
5. – The ex-boyfriend at the BBQ	232	8	.72
Sample: Offenders			
1. – Comments made by new cleaner	87	8	.78
2. – The neighbours' car	87	8	.64
3. – The unpaid debt owed by friend	87	8	.75
4.– Conditions and tasks assigned at work	87	8	.82
5. – The ex-boyfriend at the BBQ	87	8	.76
Sample: Community			
1. – Comments made by new cleaner	198	8	.78
2. – The neighbours' car	199	8	.75
3. – The unpaid debt owed by friend	193	8	.74
4.– Conditions and tasks assigned at work	194	8	.81
5. – The ex-boyfriend at the BBQ	198	8	.73

Notes: [a] number of respondents. [b] items per scale. [c] Cronbach's alpha.

Table 2. Means, Standard Deviations, and Group Differences for the Attribution of Intent

Scenario number and type of intent	Male Offenders (n =86)	Community Women (n =89)	t (d.f.) Sig.
Scenario 1 (Ambiguous intent)	3.01 (1.23)	3.08 (1.32)	$\underline{t}$ (173) = 0.35, $\underline{p}$ = .73
Scenario 2 (Accidental/benign intent)	2.38 (1.02)	2.26 (1.00)	$\underline{t}$ (173) = 0.82, $\underline{p}$ = .41
Scenario 3 (Ambiguous intent)	3.92 (0.80)	3.96 (0.75)	$\underline{t}$ (173) = 0.31, $\underline{p}$ = .76
Scenario 4 (Ambiguous intent)	3.13 (1.15)	3.38 (0.97)	$\underline{t}$ (173) = 1.59, $\underline{p}$ = .12
Scenario 5 (Hostile intent)	4.15 (0.91)	4.42 (0.75)	$\underline{t}$ (173) = 2.10, $\underline{p}$ = .04

Notes: Standard deviations in parentheses.

The next step was to assess whether male offenders would demonstrate significantly higher HABs, especially in situations where the intent of the harmdoer is unclear (ambiguous). This analysis also explored whether the two forms of HABs ('hostile' and 'malevolent' intent) could discriminate offenders from non-offenders. A series of independent sample t-tests were used. The results, the means and standard deviations can be seen in Table 3. Significant differences are in highlighted in bold.

The results showed only one significant difference. This was for regarding the behaviour of the neighbours in Scenario 2 where the offender group demonstrated a higher level of hostile intent than the community women did. This suggests that in benign situations non-offender women are less likely to infer hostility than male offenders. However, although the groups were significantly different, it is noteworthy that this difference did not represent a pronounced level of HAB for the offender sample. The mean score observed for the male offenders was within the 'perhaps no' to the midpoint ('undecided') range. Within this range this is not a clear demonstration of hostile attributional bias. It is reasonable to suggest that a clear demonstration of a pronounced HAB would be where the mean was above the midpoint and in the range where hostility was confirmed as 'perhaps yes', or 'definitely yes'.

Table 3. Means, Standard Deviations and Group Differences for the Attribution of Hostile and Malevolent Intent

Scenario and intent	Attribution	Male Offenders (n =86)	Community Women (n =89)	t (d.f.) Sig.
Scenario 1	Hostile intent	4.85 (1.76)	4.66 (1.77)	T (173) = 0.70, p = .49
(Ambiguous)	Malevolent intent	3.26 (1.19)	3.26 (1.15)	T (173) = 0.02, p = .99
Scenario 2	Hostile intent	4.71 (1.38)	4.13 (1.48)	T (173) = 2.66, p < .01*
(Benign)	Malevolent intent	3.27 (1.11)	2.90 (1.01)	T (173) = 2.29, p = .03
Scenario 3	Hostile intent	6.08 (1.54)	5.62 (1.38)	T (173) = 2.10, p = .04
(Ambiguous)	Malevolent intent	3.45 (0.94)	3.49 (0.92)	T (173) = 0.29, p = .77
Scenario 4	Hostile intent	5.24 (1.73)	5.36 (1.26)	T (155.43)=0.50, p = .62
(Ambiguous)	Malevolent intent	3.17 (1.09)	3.48 (0.96)	T (173) = 1.99, p = .05
Scenario 5	Hostile intent	8.17 (1.29)	8.03 (1.13)	T (173) = 0.77, p = .45
(Hostile)	Malevolent intent	3.52 (0.99)	3.26 (1.05)	T (173) = 1.72, p = .09

Notes: Standard deviations in parentheses. * $p < .01$.

These sets of results are contrary to prediction showing that male violent offenders were no more likely than the women non-offenders to assign a higher level of hostile and/or malevolent intent to the harmful behaviour of others.

Moreover, no significant differences were observed in the three scenarios which were specifically written to contain elements of ambiguity, namely, Scenarios 1 (the cleaner), 3 (the friend) and 4 (the supervisor).

This suggests that unlike juvenile offenders, adult male violent offenders are no more likely to demonstrate high levels of HABs in ambiguous situations than a sample of older non-offender women from the general population. The results do not support Hypothesis 1.

Testing Hypotheses 2. The next two hypotheses were designed to assess differences in aggressive and non-aggressive problem solving to the social situations presented in each of the MAPS scenarios. The results presented below report on the difference observed in all five groups (male offenders, men and women students and men and women from the community).

Hypothesis 2 was devised to test Ajzen and Fishbein's (1980) theory that there is a link between positive attitudes toward a behaviour and behavioural intentions. It was predicted that: *male offenders would report more violence based grievance resolution strategies than male students. Male students in turn would report more violence based strategies than female students and men and women from the community.*

Prior to analysis, all responses given on Part 2 for each of the five scenarios were coded according to the scoring guide (contact the author for a copy of the guide). To explore the associations between the types of strategies reported on each scenario, a series of 5 (group) x 2 (type of strategy, yes/no) two-way contingency tables were constructed. The percentages of participants in each group who stated they would use each strategy is presented in Table 4. The results from Chi-square analysis and effect size estimates based on phi-coefficients are also presented. Where results were significant they are highlighted in bold.

As can be seen in Table 4, out of the 52 different problem solving strategies provided there were 19 significant associations observed.

For Scenario 1, regarding the ambiguous interaction with the cleaner, the results showed that 4 offenders said they would use violence, whereas none of the non-offenders said they would engage in aggression. Overall, low levels of violence were considered, although a reasonable percentage of people in all groups said they would use either verbal aggression, or ambiguous assertive strategies (i.e. passive-aggression).

Five significant associations were shown for Scenario 2 (the thoughtless neighbours). These were 'do nothing', 'reactive retaliation', 'be assertive', 'say thank-you', and 'socialise'. The negative residuals showed fewer students said they would 'do nothing' than would be expected by chance.

More offenders than expected said they would engage in acts of reactive aggression, primarily revving their own cars during the day, or would consider stealing the neighbours' car.

Table 4. Aggressive and Non-Aggressive Problem solving Strategies Reported by Each Group for each Scenario (Scenarios 1 to 3)

Scenario and intent type	Resolution strategy for each scenario	N [a]	Offenders[b]	N [c]	Male Students[b]	n [c]	Female Students[b]	n [c]	Male Community[b]	N [c]	Female Community[b]	N [c]	Pearson χ^2 [d]	Sig.	ϕ [e]
1. The cleaner	Do nothing	487	21%	17	42%	36	38%	49	27%	26	20%	18	17.26	*p*<.01*	.21
(Ambiguous)	Avoidance	487	9%	7	5%	4	3%	3	6%	6	6%	5	4.45	.35	.10
	Aggression	487	5%	4	-	0	0%	0	-	0	0%	0	20.22	*p*<.01*	.20
	Reactive	487	-	0	3%	2	3%	4	-	0	-	0	7.82	.09	.13
	Verbal aggression	487	12%	10	16%	14	8%	10	9%	9	4%	4	8.29	.08	.13
	Ambiguous assertion	487	21%	17	16%	14	19%	24	19%	19	22%	20	1.20	.89	.05
	Assertive	487	27%	22	16%	14	29%	37	32%	31	34%	31	8.50	.08	.13
	Supportive	487	7%	6	3%	3	2%	3	4%	4	9%	8	6.42	.17	.12
	Talk to HR	487	1%	1	2%	2	3%	4	10%	10	19%	17	30.86	*p*<.01*	.25
	Other	487	4%	3	1%	1	3%	4	2%	2	1%	1	2.22	.69	.07
2. Neighbours	Nothing	469	52%	44	27%	21	22%	26	39%	37	53%	49	32.91	*p*<.01*	.27
(Benign)	Avoidance	469	10%	8	4%	3	1%	1	10%	10	5%	5	11.86	.02	.16
	Aggression [f]	469	-	0	-	0	-	0	-	0	-	0	-	-	-
	Reactive	469	4%	3	-	0	-	0	-	0	-	0	13.84	*p*<.01*	.17
	Verbal aggression	469	-	0	-	0	3%	3	1%	1	-	0	6.14	*.19*	.11

Table 4. (Continued)

Scenario and intent type	Resolution strategy for each scenario	N [a]	Offenders[b]	N c	Male Students[b]	n c	Female Students[b]	n [c]	Male Community[b]	N c	Female Community[b]	N c	Pearson $\chi2$ [d]	Sig.	ϕ [e]
	Ambiguous assertion	469	5%	4	5%	4	3%	3	1%	1	-	0	7.11	.13	.12
	Assertive	469	4%	3	6%	5	8%	10	-	0	-	0	15.75	*p*<.01*	.18
	Say thanks	469	25%	21	44%	35	63%	75	50%	48	45%	42	29.32	*p*<.01*	.26
	Socialise	469	4%	4	23%	18	10%	12	4%	4	3%	3	28.67	*p*<.01*	.25
	Other	469	-	0	1%	1	2%	2	-	0	-	0	4.31	.37	.09
3. The friend	Nothing	444	1%	1	1%	1	-	0	5%	4	4%	3	6.79	.15	.12
(Ambiguous)	Avoidance	444	11%	8	3%	2	2%	2	10%	9	9%	7	12.21	.02	.16
	Aggression	444	18%	13	3%	2	-	0	-	0	-	0	57.93	*p*<.01*	.36
	Reactive	444	14%	10	1%	1	4%	5	-	0	-	0	29.60	*p*<.01*	.26
	Verbal aggression	444	10%	7	14%	11	8%	10	1%	1	-	0	18.71	*p*<.01*	.21
	Ambiguous assertion	444	17%	12	26%	21	13%	16	15%	13	10%	8	9.91	.04	.15
	Assertive	444	38%	27	43%	34	69%	85	53%	47	51%	41	23.05	*p*<.01*	.22
	Temporary fix	444	8%	6	15%	12	15%	19	17%	15	24%	19	6.62	.16	.12
	Pay money	444	13%	9	7%	6	7%	9	2%	2	3%	2	9.61	.04	.15
	Other	444	3%	2	4%	3	8%	10	6%	5	14%	11	9.13	.05	.14

Scenario and intent type	Resolution strategy for each scenario	N [a]	Offenders[b]	n [c]	Male Students[b]	n [c]	Female Students[b]	n [c]	Male Community[b]	N [c]	Female Community[b]	N [c]	Pearson χ^2 [d]	Sig.	ϕ [e]
4. Supervisor	Nothing	473	23%	18	20%	17	12%	15	12%	11	13%	11	7.76	.10	.13
(Ambiguous)	Avoidance	473	8%	6	1%	1	2%	2	2%	2	1%	1	10.04	.04	.15
	Aggression	473	1%	1	-	0	-	0	-	0	-	0	4.99	.29	.10
	Reactive	473	1%	1	-	0	1%	1	-	0	-	0	2.85	.58	.08
	Verbal aggression	473	4%	3	7%	6	-	0	-	0	-	0	19.89	*p*<.01*	.21
	Ambiguous assertion	473	9%	7	2%	2	3%	4	6%	6	6%	5	5.03	.28	.10
	Assertive	473	13%	10	38%	33	52%	66	44%	41	47%	41	33.73	*p*<.01*	.27
	Talk to boss/HR	473	8%	6	5%	4	13%	17	18%	17	17%	15	10.89	.03	.15
	Quit	473	18%	14	13%	11	11%	14	20%	19	22%	19	6.31	.18	.11
	Bide time	473	11%	9	33%	28	32%	41	20%	19	33%	29	17.01	*p*<.01*	.19
	Prove self	473	22%	17	7%	6	20%	25	10%	9	3%	3	20.97	*p*<.01*	.21
	Other	473	3%	2	4%	3	4%	5	2%	2	1%	1	1.86	.76	.06
5. Ex-boyfriend	Nothing	471	10%	8	5%	4	4%	5	14%	13	13%	11	11.39	.02	.15
(Hostile)	Avoidance	471	7%	6	18%	16	34%	44	25%	23	45%	38	37.37	*p*<.01*	.28
	Aggression	471	56%	44	44%	39	5%	6	8%	7	3%	2	139.41	*p*<.01*	.54

Table 4. (Continued)

Scenario and intent type	Resolution strategy for each scenario	N [a]	Offenders[b]	n [c]	Male Students[b]	n c	Female Students[b]	n c	Male Community[b]	N c	Female Community[b]	N c	Pearson $\chi 2^d$	Sig.	ϕ [e]
	Reactive	471	-	0	6%	5	4%	5	-	0	-	0	12.96	.02	.16
	Verbal aggression	471	8%	6	5%	4	2%	3	3%	3	-	0	8.25	.08	.13
	Ambiguous assertion	471	5%	4	10%	9	2%	3	9%	8	2%	2	10.04	.04	.14
	Assertive	471	17%	13	27%	24	28%	36	28%	26	21%	18	4.81	.31	.10
	Police/legal	471	5%	4	42%	36	75%	98	39%	36	57%	48	102.20	$p<.01$*	.47
	Defend self	471	8%	6	13%	11	7%	9	9%	8	1%	1	8.63	.07	.14
	Other	471	-	0	1%	1	4%	5	-	0	5%	4	8.69	.07	.14

Notes: $*p < .01$ (adjusted alpha, 2-tail). [a] Total number of participants used for analysis. [b] Percentage of participants by group endorsing type of strategy. [c] Number of participants by group endorsing type of strategy. [d] Pearson Chi-square, using 2 d.f. [e] Phi coefficient. [f] Chi-square not calculated, no participants said they would use this strategy.

The residuals also showed that more female students would thank the neighbours while fewer offenders than expected said they would thank them. Finally, more male and female students than expected said they would purposefully get to know the neighbours better and arrange a social event like a BBQ. These results combined suggest that more offenders would just leave the matter, while more male and female students would actively develop a relationship with the neighbours.

Four significant associations were observed for Scenario 3, regarding the ambiguous actions of friend. These associations were for using 'aggression', 'reactive retaliation', 'verbal aggression' and 'assertion'. The residuals showed that more offenders than expected by chance said they would use/threaten physical aggression. More female students than expected said they use an indirect form of retaliation to solve this problem. More students and more offenders than expected said they would be verbally abusive. More female students than expected would engage in assertive communication, whereas fewer offenders said they would be assertive. Overall, more offenders said they would use violence or would engage in passive-aggressive acts and were the least likely of all the groups to be assertive in trying to sort the situation out. In this scenario, three of the significant associations had small estimated effect sizes, with phi-coefficients ranging from .21 to .26. For the strategy of 'aggression' the phi-coefficient estimated a small to medium effect; that is .36.

In Scenario 4, describing the ambiguous behaviour of the supervisor, three associations were significant. Overall, the results showed that although fewer offenders would be assertive or were willing to bide their time, they were more likely to work hard to prove to the supervisor they were good employees. In this scenario low levels of physical aggression, verbal aggression or passive-aggression were endorsed. Similar to the other scenarios discussed so far, small estimated effect sizes were observed for Scenario 4, with phi-coefficients ranging from .19 to .27.

In Scenario 5, regarding the antagonistic ex-boyfriend, three associations were significant for the strategies of 'avoidance', 'aggression' and 'police/legal'. The residuals showed that in this hostile situation more community men and women and more female students than expected said they would actively avoid further interaction with the ex-boyfriend. This usually equated to going inside, locking the doors, or making a quick escape and going home. In keeping with Hypothesis 5, the residuals for 'aggression' showed that more offenders and more male students said they engage in, or threaten, physical aggression to deal with the ex-boyfriend. In contrast, the negative residuals showed that fewer female students and fewer men and women from the community than expected by chance said they would use or threaten physical aggression. The negative residuals for the last significant association showed that fewer offenders than expected by chance said they would call the police or seek another form of legal assistance. In contrast, the residuals showed that that more female students and women from the community than expected by chance said they would call the police or get another kind of legal assistance (e.g., a violence restraining order). In Scenario 5 the largest effect size were observed. For the strategy of 'avoidance' a small effect was estimated, being .28. However for 'aggression' and 'police/legal' medium effect sizes were estimated with phi-coefficients ranging from .47 to .54.

Testing Hypothesis 3. The final hypothesis tested whether the significant findings of Slaby and Guerra (1988), using an adolescent sample was generalisable to adults. *Hypothesis 3* predicted that if a risk factor for aggression is the generation of fewer alternative problem solving strategies then: *male offenders will report a lower number of problem solving solutions than non-offenders.*

In order to test hypothesis 3 the number of alternative responses (e.g., different types) given by the participants in each group on each of the five scenarios were summed. A series of five one-way ANOVAS assessed whether the groups differed. Only those participants who provided a response on each of the scenarios were included. The number of participants per group is recorded in Table 5 below. The table also presents the mean number and standard deviations for the different alternatives given as well as the ANOVA results. Significant results are highlighted in bold.

The ANOVAs found three significant differences across the five scenarios. The first difference was for Scenario 3, and contrary to prediction, it was the offender group who generated the highest number of alternate strategies. The post hoc Scheffé tests showed that the offender group generated a significantly higher number of strategies than male and female students ($p < .05$) and men and women from the community group ($p < .001$). The male and female students were not different from the community (all tests $p > .05$).

Although the ANOVA found a significant difference for Scenario 4 the post hoc tests could not locate where the groups difference lay. All Scheffé comparisons for each of the five groups were $p > .05$. According to the post hocs, all five means formed one homogeneous subset which could not clearly distinguish one group from another. This could have occurred due to a slight difference in the mean being significant, although when looking at the estimated effect size ($\eta^2 = .03$) the effect is so small that the groups were in effect not markedly different.

The third significant difference was for Scenario 5. Here it was the male and female students and women from the community who generated the same number of strategies (all tests $p > .01$) as well as generating a higher number than the community men and the male offenders (all tests $p < .01$). The post hoc tests also showed that the community men and the male offenders were not different from each other ($p = .38$).

STUDY 2: DO OFFENDERS ENDORSE HIGHER PRO-VIOLENT AND PRO-CRIMINAL SENTIMENTS THAN STUDENTS AND THE COMMUNITY?

The objective of Study 2 was to explore whether adult male offenders convicted of serious violent index offences were more likely to endorse a higher level of pro-violent and pro-criminal attitudes and sentiments than men and women university undergraduates and men and women from the general population.

Method

The Participants, procedures and measured were described above in study 1. Of note the results reported in this study related to those using the JFV and Criminal Sentiments Scale.

Table 5. Means, Standard Deviations (in parentheses) and Group Differences in the Number of Alternative Grievance Resolution Strategies Reported

Scenario number	Male Offenders	Male Students	Female Students	Male Community	Female Community	f (d.f.) Sig, η^2 [a]
1.	1.07 (0.26)	1.03 (0.18)	1.06 (0.27)	1.09 (0.29)	1.14 (0.35)	$f\,(4, 482) = 1.94$, $p = .10$, $\eta^2 = .02$
2.	1.04 (0.18)	1.12 (0.32)	1.11 (0.31)	1.05 (0.22)	1.06 (0.25)	$f\,(4, 464) = 1.64$, $p = 16$, $\eta^2 = .01$
3.	1.32 (0.50)	1.27 (0.48)	1.16 (0.41)	1.12 (0.33)	1.08 (0.32)	$f\,(4, 439) = 4.90$, $p < .01^*$, $\eta^2 = .04$
4.	1.19 (0.40)	1.32 (0.50)	1.48 (0.70)	1.34 (0.58)	1.42 (0.56)	$f\,(4, 468) = 3.62$, $p < .01^*$, $\eta^2 = .03$
5.	1.17 (0.38)	1.72 (0.68)	1.68 (0.62)	1.35 (0.52)	1.50 (0.57)	$f\,(4, 466) = 14.71$, $p < .01^*$, $\eta^2 = .11$

Notes: * $p < .01$. [a] Results for one-way ANOVAs with eta-squared estimates η^2 for the effect size.

Results

Prior to the analyses the assumptions underlying all the statistical tests used were examined. Where the assumptions were violated, the impact of the violation upon the robustness of the test was considered and the recommendations provided by Tabachnick and Fidell (2013) for correcting the violations were applied. Due to the number of multiple tests performed a more conservative alpha level of .01 was set for evidence of significance as recommended by Coates (2009).

*Testing Hypothesis 1: Endorsement of Violent and Criminal Sentiments.*_Hypothesis 1 predicted that: male offenders would endorse a higher level of violent and criminal sentiments than the two male non-offender groups (students and community). It was also predicted that: men would endorse a higher level of justifications for violence than women. The first analysis performed explored whether there were any significant differences between the groups in their endorsement of these sentiments. The means and standard deviations by group for the VCSS can be seen in Table 6. The means observed suggest that male offenders endorsed the highest level of violent and criminal sentiments with the community women endorsing the lowest level.

A one-way between-subjects Multivariate Analysis of Variance (MANOVA) was performed to access differences in endorsement on the four dependent variables: ALCP; TLV; JFV; and ICO+. As expected, using Pillai's Trace, the MANOVA showed significant differences between the groups on the combined DVs ($F\ (16,2100) = 25.70$, $p < .001$, $\eta^2 = .17$). The univariate tests also showed highly significant differences for each of the four DVs with partial eta-squared estimating small to medium effect sizes for each.

Table 6. Means and SD by Group on the Four VCSS Subscales. (SD given in parentheses)

Variable	(n) [a]	ALCP [b]	TLV [c]	JFV [d]	ICO+ [e]
Male offender sample	87	69.07 (15.14)	31.95 (7.40)	45.95 (12.26)	32.71 (9.79)
Male student sample	96	84.23 (12.68)	26.96 (5.94)	34.54 (9.27)	22.15 (6.19)
Female student sample	139	87.00 (11.08)	23.56 (4.82)	25.81 (6.32)	18.94 (5.33)
Male Community sample	108	94.09 (11.99)	22.00 (5.45)	28.62 (6.94)	18.31 (4.94)
Female community sample	100	94.98 (10.38)	20.32 (4.65)	23.74 (6.08)	17.51 (4.81)

Notes [a] number of participants. [b] Attitudes towards law, courts and police. [c] Tolerance for law violation. [d] Justifications for violence. [e] Identification with criminal peers plus.

The results obtained were as follows: F_{ALCP} (4, 525) = 67.93, $p< .001$; $\eta^2 = .34$; F_{TLV} (4, 525) = 62.93, $p < .001$; $\eta^2 = .32$); F_{JFV} (4, 525) = 112.19, $p < .001$; $\eta^2 = .46$); and F_{ICO+} (4, 525) = 92.34, $p < .001$; $\eta^2 = .41$). As can be seen from these results, the largest estimated effect size was for justifications for violence, suggesting that this is the main discriminating variable between the five groups.

Post hoc comparisons were then performed to identify which of the subscales which groups differed from each other. To control for risk of Type I and II errors, the Scheffé test was selected. This test provides all possible comparisons but utilises a strict criterion for rejecting the null hypothesis (Coakes, 2009). The results showed that on all four VCSS subscales the offenders were clearly distinguishable from the other four non-offender groups with all comparisons being $p <.001$. The offenders endorsed a more negative opinion of the law and the justice system, were more tolerant of law violation, were more likely to justify the use of violence in various social situations and had a higher identification with criminal others than any of the male or female non-offenders they were compared with.

For the JFV subscale, as can be seen in the observed means presented in Table 6, the male offenders endorsed almost twice the number of sentiments as the community women and this observation was reflected in the results. The male offenders were clearly distinguishable from all four non-offender groups and endorsed a significantly higher level of pro-violent sentiments.

The next highest level of endorsement was by the male students who as a group demonstrated a significantly higher endorsement of JFV than female students and men and women from the community (all tests $p < .001$). Finally the results showed that men and women from the community and female students endorsed the lowest level and all three groups were not significantly different from each other (all tests $p > .01$).

The comparisons between non-offenders on the remaining subscales were as follows. For the ALCP subscale, the results showed male students and female students shared similar views about the law and the justice system ($p = .87$), although their views were significantly more negative than the community men and women ($p < .001$. The men and women from the community were shown to share similar views amount the validity of law ($p = 1.00$). For the TLV and ICO+ subscales the student men were shown to have a significantly higher tolerance for law violation and a significantly higher identification with criminal peers than the female students and men and women from the community (all tests $p < .001$). The female students and the men and women from the community sample were not significantly different from each other suggesting that on the TLV and ICO+ subscales these three groups share similar attitudes and values (all comparisons were $p >.05$).

The results from the above analyses are presented graphically in Figure 1.

Testing Hypothesis 2: The Relationships Between the Four VCSS Subscales. The second hypothesis predicted that: strong and significant relationships will be found between the original CSS subscales and the new JFV subscale. The relationships expected are where higher sentiments justifying violence will correlate with a higher disrespect for the law and criminal justice system, a greater willingness to neutralise offending behaviour, and a higher identification with criminal others. This relationship is expected to be stronger for male offenders than the four non-offender groups. To assess how the patterns of relationships between the VCSS subscales differed across the five groups a Pearson product moment correlation matrix was developed. Table 7 shows the matrix for each group.

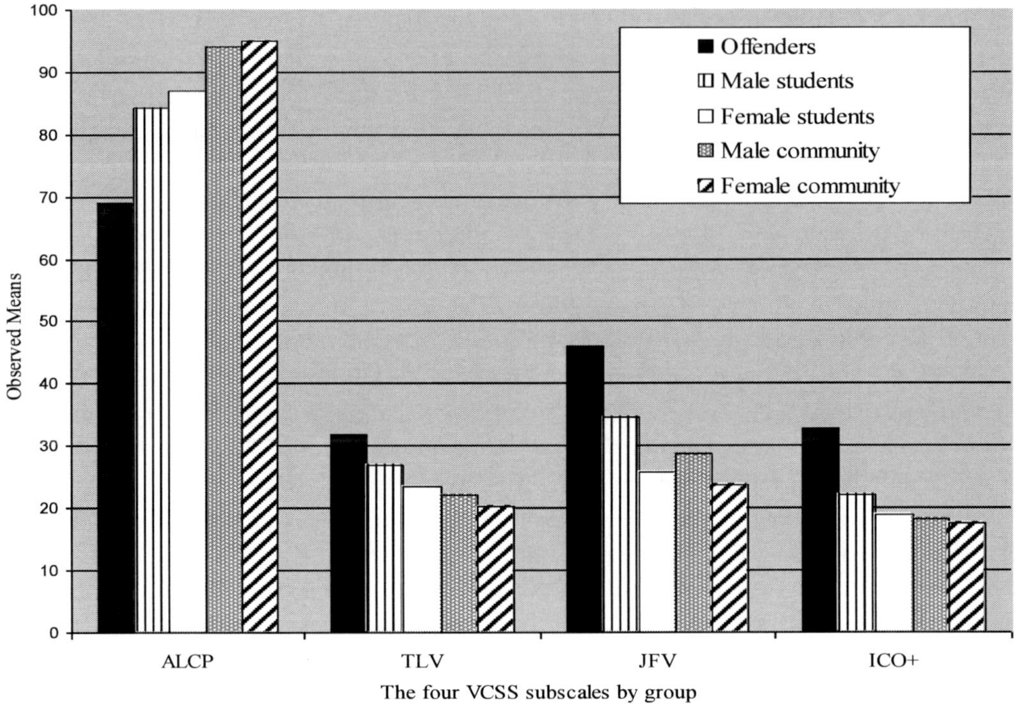

Figure 1. Profile plot for the four VCSS Subscales by group.

Table 7. Intercorrelations between the Four Subscales of the VCSS for the Offender, Student and Community Samples

Group and number of participants per group	Variable	ALCP [a]	TLV [b]	JFV [c]
Male offender sample	TLV [b]	-.564**	-	-
(n = 87)	JFV [c]	-.569**	.770**	-
	ICO+ [d]	-.493**	.704**	.748**
Male student sample	TLV	-.584**	-	-
(n = 96)	JFV	-.385**	.568**	-
	ICO+	-.531**	.620**	.528**
Female student sample	TLV	-.473**	-	-
(n = 139)	JFV	-.236**	.520**	-
	ICO+	-.368**	.664**	.478**
Male community sample	TLV	-.651**	-	-
(n = 108)	JFV	-.528**	.584**	-
	ICO+	-.457**	.551**	.466**
Female community sample	TLV	-.569**	-	-
(n = 100)	JFV	-.376**	.556**	-
	ICO+	-.304**	.531**	.498**

Notes: * $p< .05$ (2 tail).** $p< .01$ (2 tail). [a] Attitudes towards law, courts and police. [b] Tolerance for law violation. [c] Justifications for violence. [d] Identification with criminal peers plus.

As shown in Table 7, within each of the five groups the four VCSS subscales all shared highly significant relationships. As expected, the results showed that regardless of group, the more negative participants' opinion of the legal system were the more likely they were to endorse law violation, to support the use of violence and to have higher identification with criminal peers.

Overall, as can be seen in Table 7, it was the offender sample with the largest observed correlations between the subscales, especially for justifications for violence. The results also showed that even though the magnitude of the correlations observed for the two female non-offender samples were in most cases lower, the patterns themselves showed the same relationship as for the men.

DISCUSSION

The rationale for this project was to determine whether a number of cognitive variables appeared to represent dynamic criminogenic needs for adult male violent offenders. By identifying whether certain variables discriminated offenders from non-offenders, theorists and practitioners could use this knowledge to develop and deliver violence rehabilitation programs that are as effective as possible. Rehabilitation programs which have been found to be more successful are those which target dynamic criminogenic risk factors and where the risk factors have a theoretical underpinning (Howells and Day, 2002). It was therefore necessary that this project not only identify criminogenic risk factors, but present a theoretical explanation for how these variables influence violent behaviour. To achieve a more comprehensive theoretical coverage of the cognitive aspects of grievance escalation, the literature presented throughout this thesis has not just been from the disciple of psychology but has used the knowledge found in a range of disciplines including, economics, law, criminology and sociology. The primary aim of this work was to determine whether violent sentiments, HABs and violence-based grievance resolution strategies represented adult criminogenic risk factors. The project was carried out two studies. Each of the studies and their findings are summarised below. In Study 1, Part 1 of the MAPS was used to explore whether violent offenders interpreted the social behaviour of others differently compared with non-offenders. The hypothesis tested whether violent offenders would experience wider "is/ought" discrepancies and would demonstrate pronounced HABs than non-offenders. Overall, the implications from the results are that adult violent offenders do not interpret the harmful behaviour of others very differently from adult non-offenders. In contrast to the findings for adolescent offenders, these cognitive variables, especially HABs, do not appear to represent important dynamic criminogenic risk factors for adults. Although these variables did not represent clear discriminatory criminogenic factors they did appear to be influential in how and why grievances develop and escalate. Part 2 of the MAPS was used in Study 1 to test Hypothesis 2 and 3. Hypothesis 2 assessed the attitudes and behaviour link and asked whether people known to support the use of violence would be more likely to report they would use violence to deal with other people's "bad behaviour". Hypothesis 3 assessed whether adult offenders were more likely to generate only single violence-based resolutions strategies. The results showed that overall the offenders generated a similar number of strategies as the non-offenders although the offenders' strategies were more likely to be violence based. However, the offenders' use of violent strategies was selective and was only marked in two scenarios. This result was in line with the known circumstances under which many violent incidents occur; namely, that violence is more likely between parties in a relationship (as in Scenario 3: Being let down by a friend) and in hostile altercations (as in Scenario 5: The antagonistic ex-boyfriend) (AIC, 2006; Ross and Polk, 2005).

In Study 2, two hypotheses were tested assessing the differences between offenders and non-offenders in endorsement of violent and criminal sentiments using the VCSS were assessed in Hypothesis 1. Of specific interest was the score obtained on the JFV subscale. Based on JFV scores three distinct groups were observed. Group 1 were the male offenders with significantly higher JFV scores than any other group. Group 2 were the younger male students with a medium level of JFV endorsement. Group 3 were the older men from the community, female students and women from the community with the lowest level of JFVs. These results indicated that beliefs justifying violence are an important criminogenic risk factor. The difference between the groups generated a medium to large effect size (η^2 =.46). Hypothesis 2 of Study 2 explored whether violent sentiments operate in isolation or whether they are a valid addition to the criminal sentiments construct. The results showed that in all samples the JFV subscale was significantly related to endorsement of other criminal sentiments. The relationship, regardless of group, was where a negative opinion of the criminal justice system related to a higher tolerance for breaking the law, a higher level of justifying violence and a higher identification with criminal peers. It appears that violent sentiments do not operate in isolation from other criminal sentiments. The JFV subscale enhances the CSS by allowing violent sentiments to measured at the same time as other criminal sentiments. The results also showed that the VCSS is not just restricted to forensic applications but is a useful measure for applied research with both men and women. The results from this project are summarised in Figure 2 below.

Expanding Luckenbill and Doyle's Three Stage Model

The Original Model

Luckenbill and Doyle (1989) suggested that grievances escalate in a series of interrelated stages, from a perception of harm (naming) to a demand for reparation from the harmdoer (claiming) and where the reparation is unsatisfactory onto a third stage, aggression.

There is recognition that some grievances do not escalate through all three stages and that some end in the claiming stage, primarily due to reparation which is satisfactory for both parties. Grievances can end in the claiming stage even though the claim was unsuccessful because the victim decides the matter is not worth pursuing.

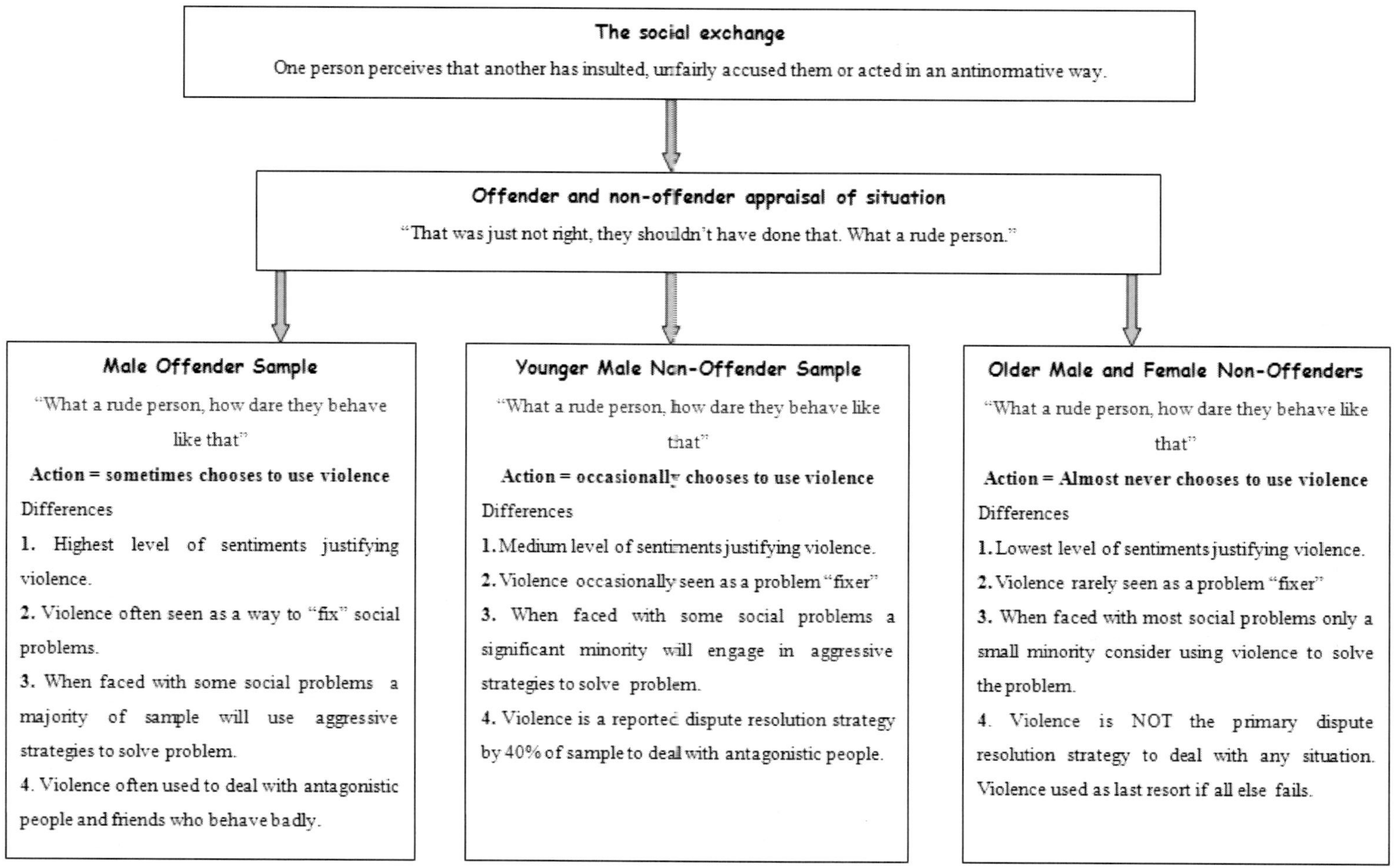

Figure 2. The empirical differences observed between offenders and non-offenders.

Despite support for the three-stage sequence (Kennedy and Forde, 1996), the model itself appeared to lack a comprehensive theory of why grievances escalate and only provided two propositions for why grievances escalate into violence. First were the two individual psychological factors. Factor one was "disputationess"; the willingness to pursue a claim and to demand reparation. Factor two was "aggressiveness"; the willingness to end grievances through violence. Both "disputationess" and "aggressiveness" were suggested to be underpinned by subcultural beliefs stating where, when and how insults or other wrongs should be responded to. The second proposition was that grievances were more likely to escalate given the nature of the interactions between the victim and the harmdoer during the "claiming" stage. Specifically, Luckenbill and Doyle stressed that grievances were more likely to escalate if the harmdoer responds inappropriately to the claim.

The Expanded Model

One rationale for doing this study was to use the findings to expand this three-stage grievance escalation model. The findings and their theoretical basis are discussed below.

The first expansion was to include the types of harm that upset people enough to make them claim. Tedeschi and Felson (1994) proposed there were four types of harm which underpin grievances: physical harm (injury or the threat of); psychological harm (lack of respect, fairness or equality); material damage (loss of goods or services) or political harm (violation of rights and freedoms by the state or organisations). This is in line with the work of interactional justice researchers, specifically, Bies and Tripp (1996), Mikula et al., (1998) and Miller (2001) who noted that it is the experience of psychological harm, especially from significant others, that upsets people the most. This suggests that it is the experience of specific types of harms that are more influential than others in why grievances escalate.

The second expansion of the "naming" stage is the inclusion of some common forms of attributional biases and social judgements people use to hold their harmdoers accountable for the harm. The common social judgement used to analyse the actions of others is suggested to be the "is/ought" discrepancy (Miller, 2001). This discrepancy occurs when we benchmark what we believe has occurred (the "is") against what we believe should have occurred (the "ought").

As "ought" beliefs are essentially the moral benchmarks we set for the behaviour of others and represent out personal beliefs about how we deserve to be treated, the wider the discrepancy between the "is" and the "ought" the more morally outraged we become and the more likely we are to demand reparation (Miller, 2001). The results in study 1 showed that the wider the discrepancy become the more likely people were to engage in two attributional biases. It was observed in Study 1 (using the MAPS) that the wider the "is/ought" discrepancy, the higher the reports of negative emotions, and the higher the levels of the fundamental attribution error and hostile and malevolent attributions of intent. The results also showed that high levels of these biases, especially HABs, were not just a phenomenon experienced by male offenders, it was a phenomenon experienced by most of the 430 non-offenders. Also observed was that the more unacceptable the behaviour of the harmdoer was considered (a wide "is/ought" discrepancy), the more negative the emotions felt and the higher the level of attributional biases, especially HABs, the less likely people were to let the matter slide.

The expansion of this model shows that it is the experience of psychological harm which is more likely to be judged as offensive and antinormative. The more offensive and antinormative the behaviour, the higher the experience of negative emotions, and the more negative the emotions, the more likely people are to use attributional biases to hold their harmdoer an inconsiderate and badly behaved "rat". The results also showed that the more antinormative the behaviour of the harmdoer was judged, the less likely people were to just let the matter slide. Of note, although "is/ought" discrepancies, HABs and the FAE did not appear to represent criminogenic risk factors for violent adults, they did appear to be influential by representing the pathway through which "naming" occurs and why "naming" escalates to "claiming".

In the current project the most significant difference between the five groups was how "claiming" proceeded to "aggression". In Study 1 it was observed that three distinct groups were formed. Group 1 were the offenders who had attitudes which supported aggression and when faced with certain situations (antagonistic people, as in Scenario 5, and "badly behaved" friends, as in Scenario 3) over 50% were prepared to use some form of "aggression" to solve the problem. For most offenders aggression (either verbal, physical or passive–aggression) were the primary strategies reported. Group 2 were the younger male students with a medium level of attitudes supporting violence with 44% of the sample prepared to use violence but only when faced with an antagonistic person. Group 3 were the older men and both female groups. They had a low level of support for violence and only very few were prepared to use violence in any of the situations assessed in this study. The implication of these results is that it is not just the interaction between the harmdoer and the victim, or whether a claim is successful or not, what appears to matter more is whether a person supports violence and is prepared to use it. It appears that women, regardless of age, neither support nor consider violence an option to solve social problems. Younger men, however, are more likely to support and use violence than older men. In Study 2, a correlation was observed showing that attitudes supporting violence in non-offender men reduced with age, although the correlation only accounted for approximately 10% of the variance. Therefore violent sentiments are not the only factor that influences younger men to behave violently and turn unsuccessful claims into acts of aggression. It is possible that another explanation for a reduction in support for violence with increasing age is the decrease in physical ability and strength to fight which therefore reduces the desire and motivation to fight. As one 59 year old community male said in response to Scenario 5 of the MAPS "I'd run like buggery. Seriously, I'd try to talk to him but at my age (I'm 59 now) I would probably run. When I was younger it would have been different, I would have had it out with the blighter".

The Applied Implications of the Results

Several of the findings have applied implications for violent offender programs.

First, one of the most important findings of this project was that HABs were a phenomenon observed in the sample of 87 adult male mainstream violent offenders at high-risk of violent recidivism and in the sample of 430 men and women non-offenders. Although some significant differences were observed between offenders and non-offenders, the actual means observed showed the difference did not equate to a pronounced HAB. That is, any differences were accompanied by such small effect sizes making any difference in the means negligible. The rationale for HAB intervention is to reduce the hypothesised tendency for offenders to assume that the harmful behaviour of others was malicious. In Serin and

Kuriychuk's (1994) Canadian violent offender program they aim to teach offenders to "pause, reflect and check the information". Serin and Kuriychuk's (1994) program was underpinned by the hypothesis that violent offenders are more likely than non-violent offenders and non-offenders to base their social information processing on hostile scripts and hostile attributional biases. As mentioned, the current project appears to be the first study to assess whether a sample of mainstream adult violent offenders actually differ on this variable from a large sample of adult non-offenders. What the current project found was that it is not just the violent offenders who did not pause, reflect or check the information, neither did the men and women non-offenders. Therefore, if non-offenders are prone to attribute malice and hostility where none exists and yet do not engage in violence then HABs in adulthood do not appear to be a dynamic criminogenic need. As effective intervention programs are those which target variables that are related to offending behaviour and discriminate offenders from non-offenders (Ogloff and Davis, 2004) then given these results the issue to be considered is whether targeting HABs warrants valuable time in adult intervention programs.

There are two possible resons for why the HAB results were so divergent from forensic text books and from what clinicians have noted. The first two reasons are based on the suggestion that the assumed low level of HABs in non-offender adults was too low. There is also a third potential reason which is partly based on this assumption in that clinicians may have assumed that non-offenders do not engage in such high levels of HABs as they have observed in offenders. As shown, in the range of situations assessed in this project, the offenders and non-offenders engaged in the same level of HABs which became more pronounced for all groups as the scenario descriptions became progressively more hostile. The results also showed that the most marked differences between offenders, younger males, and older males and women was not at the commencement of the grievance, in the "naming" stage where HABs occur, but at the end of the escalation, the "aggression" stage. It appeared that although HABs are an influential pathway in explaining why grievances escalate, what leads to violence is whether people support violence and are prepared to use it. It follows that if clinicians assume that HABs are more criminogenic than they are, when they discuss violent acts with offender, clinicians may be placing more emphasis on what the offender thought the harmdoer had done and why, rather than on the beliefs that offenders hold about why violence was considered necessary.

In the current project the two variables that appeared to represent criminogenic risk factors and which clearly discriminated offenders from non-offenders were violent and criminal sentiments and violence-based grievance resolution strategies. Intervention options for both of these variables are considered below.

It has been argued that the most important risk factor to target is criminal sentiments (Andrews, 1995). These sentiments have been found to represent the highest risk factor for recidivism for both men and women (Andrews and BONTA, 2010). At present criminal sentiments have been discussed in terms of three related constructs which share a highly significant relationship where a negative opinion of the criminal justice system is related to a higher tolerance for law violation and a higher identification with criminal peers. The results indicated that an enhancement of the criminal sentiment construct was the addition of violent sentiments (attitudes and beliefs which justify and support the use of violence given certain situations). In the current project, the endorsement of violent sentiments generated the largest effect size out of all the criminal sentiments measured (η^2 =.46). Although these sentiments are the highest risk factor, reducing their influence is a difficult task. As Bush (1995),

Simourd (1996) and Toch, (1969) have noted, high-risk adult offenders appear to have a strong commitment to criminal sentiments which they strenuously defend whenever another point of view is presented. This suggests they are highly internalised variables which are therefore enduring. Simourd (1996) also noted that there is the risk of transference when clinicians aim to reduce these sentiments. The transference risk is where clinician's levels of criminal sentiments increase as offender's levels decrease. It is therefore vital that clinical staff be supervised and debriefed during criminal sentiments interventions.

The phenomenon of transference was noted by Andrews (1980) who exposed 10 offenders to 10 community volunteers during an eight week study where the offenders and non-offenders discussed a number of issues such as the role of law in society, crime and victims, and the role of criminal justice personnel. After their exposure, the offenders reported significantly lower criminal sentiments whereas the non-offender's tolerance for law violation had increased as had their identification with criminal peers, although the non-offenders' attitudes towards the criminal justice system remained the same. Although the risk of transference is high, and has to be acknowledged, given that criminal sentiments are the highest risk factor and resistant to change practitioners may find it useful to address this criminogenic need in two different ways. The first way is to address this risk factor during structured intervention programs commonly carried out in prisons with justice departmental clinical staff. The second way is for practitioners to run adjunct exposure groups. Several Canadian studies showed significant reductions in pro-criminal sentiments for the offender participants after just 8 to 12 weeks (Andrews, 1980; Andrews and Wormith, 1990). These programs used the essence of Differential-Association as the mechanism for attitude change by exposing a group of offenders to a group of non-offenders, who were community volunteers. These Canadian programs were usually run once a week for a few hours and were conducted in an informal manner where offenders and non-offenders discussed each other's opinions about law violation, violence, victims, and crime. If these adjunct programs are implemented it is vital they be carefully supervised, especially regarding attitude transference through exposure to high-risk offenders for the non-offender group.

The final applied implication for violence rehabilitation programs concerns grievance resolution strategies. In the current project it was shown that the use of violence was most prominent in response to friends' "bad behaviour" and during hostile altercations with antagonistic people. Given that violence in response to "bad behaviour" was selective, and given that the situations where offenders were more likely to engage in violence was in line with the circumstances surrounding most reported violent crimes, it appears that programs may find it useful to tailor their interventions.

Based on the Study 1 results it could be argued that programs could be more effective by concentrating on non-violence based grievance resolution strategies to specific types of interactions. For example, most assaults and homicides occur between friends and family members, therefore helping offenders learn non-violent ways to deal with the "bad behaviour" of significant others appears valuable.

Of note, although programs often aim to show offenders non-violent grievance resolution strategies these programs are often underpinned by the theory that the offenders have attributed hostile intent and are acting violently upon their mis-attribution (Bush, 1995; Serin and Kuriychuk, 1994). What is indicated by the results in Study 1 of the current project is a slightly different approach.

Instead of looking at resolution strategies which aim to ask offenders to pause and check the information, this approach says "well ok, this person has probably behaved badly, how can we sort this problem out without using force and without you getting a jail term". This approach does not assume that offenders will have interpreted the behaviour of their harmdoer any differently from non-offenders.

What this approach does is to acknowledge openly to offenders that non-offenders will probably also have thought that the harmdoer was a "rude or inconsiderate person" but non-offenders will deal with this problem without resorting to a violent solution.

CONCLUSION

This research asked is it *how* offenders think (in the form of attributional biases) or *what* they think (in the form of violent sentiments and approval for violence-based grievance resolution strategies) that discriminates them most from non-offenders. What this research showed was that for aggressive adult offenders it is *what* they think not how they thought that is the most criminogenic. Of importance, although it appears that HABs are not a criminogenic risk factor for adult offenders, this in no way implies that HABs do not exist, or that pronounced levels of this bias were not present in the data: they were. What the data suggests is that HABs appear to be a more common attributional bias for adults than previously assumed and that most adults, regardless of being an offender or not, will probably engage in quite high levels of this bias at some point. Overall, these findings add empirical support to the prediction of Andrews that: "*what people think (antisocial attitudes) will prove more important than how they think*" (Andrews, 1995, p.51).

Criminal sentiments represent the highest risk factor for violent recidivism (Gendreau et al, 1996) yet are one of the hardest dynamic needs to change (Simourd, 1996). It appears that criminal (and now violent) sentiments are an ingrained aspect of a person's belief and value system. The question of why offender's strenuously hold onto these sentiments maybe answered by Aronson (2004) who stressed that it is through the endorsement of attitudes and beliefs (e.g., violent and criminal sentiments) that one psychological need may be met. A need that Aronson argues most people can relate to, that I am a reasonable person who does not hurt other people without just cause. It is the just cause that violent sentiments could provide for people who consistently engage in violent behaviour. After all, by justifying aggression as the right response given the circumstances, and with knowledge or a belief that friends and associates will support your behaviour, then if other people condemn you for doing what you believe to be right, it must be the condemners who are misguided, or soft.

In a final note, these results were the culmination of three and half years research. In the time taken to complete this work, based on 2006 AIC official reports, approximately 1194 Australian people will have been the victims of homicide. The economic cost of adjudicating just one of these trials in 1995 was over $1 million (Chappell, 1995). Approximately 555,202 people will have been the victims of serious non-sexual assault with roughly 166,560 of these victims requiring medical attention, often extensive. It is also vital to stress that this is an underestimation because about 30% of assaults are not reported (Carcach, 1997). Violent crime is a major social issue which has both far reaching macro and micro economic and social costs for Australia and other OCED nations. The rationale for this research was to provide practitioners with the data they would find useful when developing rehabilitation programs that are as effective as possible in reducing the level and severity of violence in our societies.

APPENDIX A. SCENARIO FROM PART 1 AND 2 OF THE MAPS

Situation 2.	
Your neighbours across the street have just bought a top-of-the-range V8 Sedan. You've met them a few times but you don't know them well. The new car has a sports exhaust, which makes it really noisy when it's revved up. Your neighbours also listen to loud music while driving. Both of them work evening shifts, and about 2am each morning you hear them coming home, revving the car as they pull into the drive. After a few weeks you decide to tell them how loud the car is. The next evening you see them about to go off to work. You quickly walk over to their house and say, "Lovely car, she is loud though, I hear you going off to work". They apologise to you for the noise, and say they didn't realise the car made so much noise. You don't hear the car after that.	

2.1. Do you think it was acceptable that the neighbours apologised and stopped revving their car? (Please circle one option)

Totally acceptable ---- A bit acceptable ---- undecided ---- a bit unacceptable ---- totally unacceptable

2.2. In general, is this how neighbours should behave once they are told they are making a noise? (Please circle)

Definitely yes --------- Perhaps yes --------- Undecided ---------- Perhaps no ---------- Definitely not

2.3. Do you think it is possible that they revved their car late at night on purpose? (Please circle one option)

Definitely yes --------- Perhaps yes --------- Undecided ---------- Perhaps no ---------- Definitely not

2.4. Do you agree or disagree with the following reasons for why they stopped revving their car: (Please answer by circling only one option per question – please answer all 6 questions)

	Strongly agree	Tend to agree	Unsuren	Tend to disagree	Strongly disagree
They just made a mistake and are now doing the right thing.	SA	A	U	D	SD
They are out for trouble; I bet they will start revving the car up again in a few weeks.	SA	A	U	D	SD

Table (Continued)

They wanted to show off their car, they only cut the noise out to save themselves getting into hassle with the neighbours.	SA	A	U	D	SD
Inconsiderate types, they probably don't know any better.	SA	A	U	D	SD
They were insulting my intelligence by lying about not knowing how loud the car was.	SA	A	U	D	SD
Probably had the music so loud they didn't know how much noise they made, they didn't mean any harm.	SA	A	U	D	SD

2.5. If this happened to you, what would you say or do about this, and why?

____
____
____
____
____
____
____
____

REFERENCES

ABS: Australian Bureau of Statistics. (2002). 2001 Census: Expanded community profile: Central metropolitan Perth, statistical district 50505. Catalogue number 2005.00, AusStats: http://www.abs.gov.au/.

AIC: Australian Institute of Criminology. (2006), Australian crime: Facts and figures 2006. Canberra, Australian Capital Territory: Australian Institute of Criminology.

Ajzen, I., and Fishbein, M. (1980). Understanding attitudes and predicting social behavior. Englewood Cliffs: NJ: Prentice-Hall.

Ajzen, I., and Madden, T. J. (1986). Prediction of goal-directed behavior: Attitudes, intentions and perceived behavioural control. *Journal of Experimental Social Psychology,* 22, 453-473.

Akers, R. L. (1997). Criminological theories: Introduction and evaluation (2nd ed.). California, CA: Roxbury Publishing.

Andrews, D. A. (1980). Some experimental investigations of the principles of differential-association through deliberate manipulations of the structure of service systems. *American Sociological Review*, 45, 448-462.

Andrews, D. A., and Bonta, J. (2010). The psychology of criminal conduct, (5th ed.). Cincinnati, OH: Anderson Publishing co.

Andrews, D. A., and Wormith, J. S. (1990). A summary of normative, reliability, and validity statistics on the criminal sentiments scale. Ottawa, Canada: Ministry of Correctional Services of Canada.

Aronson, E. A. (2004). The social animal (9th ed.). New York: Worth Publishers.

Bailey, C. A., and Ostrov, J. M. (2008). Differentiating Forms and Functions of Aggression in Emerging Adults: Associations with Hostile Attribution Biases and Normative Beliefs. *Journal of Youth and Adolescence*, 37, 713-722.

Bandura, A. (1977). Social learning theory. Englewood Cliffs, NJ: Prentice Hall.

Bell, M. L., and Forde, D. R. (1999). A factorial survey of interpersonal conflict resolution. *The Journal of Social Psychology*, 139, 369-378.

Bies, R. J., and Tripp, T. M. (1996). Beyond distrust: "Getting even" and the need for revenge. In R. M. Kramer, and T. R. Tyler (Eds.), Trust in organisations: Frontiers of theory and research. (pp.246-260). Thousand Oaks, CA: Sage Publications.

Bourgon, G., and Armstrong, B. (2005). Transferring the principles of effective treatment into a "real world" prison setting. *Criminal Justice and Behavior*, 32, 3-25.

Bush, J. (1995). Teaching self-risk management to violent offenders. In J. McGuire (Ed.), What works: Reducing reoffending: Guidelines from research and practice. Chichester, England: John Wiley and Sons.

Carcach, C. (1997). Reporting crime to the police (Trends and issues in crime and criminal justice. (Publication No. 68). Canberra, Australian Capital Territory: Australian Institute of Criminology.

Chappell, D. (1995) How violent is Australian society? In D. Chappell, and S. Egger (Eds.), Australian violence: Contemporary perspectives: Vol. 2. (pp.13-29). Canberra, Australian Capital Territory: Australian Institute of Criminology.

Coakes, S. J (2009). Spss: Analysis Without Anguish: Version 17.0 For Windows. Brisbane, Australia: John Wiley.

Copello, A. G., and Tata, P. R. (1990). Violent behaviour and interpretative bias: An experimental study of the resolution of ambiguity in violent offenders. *British Journal of Clinical Psychology*, 29, 417-428.

de Castro, O. B., Veerman, J. W., Koops, W., Bosch, J. D., Monshower, H. J. (2002). Hostile attribution of intent and aggressive behavior: A meta-analysis. *Child Development*, 73, 916-934.

Dillman, D. A., Smyth, J. D and Christian, L. M. (2008) 'Internet, Mail, and Mixed-Mode Surveys: The Tailored Design Method, (3rd Ed.). Hoboken, NJ: Wiley.

Dodge, K. A. (2006). Translational science in action: Hostile attributional style and the development of aggressive behavior problems. *Development and Psychopathology,* 18, 791–814.

Devillis, R. (1991). Scale development: theory and applications. London: Sage.

Ellis, A. (2002). Overcoming resistance: A rational emotive behavior therapy integrated approach (2nd ed.). New York: Springer Publishing Co.

Epps, J., and Kendall, P. C. (1995). Hostile attributional bias in adults. *Cognitive Therapy and Research*, 19, 159-178.

Ferguson, T. J., and Rule, B. G. (1983). An attributional perspective on anger and aggression. *Aggression,* 1, 41-74.

Gendreau, P., Little, T., and Goggin, C. (1996). A meta-analysis of the predictors of adult offender recidivism: What works. *Criminology*, 34, 575-595.

Graffam, J., Shinfield, A., Lavelle, B., and Hardcastle, L. (2005). Attitudes of employers, corrective services workers, employment support workers, and prisoners and offenders towards employing ex-prisoners and ex-offenders (Report to The Australian Criminology Research Council, grant 26.02.2003).

Hogan, R., and Emler, N. P. (1981). Retributive justice. In M. J. Lerner, and S. C. Lerner (Eds.), The justice motive in social behavior: Adapting to times of scarcity and change. (pp. 125-143). New York: Plenum Press.

Holtzworth-Munroe, A., and Hutchinson, G. (1993). Attributing negative intent to wife behaviour: The attributions of martially violent versus non-violent men. *Journal of Abnormal Psychology*, 102, 206-211.

Howells, K. (1988). The management of angry aggression. In W. Dryden and P. Trower (Eds.), Developments in cognitive psychotherapy (pp.129-153). London: Sage Publications.

Howells, K., and Day, A. (2002). Grasping the nettle: Treating and rehabilitating the violent offender. *Australian Psychologist*, 37, 222-228.

Howells, K., Watt, B., Hall, G., and Baldwin, S. (1997). Developing programs for violent offenders. *Legal and Criminological Psychology*, 2, 117-128.

Huesman, L. R. (1998). Information processing and cognitive schema model of aggression. In G. Geen, and E. Donnerstein (Eds.), Human aggression: Theories, research and implications for social policy. (pp.73-109). San Diego, CA: Academic Press.

Kelty, S. F., Hall, G., and Watt, B. D. (2010). You Have to Hit Some People! Measurement and Criminogenic Nature of Violent Sentiments in Australia. *Psychiatry, Psychology and Law*, 18, 15-32.

Kelty, S. F., Hall, G., and O'Brien-Malone (2011). You have to hit some people! Endorsing violent sentiments and the experience of grievance escalation in Australia. *Psychiatry, Psychology and Law*: DOI:10.1080/ 13218719.2011.561769.

Kennedy, L. W., and Forde, D. R. (1996). Pathways to aggression: A factorial study of "routine conflict". *Journal of Quantitative Criminology*, 12, 417-438.

Krahe, B. (2001). The social psychology of aggression. Hove, England: Psychology Press.

Luckenbill, D. F., and Doyle, D. P. (1989). Structural position and violence. *Criminology,* 27, 419-436.

Matthews, B. A., and Norris, F. H. (2002). When is believing "seeing"? Hostile attribution bias as a function of self-reported aggression. *Journal of Applied Social Psychology,* 32, 1-32.

Mikula, G., Petri, B., and Tanzer, N. (1990). What people regard as unjust: Types and structures of everyday experiences of injustice. *European Journal of Social Psychology,* 20, 133-149.

Mikula, G., Scherer, K. R., and Athenstaedt, U. (1998). The role of injustice in the elicitation of differential emotional reactions. *Personality and Social Psychology Bulletin,* 24, 769-783.

Miller, D. T. (2001). Disrespect and the experience of injustice. *Annual Review of Psychology,* 2001, 527-560.

Mukherjee, S., and Graycar, A. (1997). Crime and justice in Australia (2nd ed.). Sydney: Hawkins Press.

Ogloff, J. R. P., and Davis, M. R. (2004). Advances in offender assessment and rehabilitation: Contributions of the risk-needs-responsivity approach. *Psychology, Crime and Law*, 10, 229-242.

Polaschek, D. L. L., and Collie, R. M. (2004). Rehabilitating serious violent offenders: An empirical and theoretical stocktake. *Psychology, Crime and Law,* 10, 321-334.

Polaschek, D. L. L., and Reynolds, N. (2001). Assessment and treatment: Violent offenders. In C. R. Hollin (Ed.), Handbook of offender assessment and treatment (pp. 415-432). London: John Wiley and Sons.

Ross, S. and Polk, K. (2005). Violent crime in Australia. In D. Chappell, and P. Wilson (Eds.), Issues in Australian crime and criminal justice (pp.36-51). Chatsworth, NSW, Australia: LexisNexis Butterworths.

Seager, J. A. (2005). Violent men: The importance of impulsivity and cognitive schema. *Criminal Justice and Behavior*, 32, 26-49.

Serin, R. C., and Kuriychuk, M. (1994). Social and cognitive processing deficits in violent offenders. *International Journal of Law and Psychiatry*, 17, 431-441.

Simourd, D. J. (1996). Criminal attitudes: The silent partner in crime. In B. Wolfe, (Ed.), Proceedings of the Sixth Symposium on Violence and Aggression. Saskatchewan Canada: University of Saskatoon, Saskatchewan, Extension Press.

Simourd, D. J., and Mamuza, J. M. (2002). Hostile interpretations questionnaire: Users Manual. Ontario, Canada: Algonquin Correctional Evaluation Services Inc.

Slaby, R. G., and Guerra, N. G. (1988). Cognitive mediators of aggression in adolescent offenders: 1. assessment. *Developmental Psychology*, 24, 580-588.

South, D. (1998). General deterrence and behaviour change: A comment on the Australian Psychological Society position paper on punishment and behaviour change. *Australian Psychologist*, 33, 76-78.

Stevenson, S. F., Hall, G. and Innes, J. M. (2004). Rationalizing criminal behaviour: The influence of criminal sentiments on sociomoral development in violent offenders and non-offenders. *International Journal of Offender Therapy and Comparative Criminology,* 48, 161-174.

Tabachnick, B. G., and Fidell, L. S. (2013) 'Using Multivariate Statistics' (6th ed) Boston: Allyn and Bacon.

Tedeschi, J. T., and Felson, R. B. (1994). Violence, aggression, and coercive actions. Washington, DC: American Psychology Association.

Thomsen, S. (1997). A top night out: Social protest, masculinity and the culture of drinking violence. *British Journal of Criminology*, 37, 90-103.

Toch, H. (1969). Violent Men. Chicago: Aldine.

Vitale, J. E., Newman, J. P., Serin, R. C., and Bolt, D. M. (2005). Hostile attributions in incarcerated adult male offenders: An exploration of diverse pathways. *Aggressive Behavior*, 31, 99-115.

In: Antisocial Behavior
Editor: Justine H. Gallo
ISBN: 978-1-63321-521-4

Chapter 5

ANTISOCIAL BEHAVIOR IN CHILDREN WITH ADHD: CLINICAL PRESENTATION, EPIDEMIOLOGY, ETIOLOGY, PROGNOSIS AND TREATMENT APPROACHES

Yasaman Ahmadi-Kashani and Lily Hechtman
McGill University Health Centre/Montreal Children's Hospital

ABSTRACT

This chapter provides a review of the literature pertaining to the clinical presentation, epidemiology, etiology, prognosis and treatment of Oppositional Defiant Disorder (ODD) and antisocial behavior in children with Attention Deficit Hyperactivity Disorder (ADHD). The pervasive effects of ODD in children with ADHD may have an impact on their cognitive, behavioral, emotional and academic performances. ODD type behavior in ADHD school-aged children is characterized by talking back to adults, rejection by peers and failure in school. Followed into adolescence, some of these children may exhibit a significantly elevated risk for delinquent behaviors such as stealing and disobedient acts. The clinical presentation of antisocial behavior in adults is characterized by the progression of criminal behaviors and severe personality disturbance. A combination of genetic predispositions leading to cognitive deficits, combined with exposure to environmental risk factors contributes to the link between ADHD, ODD and antisocial behavior. Only in some cases, do children with ADHD continue to show these behaviors into adolescence and adulthood. Thus, there is generally a gradual decrease in antisocial behaviors and rates of dysfunctions and they may never be exhibited in later stages. An early intervention that aims to control the symptoms of ADHD and reduce the impact of antisocial and ODD type behavior at each developmental stage should be utilized. These interventions can consist of medication and a variety of psychosocial interventions, such as parent-child therapy, parent training, positive behavioral support, and collaborative problem solving.

Introduction

This chapter provides a comprehensive review of the literature and relevant research findings treating the link between Attention Deficit/Hyperactivity Disorder (ADHD), Oppositional Defiant Disorder (ODD) and antisocial behavior. The aim of this chapter is to provide insight into the developmental trajectory from children's ADHD symptoms of inattention, hyperactivity and ODD type symptoms, to adult antisocial behaviors and delinquency. The first section of this chapter focuses on the clinical presentation including definition and epidemiology of ADHD, ODD and Conduct Disorder (CD) at three different developmental stages, e.g. childhood, adolescence, and adulthood. The second part of this chapter presents the possible development of this comorbidity by presenting the underlying neurobiological and environmental risk factors. The third section aims to examine the progression of co-occurrence of ADHD and antisocial behavior and reviews the pathway from childhood ADHD and ODD to adolescence and adulthood CD and delinquency. The final portion of this chapter assesses the influence of both psychological and medical treatments in each stage of development during the course, as well as the outcome of ADHD, ODD and antisocial behavior.

Definition and Symptomology

Attention Deficit Hyperactivity Disorder

ADHD is a disorder characterized by six or more symptoms of pervasive developmentally inappropriate levels of inattention and/or hyperactivity/ impulsivity, an onset of symptoms prior to age 12 and clinically significant impairment in academic, occupational, and/or social functioning. Although ADHD onset is in childhood, the symptoms may continue to persist through adulthood for some individuals. It used to be thought that ADHD symptoms dissipated by adolescence. However, controlled prospective longitudinal and follow up studies indicate that ADHD continues in 85% cases into adolescence and approximately 60% of cases into adulthood (Faraone, Biederman & Mick, 2006; Hinshaw, Owens, Sami & Fargeon, 2006). Thus, the definition of ADHD has been revised in DSM-5 in a way that is more appropriate for adolescents and adults who are challenged by ADHD (American Psychiatric Association, 2013). In individuals aged 17 and over, a lower threshold of symptoms (5 vs. 6) is sufficient for practitioners to establish a reliable ADHD diagnosis (Von Polier, Vloet & Harpertz-Dahlmann, 2012).

Depending on diagnostic criteria and age group, ADHD affects approximately 5–10% of children and adolescents globally. Thus, it represents one of the most common psychiatric disorders with onset in childhood (Keenan et al., 1997, Taylor & Sonuga-Barke, 2008). Survey of DSM-IV symptoms in preschool-aged children found that parents rated 8% of boys and 4% of girls as meeting the prerequisite number of behavioral symptoms of ADHD (Gadow & Nolan, 2002). Symptoms of inattention, impulsivity, and hyperactivity may result in children's inability to respond appropriately to delay gratification, as well as follow instruction. Both inattention and impulsivity tend to persist throughout children's developmental course and affect functions in different domains throughout the life span

(Barkley, 1997b). Children with ADHD have shown significant functional problems at home, school, and social settings. They also have a higher risk for comorbidities such as aggression, ODD, and CD (Ross and Ross, 1982).

Oppositional Defiant Disorder & Conduct Disorder

ODD is characterized as defiant, disobedient, and hostile behavior directed at authority figures, expressing anger, blaming others for one's own mistakes, losing one's temper, and deliberately annoying others whereby these characteristics persist for at least 6 months (Turgay, 2009). ODD most commonly emerges in late preschool or early school-age children and it is not limited to a particular age group. Studies on ODD prevalence suggest a wide range of rates from 2 to 15% (Young & Amarasinghe, 2010).

The DSM-5 does not allow for diagnosis of ODD in adults over the age of 18 who meet the criteria for antisocial personality disorder (American Psychiatric Association, 2013). Throughout their life span, some children may continue to exhibit ODD type behavior during adolescence and adulthood and progress to antisocial behavior or conduct disorder (CD). CD is characterized by continuing patterns of behavior such as physical aggression, deception, and violation of others' rights (Loeber & Stouthamer-Loeber, 1998). CD is sometimes described as an encompassing spectrum of behaviors ranging from less serious to more severe antisocial behaviors (Stahl & Clarizio, 1999).

One of the most important gaps in the epidemiology of CD and ODD is the fact that age related changes of these disorders are not often thoroughly investigated in longitudinal community studies (Nock et al. 2007). Research shows that ODD's usual persistence is around 6 years (Polanczyk & Rohde, 2007). However, some adults diagnosed as ODD during childhood and adolescence display ODD type behavior with higher intensity and more severity in adulthood and progress towards CD. Research emphasizes the independence yet interrelatedness of ODD and CD. Thus, it is important to note that 75% of children who meet the criteria for ODD do not progress to CD diagnosis (Turgay, 2009).

Co-occurrence of ADHD, ODD & Antisocial Behavior

ADHD has been linked to several psychosocial issues, e.g. relationship and communication problems and academic failures that have a substantial impact on development (Shaw-Zirt, Popali-Lehane, Chaplin, & Bergman, 2005; Stormont, 2001). In addition to displaying earlier symptoms such as poor attention and impulsivity (Fischer, Barkley, Fletcher & Smallish, 1993), some individuals with ADHD present what is referred to as secondary problems or emergence of comorbidities such as ODD and CD (Angold, Costello, & Erkanli, 1999; Hinshaw & Anderson, 1996; Mannuzza, Klein, & Moulton, 2003; Slomkowski, Klein & Mannuzza, 1995). The trajectory from childhood ADHD and ODD to adolescent and adult antisocial behavior and CD, signifies the need for a better understanding of the progression from childhood disorderly behavior, to criminal and maladaptive behavior in adults with ADHD.

In follow-up studies of children (Biederman et al., 2008) and adolescents (Barkley, Fischer, Edelbrock, & Smallish, 1990; Kuhne, Schachar, & Tannock, 1997) ADHD children with ODD often show persistent disruptive behavior that affects diverse domains of their functioning. These disruptive behaviors and ODD in the presence of environmental risk factors such as delinquent peers, poor parental mentoring, and supervision, put children with ADHD at risk for delinquent antisocial behavior in adolescence and adulthood (Reimherr, Marchant, Olsen, Wender, & Robison, 2013) For instance, the progression from ODD to CD is often influenced by the child with ADHD and ODD teaming up with a delinquent peer group, who expose the child to more severe antisocial behavior (O'Donnell, Hawkins, Abbott, 1995; Patterson, 1982).

Clinical Presentation in Childhood

ODD in school-aged children is characterized by lying, talking back to adults, physical fights, bullying, rejection by peers and failure in school (Mrug, Hoza, Pelham, Gnagy, & Greiner, 2007). ADHD children with ODD often show oppositional problems, social aggression and antisocial behavior due to their impulsivity and inability to follow rules and instructions (Barkley, 1997a; Hinshaw, 1987). Such behaviors may have short-term and long-term negative social consequences for these children (Whalen & Henker, 1985). Serious problems with peers and interaction problems with their family members have been consistently documented (Barkley et al., 1990). Children with ADHD with comorbid ODD have a tendency to be loud, forceful and indiscreet in social interactions, which may lead them to be perceived as aggressive, and to be rejected by other children (Flicek, 1992; Pope, Bierman & Mumma, 1987). Moreover, they may present more impaired social problem-solving skills and aggressive responses in conflict situations than children with ADHD alone (Gadow & Nolan, 2002; Matthys, Cuperus & Engeland, 1999). Their difficulty in maintaining attention on a task and finishing it, along with disruptive behaviors in the classroom may contribute to their classroom challenges and poor academic performance (Cantwell, 1986).

Clinical Presentation in Adolescence

Followed into adolescence, children with ADHD, predominantly those with comorbid ODD, have a significantly higher risk for developing CD with delinquent and antisocial activities (August, Stewart, & Holmes, 1983; Barkley et al., 1990; Klein & Mannuzza, 1991). Despite possible overall improvement in functioning by adolescence, in some children with ADHD, ODD may persist into later life stages followed by social and academic problems (Faigel et al., 1995). Some may continue to have difficulties in their social interactions and demonstrate poor social skills, which may lead to underachievement in the academic domain, problems at home and rejection by peers (Young & Amarasinghe, 2010). They may then gravitate to a delinquent peer group and thus exhibit a significantly elevated risk for delinquent behaviors such as stealing, disobedient acts, temperamental outbursts, substance use and abuse, and fire-setting (Fischer & Barkley, 2003). These individuals may be involved in fewer social and organized activities, have fewer friends, and exhibit a lower level of social competence compared to the control group (Fischer & Barkley, 2003). They also showed more deficiency in internalizing and externalizing their thoughts and emotions as rated by parents and teachers (Barkley, Anastopoulos, Guevremont & Fletcher, 1991).

Clinical Presentation in Adulthood

Childhood ADHD has been linked to various manifestations of risk-taking and antisocial behaviors in adulthood (Carlotta, Borroni, Maffei & Fossati, 2011). Long-term longitudinal studies on the adult outcome of childhood ADHD consistently exhibit a significant link between childhood ADHD with ODD and conduct problems in adolescence and antisocial behavior in adulthood (Mannuzza, Klein, Bessler, Malloy & LaPadula, 1998). Despite the fact that by adulthood many of the hyperactivities disappear and the ODD symptom patterns improve (Ingram, Hechtman & Morgenstern, 1999), some adults particularly those who developed antisocial behaviors during adolescence continue to exhibit difficulties and demonstrate deficits. These difficulties include impaired social relationships, low self-esteem, substance abuse (Biederman et al., 1997; Lambert & Hartsough, 1998), educational and occupational problems (Weiss and Hechtman, 1993), and a higher risk of being arrested (Satterfield, Swanson, Schell, & Lee, 1994).

Another study by Marks, Newcorn & Halperin (2006) shows that in comparison to controls, a significantly higher portion of adults with ADHD and CD reported that they had partaken in physically dangerous acts, frequently did not appear to listen, had difficulty waiting their turn, and struggled to remain seated. Many of these individuals exhibited poor parenting methods and had a higher rate of divorce and separation (Retz & Rosler, 2009). The clinical presentation of CD in adults with ADHD, usually for those who show antisocial behavior and CD in adolescence, is also characterized by the progression of criminal behaviors, severe personality disturbance, violent offenses, (Flory, Molina, Pelham, Gnagy & Smith, 2006; Mannuzza et al., 2008) as well as taking higher risks in daily functioning (Barkley, 2000). They are often overrepresented in reckless driving, accidents, disregard for traffic rules and severe cases of injury due to accidents at home, school, and work (Kaya et al., 2008). According to Jerome, Habinski, and Segal (2006), a higher frequency of accidents, speeding, driving under the influence of alcohol, and driving without a license is evident among adults with ADHD and CD. It must be stressed that these do not constitute the majority of adults with ADHD who have attention and behavioral problems and are not significantly involved in antisocial or criminal behaviors.

Etiology

In the past few decades, reaearch has focused on the role of "nature" versus "nurture" with regards to children with ADHD who exhibit comorbidity with ODD. This has been followed by research on the interaction between genetic and environmental influences on the development of this comorbidity (Raine, 2002). Research has focused on the genetic, neurobiological, and environmental underpinnings of ADHD, ODD, CD, and antisocial behavior (Retz & Rosler, 2009).

Neurobiology

Several recent studies have linked ADHD, CD, and ODD to shared genetic risk factors (Dick, Viken, Kaprio & Rose, 2005; Nadder, Rutter, Silberg, Meas & Eaves, 2002). As such, genes that are linked to the presence of ADHD symptoms may also be the same genes that are associated with antisocial behavioral phenotypes (Beaver et al., 2007). Two genetic polymorphisms have been identified as major contributors to antisocial phenotypes: dopamine D2 receptor gene (DRD2) and the dopamine D4 receptor gene (DRD4). DRD2 codes are located throughout the body and more so in the striatum, the pituitary gland and the amygdala (Beaver et al., 2007). Genetic association studies show that D2 and D4 dopamine receptors are consistently associated with conduct disorder and antisocial behavior such as compulsive gambling and alcohol consumption (Beaver et al., 2007; Congdon, Lesch, & Canli, 2008). On the other hand, research also shows that the same dopaminergic polymorphisms have been implicated in ADHD, and impulsivity. Sagvolden et al. (2005) proposed a developmental behavioral theory to elaborate on how these two polymorphisms underpin the emergence of ADHD. They suggested that a "hypofunctioning mesolimbic dopamine system is largely responsible for producing alterations in behavioral reinforcement and extinction, which, in turn, disrupts learning processes. These disrupted learning processes coupled to a hypofunctioning mesocortical dopamine pathway can cause the emergence of ADHD and ADHD-like symptoms" (Beaver et al., 2007, p. 6). Sagvolden et al.'s (2005) theory also sheds light on how altered dopaminergic levels may lead to behavioral disinhibitation and an inability to control impulsivity, which are associated with antisocial behavior such as aggression and violence. However, it is important to note that the dopamine genes have been identified and implicated as risk factors for many other psychological conditions such as anxiety and depression which makes the connection between the dopamine neurotransmitter and the presence of ADHD and ODD less specific. Thus, further research is necessary to clarify the impact (Beaver et al., 2007).

It has also been shown that dysfunction of the amygdala may contribute to antisocial development, ODD and CD (Fairchild et al., 2011; Raine, 2011). The amygdala, which is connected to the prefrontal cortex, is a part of the limbic system essential for emotion processing and fear conditioning (Olson, Plotzker, & Ezzyat, 2007; Weber, Habel, Amunts, & Schneider, 2008). Malfunction in the amygdala leads to problems with inhibition, affects regulation, anticipation of punishment and reward, social cognition, and reaction in general. This is in line with research findings showing that emotional provocation leads to increase in activity of the amygdala in children with the early-onset subtype of ADHD (Herpertz et al., 2001) and that antisocial children are characterized by an increased sensitivity to negative emotional cues when compared with a control group (van Goozen, Fairchild, Snoek, & Harold, 2007). In conflict with these findings, Sterzer et al.'s (2005) research shows decreased responsiveness of the left amygdala to negative pictures in children with CD compared with control subjects. It has been argued that although ADHD is associated with different neural circuits, neuroimaging data suggest abnormal frontostriatal processing in ADHD individuals who exhibit antisocial behavior (Connor, 2002; Raine, 2002; van Polier, Vloet, Herpertz- Dahlmann, 2012). More research is needed to clarify the impact of the neurotransmitters and brain regions involved in the complex comorbidity of ADHD and ODD.

Environment

Research suggests that family environments may have an impact on the development of delinquent and antisocial behavior (Schmitz, 2003). Family problems, poor parenting, parental pathology, and unstable family situations may all effect the development and progression of ODD and CD in children with ADHD. Families of many ADHD adolescents tend to be more disharmonious than controls (Barkley et al., 1991). Research on parental psychopathology provides evidence that parents of children with ADHD and ODD more often suffer from psychiatric disorders such as schizophrenia, substance abuse, depression, antisocial personality disorder, (Pfiffner, McBurnett, Rathouz, & Judice, 2005) and exhibit a high prevalence of sociopathy, hysteria, and alcoholism (Morrison, 1980).

Other environmental risk factors related to parental factors that increase the occurrence of antisocial behavior in children with ADHD includes low parental intelligence (Rosler et. al, 2008), negativity and lack of warmth (Kashdan et al., 2004; Pfiffner et al., 2005), inconsistency, (Taylor, Schachar, Thorley, & Wieselberg, 1986) as well as lack of responsiveness (Johnston, Murray, & Hinshaw, 2002; Seipp & Johnston, 2005). Deault (2010) suggests that poor and inconsistent parenting such as inappropriate and harsh punishment and lack of control and supervision that at times occur among parents with ADHD, often act as a situational stressor and risk factor for ODD. In addition, parents as role models may positively or negatively reinforce violence and antisocial behavior or reward selfish and aggressive behavior (Bornovalova et al., 2010; Deault, 2010).

Both ODD and CD are associated with negative parenting practice (Pfiffner et al., 2005) and overt parenting disagreement (Conner & Doerfler, 2007). Compared with children diagnosed with ADHD alone, children with ODD comorbidity often experience less parenting effectiveness and agreement between parents (Conner & Doerfler, 2007). When analyzed by age, exhibition of ODD-like symptoms in ADHD children such as overt aggression and impulsivity has been associated with more overt parenting disagreement. However, parental disagreement may decrease in adolescence. Aggression may become more covert and parents become less aware of their children's behaviors, which lead to less parental disagreement and conflict (Connor, 2002; Conner & Doerfler, 2007).

Research findings shed light on the importance of parenting in the continuity of children's behavioral problems and their developmental course. For instance, Heller and Baker (2000) have found a link between the frequency of maternal commands during pre-school parent–child interaction and third grade diagnoses of ADHD, exhibiting ODD and CD in later developmental stages. Moreover, a longitudinal study has shown a high positive correlation between negative maternal behaviors and aggressive and antisocial behavior among preschool children (Campbell, March, Pierce, Ewing, & Szumowski, 1991). It is important to note that researchers frequently face methodological difficulties in determining whether family and parental problems are contributing factors to the presence of ODD and CD symptoms in ADHD or if they are the outcome posed by the emergence of ODD and CD (Johnston & Mash, 2001).

Interaction of Genes & Environment

The core of symptomology among individuals with ADHD who exhibit ODD, CD, and antisocial behavior may be linked to genetic underpinnings influenced by reciprocal interaction with environmental factors (Goodman & Stevenson, 1989; Hinshaw & Renfro, 1999). Recent studies show that ADHD children with low monoamine oxidase A (MAO-A) activity who experienced maltreatment in childhood exhibit antisocial and violent behavior (Caspi et al., 2002; Foley et al., 2004). According to Retz & Rosler (2009), "High MAO-A activity, i.e. long MAOA alleles, protected against the development of violent behavior in the presence of childhood maltreatment, whereas short MAOA alleles predisposed towards violent behavior, at least in case of exposure to childhood maltreatment. Likewise, low-activity MAOA alleles could be found more often in conduct disorder exclusively in the presence of adverse childhood environment" (p. 239). These results are confirmed with another study on a Swedish sample where short MAOA allele interacted with adverse psychosocial risk factors during adolescence and was associated with conduct and criminal behavior. MAO-A genotype has also been shown to mediate amygdala volume and prefrontal and amygdala activation in response to emotional stimuli (Meyer-Lindenberg et al., 2006). Moreover, in their recent study, Brennan et al. (2011) examined the catechol-O-methyltransferase (COMT) Val108/158Met polymorphism and the outcome of this study suggests a significant link between genetic predisposition and environmental risk factor such as maternal cigarette smoking during pregnancy to predict participants' antisocial and aggressive behavior among adolescents (Peris & Hinshaw, 2003). Further studies are necessary to determine the extent of environmental risk factors' impact on MAOA malfunction that may contribute to the persistence and progression of ODD among ADHD children throughout the developmental course.

Studies concerning the association between the 5HTTLPR genotype, and childhood psychosocial adversity with ADHD and violent behavior, provide evidence supporting the notion of gene and environment interactions in the occurrence of ADHD, ODD, and antisocial behavior. Although research shows that in carriers of 5-HTTLPR LL-genotype, the risk for ADHD was usually higher and prevalence of antisocial behavior and aggression was lower in carriers, carriers of the 5-HTTLPR SS/SL-genotype had a low risk for both ADHD and violent behavior in absence of psychosocial adversity and a significantly higher risk of ADHD and violent behavior if psychosocial adversity was present (Retz & Rosler, 2009). Furthermore, Cadoret et al.'s (2003) study was also able to detect an association between 5HTTLPR, ODD and ADHD only when the confounding environmental variables like parental anti-sociality were taken into consideration.

To sum up, antisocial behavior, ODD, and CD is not inevitably associated with ADHD, but co-occurrence depends on particular genetic and environmental interactions. In order to determine the factors involved in the development of ODD, CD, and antisocial behavior in individuals with ADHD in general, it is important to also focus on the interplay between genetic and environmental influences. Genes may not linearly influence human behavior and it is necessary to assess pleiotropic genetic risk factors in the presence of different environmental and psychosocial conditions (Derks, Dolan, Hudziak, Neale & Boomsma, 2007; McEwen, 2008; Robinson, Fernald, & Clayton, 2008)

Prognosis

There is a common tendency in perceiving ODD as a predictor of CD, emergence of antisocial behavior, and the presence of antisocial personality disorder. Thus, studies mostly explored the progression of ODD in combination with CD under one category (Angold & Costello, 2006). Although ODD and CD share many similar correlates, significant differences emerge on some variables that support distinctiveness between these diagnoses. On the one hand, some longitudinal studies find no evidence that ODD behavior in childhood predicts later CD, which supports the concept of separate disorders (Achenbach, 1991; Loeber et al., 2000; Mannuzza, Klein, Abikoff, & Moulton, 2004). Some cross-sectional studies using clinical ADHD samples have supported the distinctiveness of ODD from CD regarding the intensity of antisocial symptoms (Kuhne, Schachar, & Tannock, 1997) where ADHD alone has the least severity, comorbid with ODD has intermediate severity, and ADHD with CD has the most severity (Ercan et al., 2013). On the other hand, research suggests that onset ODD may serve as a developmental foundation to CD, thus supporting the notion of ODD as a mild form and predictor of CD (Biederman et al., 1995; Kuhne et al., 1997, Loeber et al., 2000). It is important to note that these studies suggest that regardless of the possible associations between ODD and CD, they need to be studied and understood separately in order for the treatment and interventions to be effective (Nock, Kazdin, Hiripi & Kessler, 2007)

In addition to distinguishing ODD from CD in ADHD children, there have been debates as to whether or not ADHD alone or with comorbid ODD predict antisocial behavior in later stages of development (Angold, Costello, & Erkanli, 1999; Loeber, Green, Keenan, & Lahey, 1995). The majority of studies suggested that ODD and CD alone and not ADHD predict adult antisocial behavior (Lahey, Loeber, Burke, & Applegate, 2005; Satterfield et al., 2007). To validate this claim, they reported findings in clinically referred boys, showing that ODD was a more reliable and accurate predictor of the later onset of CD than ADHD was (Lahey, Loeber, Burke, Rathouz, & McBurnett, 2002; Loeber, Green, Lahey, Frick, & McBurnett, 2000). Further studies support the notion that for conduct problems, hyperactivity and/or impulsivity, but not inattention, underpin the risk of delinquent and antisocial behavior (Loeber et al., 2000). As such, taking ODD and ADHD into account simultaneously, the association between ADHD and CD in particular, becomes less evident, suggesting a dominance of ODD over ADHD in exhibiting antisocial behavior.

Research suggests that about 67% of children with ODD no longer meet the criteria for the diagnosis after a 3-year follow-up (Connor, 2002; Loeber et al., 2000). An earlier age at onset of ODD symptoms suggests a poorer prognosis in terms of progression to CD and 40% may eventually progress to antisocial personality disorder (Zoccolillo et al., 1996). There has been much debate about how some children desist from this progression and some do not. Interplay of several factors has been identified as to why some ADHD children tend to continue presenting ODD, CD, and antisocial behaviors (Lahey & Waldman, 2003; Moffitt, 1990). First, dysfunctional parenting practices and negative parent-child communications in preschool-aged children have been consistently linked to the continuity of children's present and future oppositional-defiant and conduct problems (Eiden, Edwards, & Leonard, 2007; Keown & Woodward, 2002). Second, it has been suggested that mutual interactions between child behavior and family experiences may contribute to the continuation of ODD type behaviors (Patterson, 1982). Family adversities such as low socio-economic status and poverty have been identified as correlates of conduct problems in children (AACAP, 2007; Harvey & Metcalfe, 2012). Preschool children who live in poverty are at a higher risk for the progression of conduct problems and ODD, than are children from higher socio-economic backgrounds (Qi & Kaiser, 2003). However, it has also been suggested that there is not sufficient evidence on possible differences in the prevalence of ODD and CD in rural and urban areas and prevalence rates of ODD and CD in the disadvantaged neighborhoods, compared with advantaged neighborhoods which have not been adequately investigated (Angold & Costello, 2006; Loeber, Burke, Lahey, Winters & Zera, 2000). Thus, more research is necessary in order to clarify and determine the extent and intensity of socio-economic adversity and its impact on the progression and continuity of ODD and CD among individuals with ADHD.

TREATMENT

In children with ADHD, the presence of comorbid disorder of ODD may complicate the application of effective interventions. In order to address associated cognitive, behavioral, and psychosocial dysfunctions, a successful treatment plan should be comprehensive, involving the patient's education system, psychotherapy, family relationships, parent training, and pharmacotherapy (Wender, 1995). The treatment reasoning is that by early intervention, in order to address present behavioral and cognitive problems as well as improve functioning early in life, children will develop fewer primary and secondary difficulties later in life (Ingram, Hechtman, & Morgenstern, 1999). Such treatment can diminish the risks for both concurrent ODD type behavior and later antisocial conduct (Fischer, & Barkley, 2003).

Pharmacotherapy

Most of the information regarding the pharmacotherapy of ODD is based on comorbidity studies of ODD with ADHD (Turgay, Joseph, Nag et al., 2003). As such, there is a significant overlap in treatment and use of stimulants in treating ADHD with ODD. The long acting psycho-stimulants such as Concerta and Adderall XR are suggested to be more effective medications for patients with ADHD and ODD due to higher remission and compliance rates when compared to short-acting stimulants such as methylphenidate (Banaschewski et al., 2006)

There is strong evidence that medication is helpful in improving impulsive, aggressive, and disruptive behavior short term. A longitudinal study conducted by Beiderman et al. (2009) showed that stimulant-treated children developed fewer disruptive and other psychiatric disorders, and exhibited less school failure. However, the major issue is the continuity and maintenance of the medication treatment. Research shows that of those patients with ADHD who are prescribed medication, only 18 to 50% continue with this treatment for two or three years (Hechtman, 2006; Schubert, Koster, & Lehmkuhl, 2010). Thus, the effect of medication on long-term outcome is difficult to establish. It has also been suggested that the improvement in ODD symptoms might not be directly associated to the effectiveness of the medication but rather the possible control of ADHD symptoms as a result of medication (Turgay, 2009). A recent review on the treatment of children with ODD concludes that many children and adolescents show positive responses to typical medications used for ADHD, but for a substantial group these medications alone are not adequate (Connor, Steeber, & McBurnett, 2010). These results confirm the clinical notion that while stimulant medication may be effective, often pharmacotherapy alone is not deemed sufficient (Reimherr, Marchant, Olsen, Wender, & Robison, 2013).

Psychosocial Interventions

Children with ADHD and comorbid ODD may require extra attention in treatment planning. Clinicians assessing children with ADHD and either ODD or CD should be aware that these children may require a multimodal treatment program which increases clinical attention to parenting support, management strategies, and enhanced school supports. Psychosocial interventions consist of cognitive interventions, skills training, conflict resolution, anger management and academic preparations that appear to reduce disruptive behaviors in the present and prevent future delinquency (Burke, Loeber & Birmaher, 2002; Connor, 2002; Eckenrode et al., 2000).

In the Multisite Multimodal Treatment study of ADHD (MTA), 576 children with ADHD of whom 40% had ODD, aged 7–9 years were randomized to four different treatment modalities for 14 months: medication management (mostly methylphenidate), intensive behavioral therapy, a combination of both, and standard community care selected by the child's family. The MTA study examined the moderating effects of ODD co-morbidity on ADHD treatment response, as well as the response of ODD symptoms to ADHD treatment (Turgay, 2009). Based on the teacher ratings and parent-child interaction (Murray et al., 2008), the overall result of this follow up longitudinal study indicated that children with ADHD with comorbid ODD benefited more from combined therapy, whereas children with ADHD without ODD, both medication alone and combined treatments were equally effective for ADHD symptoms (Jensen et al., 2001). The comorbidity of ODD did not alter the overall pattern of findings, indicating a relative superiority of medication treatment over psychosocial or community standard interventions despite 66% of whom received medication. Secondary analysis of the MTA study suggests that the effectiveness of the treatment of ODD with comorbid ADHD improved by approximately 20% when psychosocial treatment was added to medication management (Richters, Arnold, Jensen, et al. 1995; Swanson, Kraemer, Hinshaw, et al., 2001). Further studies on the comparative effectiveness of pharmacotherapy and psychosocial interventions and/or their combination in the management of ODD with or without ADHD comorbidity may clarify the most effective treatment alternatives for ODD. This may also aid in formulating prevention strategies for more serious psychopathologies including CD and antisocial personality disorder later on in developmental stages.

Conclusion

Studies on the adult outcome of childhood ADHD consistently exhibit a significant link between childhood ADHD with ODD, and antisocial behavior in adulthood. ADHD children with ODD show persistent disruptive behavior that affects diverse domains of their functioning. Although research consistently suggests that ADHD increases the likelihood of later antisocial behavior, there is still an ongoing debate as to whether this is due to ADHD itself, or to ADHD comorbidity with other disorders such as ODD and CD. It is important to note that although early conduct problems and ODD type behavior may be better indicators of adolescent and adult antisocial behavior than is an early onset of ADHD, children with ADHD are a feasible sample for the study of risk factors for antisocial behavior, when taking into consideration the role of ADHD in the occurrence of early conduct problems. However, many analyses of the predictability of later antisocial behavior from childhood ADHD have been influenced by significant comorbidity of ADHD with conduct problems. Further research is necessary in order to distinguish ODD from CD in ADHD children, and to clarify as to whether or not ADHD alone or with comorbid ODD predict antisocial behavior in later stages of development. The link between ADHD and antisocial behavior is increased by several risk factors such as parental psychopathology, socio-economic status, parenting style, and neurocognitive impairment. The association between increased ADHD symptom severity and the presence of ODD or CD, implies that children with these comorbid disorders may require more specific and earlier interventions than children with ADHD alone. These children may need a more prolonged and intensive combined treatment of medication and psychosocial treatment starting at early ages and extending into adolescence. The common path from childhood ADHD and ODD, to adult antisocial behavior and CD, suggests the need for an enhanced understanding of development from childhood disorderly behavior to criminal and maladaptive behavior in adults with ADHD. Further research is needed to determine risk factors, effective interventions, and consistent prevention methods, to ensure a more positive development course for children with ADHD.

References

AACAP. (2007). Practice parameter for the assessment and treatment of children and adolescents with oppositional defiant disorder. *Journal of the American Academy of Child & Adolescent Psychiatry*, *46*, 126–141.

Achenbach, T. M. (1991). *Manual for child behavior checklist/4-18 and 1991 profile*. Burlington, VT: University of Vermont, Department of Psychiatry.

American Psychiatric Association. (2013). Diagnostic and statistical manual of mental disorders (5th ed.). Arlington, VA: American Psychiatric Publishing.

Angold, A. & Costello, E. J. (2006). Toward establishing an empirical basis for the diagnosis of oppositional defiant disorder. *Journal of the American Academy of Child & Adolescent Psychiatry*, *35*, 1205–1212.

Angold, A., Costello, E. J. & Erkanli, A. (1999). Comorbidity. *Journal of Child Psychology and Psychiatry*, *40*, 57–87.

August, G. J., Stewart, M. A. & Holmes, C. S. (1983). A four–year follow–up of hyper-active boys with and without conduct disorder. *British Journal of Psychiatry*, *143*, 192–198.

Banaschewski, T., Coghill, D., Santosh, P., Zuddas, A., Asherson, P., Buitelaar, J., Danckaerts, M., Dopfner, M., Faraone, S. V., Rothenberger, A., Sergeant, J., Steinhausen, H. C., Sonuga-Barke, E. J. & Taylor, E. (2006). Long-acting medications for the hyperkinetic disorders. A systematic review and European treatment guideline. *European Journal of Child and Adolescent Psychiatry*, *15*(8), 476–495.

Barkley, R. A. (1997a). *Attention deficit hyper- activity disorder: A handbook for diagnosis and treatment* (2nd. Ed.). New York: Guilford.

Barkley, R. A. (1997b). Attention-deficit/hyperactivity disorder. In E. J. Mash & L. Terdal (Eds.), *Assessment of Childhood Disorders*. New York: Guilford.

Barkley, R. A. (2000). Commentary on the multimodal treatment study of children with AD/HD. *Journal of Abnormal Child Psychology*, *28*, 595-598.

Barkley, R. A., Anastopoulos, A. D., Guevremont, D. C. & Fletcher, K. E. (1991). Adolescents with attention deficit hyperactivity disorder: Patterns of behavioral adjustment, academic functioning, and treatment utilization. *Journal of the American Academy of Child and Adolescent Psychiatry*, *30*, 752- 761.

Beaver, K. M., Wright, J. P., DeLisi, M., Walsh, A., Vaughn, M. G., Boisvert, D. & Vaske, J. (2007). A gene x gene interaction between DRD2 and DRD4 is associated with conduct disorder and antisocial behavior in males. *Behavioral and Brain Functions*, *3*(30).

Biederman, J., Petty, C. R., Ten Haagen, K. S., Small, J., Doyle, A. E., Spencer, T., Mick, E., Monuteaux, M. C., Smoller, J. W. & Faraone, S. V. (2009). Effect of candidate gene polymorphisms on the course of attention deficit hyperactivity disorder. *Psychiatry Research*, *170*, 199–203.

Biederman, J., Petty, C. R., Wilens, T. E., Fraire, M. G., Purcell, C. A., Mick, E., et al. (2008). Familial risk analyses of attention deficit hyperactivity disorder and substance use disorders. *American Journal of Psychiatry*, *165*, 107-115.

Biederman, J., Wilens, T., Mick, E., Faraone, S., Weber, W., Curtis, S., Thornell, A., Pfister, K., Jetton, J. & Soriano, J. (1997). Is ADHD a risk for psychoactive substance use disorder? Findings from a four year follow-up study. *Journal of the American Academy of Child and Adolescent Psychiatry*, *36*, 21–29.

Biederman, J., Wilens, T. E., Mick, E., Milberger, S., Spencer, T. J. & Faraone, S. V. (1995). Psychoactive substance use in adults with attention deficit hyperactivity disorder (ADHD: effects of ADHD and psychiatric comorbidity). *American Journal of Psychiatry*, *152*, 1652–1658.

Bornovalova, M. A., Hicks, B. M., Iacono, W. G. & McGue, M. (2010). Familial transmission and heritability of childhood disruptive disorders. *The American Journal of Psychiatry*, *167*(9), 1066–1074.

Brennan, P. A., Hammen, C., Sylvers, P., Bor, W., Najman, J. Ph.D., Lind, P., Montgomery, G., & Smith, A. K. (2011). Interactions between the *COMT* Val108/158Met polymorphism and maternal prenatal smoking predict aggressive behavior outcomes. *Biological Psychology*, *87*, 99–105.

Burke, J. D., Loeber, R. & Birmaher, B. (2002). Oppositional defiant and conduct disorder: a review of the past 10 years, part II. *Journal of the American Academy of Child and Adolescent Psychiatry*, *41*, 1275-1293.

Cadoret, R. J., Langbehn, D., Caspers, K., Troughton, E. P., Yucuis, R., Sandhu, H. K., et al. (2003). Associations of the serotonin transporter promoter polymorphism with aggressivity, attention deficit, and conduct disorder in an adoptee population. *Comprehensive Psychiatry*, *44*, 88-101.

Campbell, S. B., Pierce, E. W., March, C. L., Ewing, L. J. & Szumowski, E. K. (1991). Hard-to-manage preschool boys: Family context and the stability of externalizing behavior. *Journal of Abnormal Child Psychology*, *19* (3), 301-318.

Cantwell, D. P. (1986). Attention deficit and associated childhood disorders. In T. Mellon & G. L. Klerman (Ed.), *Contemporary directions in psychopathology: toward DSM-IV*. New York: Guilford Press.

Carlotta, D., Borroni, S., Maffei, C. & Fossati, A. (2011). The role of impulsivity, sensation seeking and aggression in the relationship between childhood AD/HD symptom and antisocial behavior in adolescence. *Neurology, Psychiatry and Brain Research*, *17*, 89–98.

Caspi, A., McClay, J., Moffitt, T. E., Mill, J., Martin, J., Craig, I. W., et al. (2002). Role of genotype in the cycle of violence in maltreated children. *Science*, *297*, 851-854.

Congdon, E., Lesch, K. P. & Canli, T. (2008). Analysis of DRD4 and DAT polymorphisms and behavioral inhibition in healthy adults: implications for impulsivity. *American Journal of Medical Genetics. Part B, Neuropsychiatric Genetics*, *147*, 27–32.

Connor, D. F. (2002). *Aggression and antisocial behavior in children and adolescents: Research and treatment*. New York: Guilford.

Connor, D. F. & Doerfler, L. F. (2007). ADHD with comorbid oppositional defiant disorder or conduct disorder: Discrete or nondistinct disruptive behavior disorders? *Journal of Attention Disorders*, *12* (2), 126-134.

Connor, D. F., Steeber, J. & McBurnett, K. (2010). A review of attention-deficit/hyperactivity disorder complicated by symptoms of oppositional defiant disorder or conduct disorder. *Journal of Developmental and Behavioral Pediatrics*, *31*(5), 427-440.

Deault, L. C. (2010). A systematic review of parenting in relation to the development of comorbidities and functional impairments in children with attention-deficit/hyperactivity disorder (ADHD). *Child Psychiatry and Human Development*, *41*(2), 168–192.

Derks, E. M., Dolan, C. V., Hudziak, J. J., Neale, M. C. & Boomsma, D. I. (2007). Assessment and etiology of attention deficit hyperactivity disorder and oppositional defiant disorder in boys and girls. *Behavior Genetics*, *37*, 559–566.

Dick, D. M., Viken, R. J., Kaprio, J., Pulkkinen, L. & Rose, R. J. (2005). Understanding the covariation among childhood externalizing symptoms: Genetic and environmental influences on conduct disorder, attention deficit hyperactivity disorder, and oppositional defiant disorder symptoms. *Journal of Abnormal Child Psychology*, *33*, 219-226.

Eckenrode, J., Ganzel, B., Henderson, C. R., Smith, E., Olds, D. L., Powers, J., Cole, R., Kitzman, H. & Sidora, K. (2000). Preventing child abuse and neglect with a program of nurse home visitation: the limiting effects of domestic violence. *Journal of the American Medical Association*, *284*, 1385-1391.

Eiden, R. D., Edwards, E. P. & Leonard, K. E. (2007). A conceptual model for the development of externalizing behavior problems among kindergarten children of alcoholic families: Role of parenting and children's self-regulation. *Developmental Psychology*, *43*, 1187– 1201.

Ercan, E. S., Kandulu, R., Uslu, E., Ardic, U. A., Yazici, K. U., Basay, B. K., Aydın, C., Rohde, L. A., et al. (2013). Prevalence and diagnostic stability of ADHD and ODD in Turkish children: a 4-year longitudinal study *Child and Adolescent Psychiatry and Mental Health*, *2013*, *7*, 30.

Faigel, H. C., Sznajderman, S., Tishby, O., Turel, M. & Pinus, U. (1995). Attention deficit disorder during adolescence: A review. *Journal of Adolescent Health*, *16*, 174–184.

Fairchild, G., Passamonti, L., Hurford, G., Hagan, C. C., von dem Hagen, E. A., van Goozen, S. H., Goodyer, I. M. & Calder, A. J. (2011). Brain structure abnormalities in early-onset and adolescent-onset conduct disorder. *The American Journal of Psychiatry*, *168*(6), 624–63.

Faraone, S. V., Biederman J. & Mick, E. (2006). The age-dependent decline of attention deficit hyperactivity disorder: A meta-analysis of follow-up studies. *Psychological Medicine*, *36*, 159–165.

Fischer, M. & Barkley, R. A. (2003). Childhood ADHD and Later Antisocial Behavior and Drug Use. *The ADHD Report*, *11*(2), 6-16.

Fischer, M., Barkley, R. A., Fletcher, K. & Smallish, L. (1993). The stability of dimensions of behavior in ADHD and normal children over an 8 year period. *Journal of Abnormal Child Psychology*, *21*, 315-337.

Flicek, M. (1992). Social status of boys with both academic problems and attention deficit hyperactivity disorder. *Journal of Abnormal Child Psychology*, *20*, 353–366.

Flory, K., Molina, B. S. G., Pelham, W. E., Gnagy, E. & Smith, B. (2006). Childhood ADHD predicts risky sexual behavior in young adulthood. *Journal of Clinical Child Adolescent Psychology*, *35*, 571–577.

Foley, D. L., Eaves, L. J., Wormley, B., Silberg, J. L., Maes, H. H., Kuhn, J., et al. (2004). Childhood adversity, monoamine oxidase a genotype, and risk for conduct disorder. *Archives of General Psychiatry*, *61*, 738-744.

Gadow, K. D. & Nolan, E. E. (2002). Differences between preschool children with ODD, ADHD, and ODD+ADHD symptoms. *Journal of Child Psychology and Psychiatry*, *43*(2), 191–201.

Goodman, R. & Stevenson, J. (1989). A twin study of hyperactivity: An examination of hyperactivity scores and categories derived from the Rutter teacher and parent questionnaires. *Journal of Child Psychology and Psychiatry*, *30*, 671–689.

Harvey, E. A. & Metcalfe, L. (2012). The interplay among preschool child and family factors and the development of ODD symptoms. *Journal of Clinical Child & Adolescent Psychology*, *41*(4), 458–470.

Hechtman, L. (2006). Long-term treatment of children and adolescents with attention deficit/hyperactivity disorder (*ADHD*). *Current Psychiatry Reports*, *8*(5), 398–408.

Heller, T. L. & Baker, B. L. (2000). Maternal negativity and children's externalizingbehavior. *Early Education and Development*, *11*, 483-498.

Herpertz S. C., Wenning B., Mueller B., Wunaibi M., Sass H., Herpertz-Dahlmann B. (2001). Psychophysiological responses in ADHD boys with and without conduct disorder: implications for adult antisocial behavior. *Journal of the American Academy of Child & Adolescent Psychiatry*, *40*, 1222–1230.

Hinshaw, S. P. (1987). On the distinction between attentional deficits/ hyperactivity and conduct problems/aggression in child psychopathology. *Psychological Bulletin*, *101*, 443–463.

Hinshaw, S. P., Owens, E. B., Sami, N. & Fargeon, S. (2006). Prospective follow-up of girls with attention-deficit/hyperactivity disorder into adolescence: Evidence for continuing cross-domain impairment. *Journal of Consulting and Clinical Psychology*, *74*, 489–499.

Hinshaw, S. P. & Renfro, R. (1999). *Social behavior observation system*. Unpublished manuscript, University of California, Berkeley, CA.

Ingram, S., Hechtman, L. & Morgenstern, G. (1999). Outcome issues in ADHD: Adolescent and adult long-term outcome. *Mental Retardation and Developmental Disabilities Research Reviews, 5, 243–250.*

Jensen, P. S., Hinshaw, S. P., Kraemer, H. C., Lenora, N., Newcorn, J. H., Abikoff, H. B., March, J. S., Arnold, L. E., Cantwell, D. P., Conners, C. K., Elliott, G. R., Greenhill, L. L., Hechtman, L., Hoza, B., Pelham, W. E., Severe, J. B., Swanson, J. M., Wells, K. C., Wigal, T. & Vitiello, B. (2001). ADHD comorbidity findings from the MTA study: comparing comorbid subgroups. *Journal of the American Academy of Child and Adolescent Psychiatry*, *40*(2), 147–158.

Jerome, L., Segal, A. & Habinski, L. (2006). What we know about ADHD and driving risk: Literature review, meta-analysis and critique. *Journal of the Canadian Academy of Child and Adolescent Psychiatry*, *15*(3), 105-125.

Johnston, C. & Mash, E. J. (2001). Families of children with attention deficit/hyperactivity disorder: Review and recommendations for future research. *Clinical Child and Family Psychology Review*, *4*, 183–207.

Johnston, C., Murray, C. & Hinshaw, S. P. (2002). Responsiveness in interactions of mothers and sons with ADHD: Relations to maternal and child characteristics. *Journal of Abnormal Child Psychology*, *30*, 77–88.

Kashdan, T. B., Jacob, R. G., Pelham, W. E., Lang, A. R., Hoza, B., Blumenthal, J. D. & Gnagy, E. M. (2004). Depression and anxiety in parents of children with ADHD and varying levels of oppositional-defiant behaviors: Modeling relationships with family functioning. *Journal of Clinical Child and Adolescent Psychology*, *33*, 169–181.

Kaya, A., Taner, Y., Guclu, B., Taner, E., Kaya, Y., Bahcivan, H. G., et al. (2008). Trauma and adult attention deficit hyperactivity disorder. *Journal of International Medical Research*, *36*, 9–16.

Keenan, K., Shaw, D. S., Walsh, B., Delliquadri, E. & Giovannelli, J. (1997). DSM-III-R disorders in preschool children from low-income families. *Journal of the American Academy of Child & Adolescent Psychiatry*, *36*, 620–627.

Keown, L. & Woodward, L. J. (2002). Early parenting and family relationships of preschool children with pervasive hyperactivity. *Journal of Abnormal Child Psychology*, *30*, 541–553.

Klein, R. & Mannuzza, S. (1991). Long–term outcome of hyperactive children: A review. *Journal of the American Academy of Child and Adolescent Psychiatry*, *30*, 383–387.

Kuhne, M., Schachar, R. & Tannock, R. (1997). Impact of comorbid oppositional or conduct problems on attention-deficit hyperactivity disorder**.** *Journal of the American Academy of Child and Adolescent Psychiatry*, *36* (12), 1715-25.

Lahey, B. B., Loeber, R., Burke, J. D. & Applegate, B. (2005). Predicting future antisocial personality disorder in males from a clinical assessment in childhood. *Journal of Consulting and Clinical Psychology*, *73* (3), 389–399.

Lahey, B. B., Loeber, R., Burke, J., Rathouz, P. J. & McBurnett, K. (2002). Waxing and waning in concert: Dynamic comorbidity of conduct disorder with other disruptive and emotional problems over 7 years among clinic-referred boys. *Journal of Abnormal Psychology*, *111*, 556–567.

Lahey, B. B. & Waldman, I. D. (2003). A developmental propensity model of the origins of conduct problems during childhood and adolescence. In B. B. Lahey, T. E. Moffitt & A. Caspi (Eds.), *Causes of conduct disorder and juvenile delinquency* (76–117). New York, NY: Guilford.

Lambert, N. L. & Hartsough, C. S. (1998). Prospective study of tobacco smoking and substance dependencies among samples of ADHD and non-ADHD participants. *Journal of Learning Disabilities*, *31*(6), 533-544.

Loeber, R., Burke, J. D., Lahey, B. B., Winters, A. & Zera, M. (2000). Oppositional defiant and conduct disorder: A review of the past 10 years, part I. *Journal of the American Academy of Child and Adolescent Psychiatry*, *39*(12), 1468-1484.

Loeber, R., Green, S. M., Keenan, K. & Lahey, B. B. (1995). Which boys will fare worse? Early predictors of the onset of conduct disorder in a six-year longitudinal study. *Journal of the American Academy of Child and Adolescent Psychiatry*, *34*, 499–509.

Loeber, R. & Stouthamer Loeber, M. (1998). Development of juvenile aggression and violence: Some common misconceptions and controversies. *American Psychologist*, *53*, 242–259.

Mannuzza, S., Klein, R. G., Abikoff, H. & Moulton, J. L.(2004). Significance of childhood conduct problems to later development of conduct disorder among children with ADHD: A prospective follow-up study. *Journal of Abnormal Child Psychology*, *32* (5), 565-73.

Mannuzza, S., Klein, R. G., Bessler, A., Malloy, P. & LaPadula, M. (1998). Adult psychiatric status of hyperactive boys grown up. *American Journal of Psychiatry*, *155*, 493–498.

Mannuzza, S., Klein, R. G. & Moulton, J. L. (2003). Persistence of attention deficit/hyperactivity disorder into adulthood: What have we learned from the prospective follow-up studies? *Journal of Attention Disorders*, *7*, 93–100.

Mannuzza, S., Klein, R. G., Truong, N. L., Moulton, J. L., Roizen, E. R., Howell, K. H. & Castellanos, F. X. (2008). Age of methylphenidate treatment initiation in children with ADHD and later substance abuse: Prospective follow-up into adulthood. *American Journal of Psychiatry*, *165*, 604–609.

McEwen, B. S. (2008). Understanding the potency of stressful early life experiences on brain and body function. *Metabolism Clinical and Experimental*, *57*, S11-S15.

Meyer-Lindenberg, A., Buckholtz, J. W., Kolachana, B., Hariri, R., Pezawas, L., Blasi, G., et al. (2006). Neural mechanisms of genetic risk for impulsivity and violence in humans. *Proceedings of the National Academy of Sciences of the USA*, *103*, 6269-6274.

Marks, D. J., Newcorn, J. H. & Halperin, J. M. (2006). Comorbidity in adults with attention-deficit/hyperactivity disorder. *Annals of the New York Academy of Sciences*, *931*, 216-238.

Matthys, W., Cuperus, J. M. & Engeland, H. V. (1999). Deficient social problem-solving in boys with ODD/ CD, with ADHD, and with both disorders. *Journal of the American Academy of Child and Adolescent Psychiatry*, *38*, 311–321.

Moffitt, T. E. (1990). Juvenile delinquency and attention deficit dis- order: Boys' developmental trajectories from age 3 to age 15. *Child Development*, *61*, 893–910.

Morrison, J. R. (1980). Adult psychiatric disorders in parents of hyperactive children. *American Journal of Psychiatry*, *137*, 825–827.

Mrug, S., Hoza, B., Pelham, W. E., Gnagy, E. M. & Greiner, A. R. (2007). Behavior and peer status in children with ADHD: Continuity and change. *Journal of Attention Disorders*, *10*, 359-371.

Murray, D. W., Arnold, L. E., Swanson, J., Wells, K., Burns, K., Jensen, P., Hechtman, L., Paykina, N., Legato, L. & Strauss, T. (2008). A clinical review of outcomes of the multimodal treatment study of children with attention-deficit/hyperactivity disorder (MTA). *Current Psychiatry Reports*, *10* (5), 424–431.

Nadder, T. S., Rutter, M., Silberg, J. L., Maes, H. H. & Eaves, L. J. (2002). Genetic effects on the variation and covariation of attention deficit-hyperactivity disorder (ADHD) and oppositional-defiant disorder/ conduct disorder (ODD/CD) symptomatologies across informant and occasion of measurement. *Psychological Medicine*, *32*, 39-53.

Nock, M. K., Kazdin, A. E., Hiripi, E. & Kessler, R. C. (2007). Lifetime prevalence, correlates, and persistence of oppositional defiant disorder: Results from the National Comorbidity Survey Replication. *Journal of Child Psychology and Psychiatry*, *48*, 703–713.

O'Donnell, J., Hawkins, J. D. & Abbott, R. D. (1995). Predicting serious delinquency and substance abuse among aggressive boys. *Journal of Consulting & Clinical Psychology*, *63*(4), 529–537.

Olson, I. R., Plotzker, A. & Ezzyat, Y. (2007). The Enigmatic temporal pole: a review of findings on social and emotional processing. *Brain*, *130*, 1718–1731.

Patterson, G. R. (1982). *A social learning approach: Coercive family process*. Eugene, OR: Castalia.

Peris, T. S. & Hinshaw, S. P. (2003). Family dynamics and preadolescent girls with ADHD: the relationship between expressed emotion, ADHD symptomatology, and comorbid disruptive behavior. *Journal of Child Psychology and Psychiatry*, *44* (8), 1177–1190.

Pfiffner, L. J., McBurnett, K., Rathouz, P. J. & Judice, S. (2005). Family correlates of oppositional and conduct disorders in children with attention deficit/hyperactivity disorder. *Journal of Abnormal Child Psychology*, *33*(5), 551–563.

Polanczyk, G. & Rohde, L. A. (2007). Epidemiology of attention-deficit/hyperactivity disorder across the lifespan. *Current Opinion in Psychiatry*, *20*, 386–392.

Pope, A. W., Bierman, K. L. & Mumma, G. H. (1987). Peer relations of hyperactive and aggressive boys. Paper presented at the Annual Meeting of the Society of Behavioral Pediatrics, Anaheim, CA.

Qi, C. & Kaiser, A. P. (2003). Behavior problems of preschool children from low-income families: Review of the literature. *Topics in Early Childhood Special Education*, *23*, 188–216.

Raine, A. (2011). An amygdala structural abnormality common to two subtypes of conduct disorder: a neurodevelopmental conundrum. *The American Journal of Psychiatry*, *168*(6), 569–571.

Raine, A. (2002). Annotation: the role of prefrontal deficits, low autonomic arousal and early health factors in the development of antisocial and aggressive behavior in children. *Journal of Child Psychology and Psychiatry*, *43*, 417- 434.

Reimherr, F. W., Marchant, B. K., Olsen, J. L., Wender, P. H. & Robison, R. J. (2013). Oppositional defiant disorder in adults with ADHD. *Journal of Attention Disorders*,*17*, 102-113.

Retz, W. & Rösler, M. (2009). The relation of ADHD and violent aggression: What can we learn from epidemiological and genetic studies? *International Journal of Law and Psychiatry*, *32*, 235–243.

Richters, J. E., Arnold, L. E., Jensen, P. S., et al. (1995). NIMH collaborative multi-site multimodal treatment study of children with ADHD: Background and rationale. *Journal of American Academy of Child and Adolescent Psychiatry*, *34*, 987-1000.

Robinson, G. E., Fernald, R. D. & Clayton, D. F. (2008). *Genes and Social Behaviour Science*, *322*, 896-900.

Ross, D. M. & Ross, S. A. (1982). *Hyperactivity: current issues, research and theory* (2nd Ed.). New York: Wiley & Sons.

Rösler, M., Retz, W., Retz-Junginger, P., Stieglitz, R. D., Kessler, H., Reimherr, F., Wender, P. H., Nervenarzt. (2008). Attention deficit *Nervenarzt*, *79*(3), 320-327.

Sagvolden, T., Johansen, E. B., Aase, H. & Russell, V. A. (2005). A dynamic developmental theory of attention-deficit/hyperactivity disorder (ADHD) predominantly hyperactive/impulsive and combined subtypes. *Behavioral and Brain Sciences*, *28*, 397-468.

Satterfield, J. H., Faller, K. J., Crinella, F. M., Schell, A., Swanson, J. M. & Homer, L. D. (2007). A 30-year prospective follow-up study of hyperactive boys with conduct problems: Adult criminality. *Journal of the American Academy of Child & Adolescent Psychiatry*, *46* (5), 601-610.

Satterfield, J., Swanson, J. M., Schell, A. & Lee, F. (1994). Prediction of antisocial behavior in attention-deficit hyperactivity disorder boys from aggression/defiance scores. *Journal of the American Academy of Child and Adolescent Psychiatry*, *33*, 185-190.

Schmitz, M. F. (2003). Influences of race and family environment on child hyperactivity and antisocial behavior. *Journal of Marriage and Family*, *65* (4), 835-849.

Schubert, I., Koster, I. & Lehmkuhl, G. (2010). The changing prevalence of attention-deficit/hyperactivity disorder and methylphenidate prescriptions: A study of data from a random sample of insures of the AOK Health Insurance Company in the German State of Hesse, 2000–2007. *Deutsches Aerzteblatt International*, *107*(36), 615–621.

Seipp, C. M. & Johnston, C. (2005). Mother–son interactions in families of boys with Attention Deficit Hyperactivity Disorder with and without oppositional behavior. *Journal of Abnormal Child Psychology*, *33*, 87–98.

Shaw-Zirt, B., Popali-Lehane, L., Chaplin, W. & Bergman, A. (2005). Adjustment, social skills, and self-esteem in college students with symptoms of ADHD. *Journal of Attention Disorders*, *8*, 109–120.

Slomkowski, C., Klein, R. G. & Mannuzza, S. (1995). Is self-esteem an important outcome in hyperactive children? *Journal of Abnormal Child Psychology 23*, 303–315.

Stahl, N.D. & Clarizio, H. F. (1999). Conduct disorder and comorbidity. *Psychology in the Schools*, *36*, 41-50.

Sterzer, P., Stadler, C., Krebs, A., et al. (2005). Abnormal neural responses to emotional visual stimuli in adolescents with conduct disorder. *Biological Psychiatry*, *57*, 7 -15.

Stormont, M. (2001). Social outcomes of children with ADHD: Contributing factors and implications for practice. *Psychology in the Schools*, *38*, 521–531.

Swanson, J. M., Kraemer, H. C., Hinshaw, S. P., et al. (2001). Clinical relevance of the primary findings of the MTA: Success rates based on severity of ADHD and ODD symptoms at the end of treatment. *Journal of American Academy of Child and Adolescent Psychiatry*, *40*, 168-179.

Taylor, E., Schachar, R., Thorley, G. & Wieselberg, M. (1986). Conduct disorder and hyperactivity: Separation of hyperactivity and antisocial conduct in British child psychiatric disorders. *British Journal of Psychiatry*, *149*, 760–767.

Taylor, E. A. & Sonuga-Barke, E. J. S. (2008). Disorders of attention and activity. In M. Rutter, D. Bishop, D. Pine, S. Scott, J. S. Stevenson, E. A. Taylor, & A. Thapar (Eds.), *Rutter's child & adolescent psychiatry* (5th ed., 521–542). UK: Wiley-Blackwell.

Turgay, A. (2009). Psychopharmacological treatment of oppositional defiant disorder. *CNS drugs*, *23*, 1-17.

Turgay, A., Jain, U., Bedard, A. C., et al. (2008). Canadian AD/HD practice guidelines. Canadian AD/HD Resource Alliance: Toronto (ON).

Turgay, A., Joseph, L., Nag, S. A., et al. (2003). Oppositional defiant disorder, conduct disorder and ADHD relationships. Ontario Psychiatric Association Annual Scientific Conference: Toronto (ON).

van Goozen, S. H. M., Fairchild, G., Snock, H. & Harold, G. T. (2007). The evidence for a neurobiological model of childhood antisocial behavior. *Psychological Bulletin*, *133*, 149-182.

von Polier, G. G., Vloet, T. D. & Herpertz-Dahlmann, B. (2012). ADHD and delinquency – a developmental perspective behavioral sciences and the law behavior science . *Law*, *30*, 121–139.

Weber, S., Habel, U., Amunts, K. & Schneider, F. (2008). Structural brain abnormalities in psychopaths: A review. *Behavioral Sciences & the Law*, *26*, 7–28.

Weiss, G. & Hechtman, L. T. (1993). *Hyperactive children grown up*. New York: Guilford Press.

Wender, P. H. (1995). *Attention deficit hyperactivity disorder in adults*. Oxford University Press. New York.

Whalen, C. K. & Henker, B. (1985). *The social worlds of hyperactive children. Clinical Psychology Review*, *5*, 1-32.

Young, S. & Amarasinghe, J. M. (2010). Practitioner review: Non-pharmacological treatments for ADHD: A lifespan approach. *Journal of Child Psychology and Psychiatry* *51*(2), 116–133.

Zoccolillo, M., Tremblay, R. & Vitaro, F. (1996). DSM- III-R and DSM-III criteria for conduct disorder in preadolescent girls: Specific but insensitive. *Journal of the American Academy of Child and Adolescent Psychiatry*, *35*, 461–470.

In: Antisocial Behavior
Editor: Justine H. Gallo

ISBN: 978-1-63321-521-4

Chapter 6

REMISSIONS OF DRUG ADDICTS UNDER CONDITIONS OF PENAL ISOLATION: CURRENT RESEARCH IN SIBERIA

***N. A. Bokhan*[1] *and S. I. Gusev*[2]**
[1]Mental Health Research Institute SB RAMSci, Tomsk, Russia
[2]Kemerovo State University of Culture and Arts, Kemerovo, Russia

ABSTRACT

In the chapter, theoretic, methodological, organizational aspects and regularities of course of drug dependence in persons under conditions of restraint of freedom will be considered. Pathogenetic aspects of deviant, delinquent and aggressive behavior associated with substance use will be studied. Social-psychological and subcultural aspects of behavior of drug addicted convicts will be described. Comparative analysis of factors contributing to formation of antisocial and asocial activity of the personality during drug use will be introduced. Variants of structure and dynamic of formation of remissions of drug dependence in convicts under penal system conditions and clinical dynamic of comorbid mental disorders will be distinguished. A special attention will be paid to principles of rehabilitation in convicts under specific conditions of penal system, study of predictors of breakdown and relapse in the process of course of remissions including young offenders as well to possibilities of clinical-mathematical prognosis of stability and length of remission. Measures of prevention of criminal behavior associated with drug dependence as well as breakdowns and relapses in convicts, issues of improvement of addictological help under current conditions of restraint of freedom will be defined.

INTRODUCTION

In recent years at penal institutions, the specific weight of convicts suffering from mental and behavioral substance use related disorders is growing. It is indicated that most offences are committed in the period of constant use of drugs. The leading motive of committing the offence for persons, dependent on psychoactive substances - getting the money for consumption of drugs (Tsubera A. I., 1992). In native and foreign literature, a number of social and medical consequences of drug abuse have been described. Low part of employment, high per cent of criminogenic behavior and criminal records, disturbance of family ties is noted (Egorov V. F., Koshkina E. A., Korchagina G. A., Shamota A. Z., 1998; Igonin A. L., Tuzikova Yu. B., Irishkin D. A., 2003; Bravender T., Knight J. R., 1998; Garcia L. M., McGeary K. A., Shultz J. M. et al., 1999). Absence of complex investigations (medical, social, psychological, criminological) among convicts, insufficient scrutiny of course of mental disorders, remission of alcohol and drug dependences in convicts under conditions of isolation – all these complicate their diagnosis, carrying out the therapy, rehabilitation and prevention. As basic problem in achievement of lasting remission in drug dependence establishment of long-term compliance with patients in remote period, after stopping the withdrawal and post-withdrawal disorders is regarded when against the background of relative well-being, slips and relapses appear (Pyatnitskaya I. N., Naidenova N. G., 2002).

For the purpose of study of features of formation and specifics of course of remission under conditions of penal institutions, examination of juvenile and adult convicts, kept in juvenile correctional facility and special-regime penal colony has been carried out. During investigation, specifics of contingent of patients and conditions of places of imprisonment with use of differentiated approach to assessment of a number of social, psychological and clinical factors have been taken into account. In general structure of sickness rate at penal institutions of Kemerovo Region, mental disorders occupy the leading position (37,3 %). Among mental disorders, the first place is occupied by drug addictions (39,7 %), the second place – by alcoholism (16,7 %). In structure of the newly revealed sickness rate, drug addictions also occupy the first place (39,4 %), alcoholism – the second one (17,4 %). Index of prevalence of drug addiction among convicts in 2004 has constituted 13,178.1 (per 100,000 convicts) that exceeded all-Russian index by 55 times (240.2 per 100,000 of the population). Repeated analysis of index of prevalence of drug addiction in 2008 has shown that prevalence of drug addiction in Russian Federation has constituted 252.2 per 100,000 of the population, and among convicts of Kemerovo Region – 16,898.2 (higher by 67 times). This reflects predominance of drug dependence among convicts as compared with analogous index among population of Russia and testifies to significant increase of drug addiction among offenders for analyzed period.

Index of newly revealed sickness rate among convicts in 2008 has constituted 821.7 per 100,000 of the population (in Russian Federation – 18,7). More significant differences in newly revealed sickness rate with drug addiction are observed among adolescents. Newly revealed sickness rate with drug addictions in convicted adolescents in 2008 has constituted 14, 960.0 per 100,000 of juvenile convicts that is higher than all-Russian index by 1,290 times (11.6 per 100,000 of adolescent population). These indices reflect real situation when significant part of offences is committed by persons, dependent on drugs (theft, robbery, drug trafficking). Basic cause to commit offences is search for money needed to buy drugs as a consequence of severity of primary pathological craving and states of withdrawal.

Dispersion analysis has shown that the earliest terms of onset of use of drugs are observed in groups of juvenile persons whose conditions of upbringing were non-systematic and demands were excessive. Per cent of the examined persons convicted for violent offences, in group of juvenile offenders (62,7 %) is statistically significantly higher ($p<0,01$), than in group of adults (49,2 %). At the same time, adults more often (16,9 %), than juvenile offenders (8,0 %), have committed crimes associated with drug trafficking.

So, in group of juvenile persons dependent on opioids, the lowest age of onset of drug use (12,3 years) and onset of formation of dependence that is reliably lower than in adult convicts dependent on opioids (16,2 years) have been documented. During analysis of mean age of disease it is noted that it is reliably higher in group of adult convicts (16,8 years), than in convicted adolescents (13,1 years in all groups of adolescents).

It is important to note that more than 60,7 % of examined adolescents have committed violent offences being in state of alcohol or drug intoxication. Adolescents dependent on cannabinoids in 41,3 % of cases have committed violent offences, on opioids – in 32,4 %, dependent on several psychoactive substances – in 24,4 %. Difficulty of qualification of state of intoxication is associated with rare administration and carrying out of examination to establish the fact of drug use or drug intoxication. As a rule, in case materials, sentences of the court, only state of alcohol intoxication is indicated, whereas during clinical examination of adolescents is clarified that they used not alcohol but drugs or several psychoactive substances simultaneously. Among adults, offences of all kinds were committed in drug intoxication (21,6 %) more frequently ($p<0,01$), than among adolescents (6,7 %). In group of adults in drug intoxication more frequently than in group of adolescents offenses have been committed. These data are explained by that in most cases the basic aim of commitment of offences was obtaining money to buy drugs.

In the course of investigation we have distinguished basic stages of dynamic of psychopathological disorders in period of remission of drug dependence in convicts. *The first stage* – of acute withdrawal disorders (withdrawal syndrome). During detention, drug use is stopped and possibility of their buying is absent. In period up to 3 days, clinic of withdrawal syndrome develops. This period differs by acuteness of development of clinical symptoms and quick dynamic, is experienced by adolescents most hardly and is associated both with mental and somatic symptoms. For adolescents dependent on cannabinoids, it flows milder and shorter, clinical picture is characterized predominantly by sluggishness, anorexia, vegetative liability. In group of adolescents with diagnosis poly-drug addiction, there is a trend to lingering course.

The second stage – post-withdrawal disorders (post-withdrawal state). It is characterized by smoothing of acute symptoms of withdrawal and predominance of psychopathological symptoms. The clinic is characterized predominantly by psychopath-like symptoms with quick exhaustibility of affective outbreaks, asthenic and hypochondriac symptoms. Affective liability and low mood have the level of sub-depression without achievement of the level of classical depression. Length of course is up to 1 month.

The third stage – period of remission of drug dependence (length 1—3 years with wavy course). Leading syndromes in remote period of remission were asthenic-hypochondriac symptoms with sluggishness, apathy and periodical exacerbation of pathological craving for drugs. Low level of awareness of the illness is noted throughout all stages of course of remission in convicts up to anosognosia (49,3 %) and formal insight (26,0 %). During analysis across groups, anosognosia in dependent on cannabinoids is the most severe – 53,3 %, while superficial insight is the least expressed one in group of adolescents with poly-drug addiction. The most typical index is reliable predominance of open strive to use drugs in 19,5 % of persons with poly-drug dependence. Most convicts had not motivation to stop drug use (up to 85,0 % in group of persons with poly-drug dependence). They stopped drug use only in situation of forced abstinence – during detention. Strive to stop drug use really is noted only in 4,0 % of dependent on cannabinoids, in 20,6 % of dependent on opioids, in cases of poly-drug addictions – in 12,2 % of cases.

In practice, associated with discontinuation of administration by investigators of carrying out of substance use examination, pathology in the kind of alcoholism and drug addictions at the stage of investigation is legally not identified and not reflected in criminal cases. Thus, possibility of identification of fact both of single cases of alcohol and drug intoxication and states of dependence and their role in commitment of offences decreases sharply.

During combination of drug dependence and another mental pathology it is necessary to use wider possibilities of application of outpatient compulsory treatment and observation of the psychiatrist. However, as practice shows, such cases are found rarely. In the examined contingent, despite of diagnosed mental pathology and drug dependence in 81 adolescents, compulsory measures were recommended during carrying out the examination only for 1 adolescent (1,2 %). Of 320 adult convicts, outpatient observation by the psychiatrist was administered also only to 1 convict (0,3 %). In the examined convicts, the diagnoses of comorbid mental pathology were as follows: personality disorders were revealed in the range from 8,8 to 10,7 % of cases, organic brain disease was revealed from 27,8 to 30,7 % of cases. Mental retardation was relatively rare among adult convicts (3,4 %). However, in adolescents with opioid dependence, mental retardation was found already in 11,8 % of cases and in poly-drug dependence – in 21,9 %. It is obvious that low level of intellectual abilities combined with compulsive craving for drugs results in indiscrimination during use of different psychoactive substances and quick formation of poly-drug dependence.

As compared with 2004, in 2005 number of juvenile convicts under treatment of alcoholism increased by more than 2 times, and under treatment of drug dependence – almost by 6 times. At the same time among adult convicts number of persons wishing voluntary treatment in 2005 was visually lower than in adolescents with alcohol (14,5 %) and drug (28,0 %) dependences that is associated with more severe deformation of personality, increase of symptoms of anosognosia and severity of basic disease among these convicts. And if drug dependent adolescents passed voluntary and compulsory treatment without any problems, so in adult convicts 11,6% of cases refused treatment associated with greater degree of severity of symptoms of dependence and anosognosia, more severe changes of personality. In addition, even under conditions of isolation and unavailability of drugs breakdowns in the period of treatment (in 1,6%) of cases have been revealed. At the same time, indices of stability of remission in adult convicts constitute 55,9% of cases that with account for severity and depth of existing pathology is a good outcome. It has been established that in structure of remission for convicted adolescents with cannabinoid dependence, non-chemical forms of dependent behavior are the most typical ones. Among them workaholism (participation in various forms of occupational therapy) is found most frequently – in 24,0% of cases; creative hobbies (participation in hobby groups of artistic and humanitarian direction, sports) have been noted in 18,7% of adolescents. This is the most adapted group of persons with socially accepted forms of adaptation and relatively better perspectives of rehabilitation. Persons with opioid dependence were characterized by chemical form of addictive behavior (41,2%), including search for and use of analgesics, other medications; in 11,8%, use of strong tea decoction (chifir') has been revealed. In polydrug dependence, chemical form of addictive behavior (68,3%) predominated. More frequently this was transition to use of chifir' (43,9%) or search and attempts of use of not prescribed medications. Rather high indices of addictive behavior associated with gambling (17,1%) and sexual deviations (12,2%) have been noted in adolescents with polydrug dependence. Therefore this is one of the most problematic risk groups for HIV-infection, addiction to new hard drugs. In adult convicts with opioid dependence, picture of vicarious forms as a whole resembles picture in group of convicted adolescents with opioid dependence. So, leading form in them is also the chemical one (59,1% of cases). In particular, this was search and attempts of use of various medications (36,6%) and chifir' (15,3%). Whereas non-chemical form of dependent behavior has constituted 29,4%, was not persistent and was easily included into the structure of formation of stable remission.

All above mentioned is confirmed by data about formation of stable remission both in juvenile convicts with drug dependence and in adult convicts. Persons with cannabinoid dependence show the highest indices of stable remission (89,3%), whereas adolescents with opioid dependence have stable remission only in 73,5% of cases; this index is more decreased in polydrug dependence (65,9%). In adult convicts with opioid dependence, severity of clinical course of dependence, length of period of drug use and less stable character of remission are confirmed by high indices of forced character of remission in 44,1% of convicts despite of active carrying out of complex of therapeutic, rehabilitative activities, administration of compulsory treatment. At the same time, taking into account criminal changes of the personality, asocial behavior, length of use of hard drugs and low level of social adaptation (absence of the family, education, profession etc.), formation of stable remission in 55,9% of cases should be considered a good outcome. Creation of clinical-mathematical model of prediction of course of drug addictions allows predicting length of remission of drug dependence in convicts with multiple linear regression analysis. In structure of distinguished factors, beyond clinical, mutually conditioning combination of a number of social-psychological indices influencing formation and length of remission in drug dependence in the convicts is of significance. This is presence of dysphoria, mimic reactions in structure of primary craving, early age of onset of drug use ($p<0,003$), criminal record according to articles 105 and 111 of Criminal Code of Russian Federation ($p<0,007$), weight, age at the moment of examination, presence of motive of relapse of drug use.

CONCLUSION

Subculture and rituals of drug use are superimposed on subculture and rituals of criminal world with mutual reinforcement of negative effect. Onset of drug dependence to major extent misadjusts criminal personality because, on the one hand, requires increasing means for buying the drug, and on the other hand - decreases possibility of legal and illegal acquisition of these means. As far as progressing of drug or alcohol illness, professional qualification of thief, cheat decreases; the major part of their time is occupied by search for drug, mental and physical experiencing of withdrawal.

As it turned out, most violent offences are closely associated with mental and behavioral disorders in result of substance abuse. Affective-dysphoric and dysthymic disturbances as well as presence of explosive reactions, liability of affect in personal history should be regarded as leading psychopathological disorders. Presence of group environment, creating and directing the behavioral motives, changes of personality, affective disturbances, heightened aggressiveness, giving positive reward of realization of violent behavior should be recognized as one of important conditions. Basic diagnostic criteria and indications for administration of compulsory treatment, order and place of carrying out the treatment for alcoholism and drug addiction depending on custodial control have been defined. With account for ICD-10, diagnoses in substance use disorders and stages of disease are made. Many-year practice shows that the fact of administration of coercive and now compulsory treatment may become the motive to begin the therapy. Taking into account traits of criminal contingent with personality disorders, asocial purposes, and voluntary willingness of the convict to proceed to anti-alcohol or antidrug therapy gives the possibility to carry out further therapeutic and rehabilitative activities creating favorable ground for destruction of symptoms of anosognosia and overcoming the resistance. In fact, follow-up confirms our rightness: in the future, formation of patients' attitude toward voluntary treatment occurs.

During follow-up investigations after one year, formation of stable remission in most examined adolescents, who in the future passed a complex of therapeutic and rehabilitative activities, has been revealed clinically. Stability of remission is confirmed by absence of breakdowns and relapses (including also identification by randomized monthly test-control for availability of drugs in the urine with screening-systems). It has been noted, that formation of remission occurs worst in juvenile persons with polydrug dependence and in adult convicts. For the specified contingent, absence of firm attitude toward the life without drugs, recurrence of psychopathological symptoms, renewal of primary craving, absence of attitude toward stopping the drug use are typical.

In places of imprisonment, in fact access to drugs is excluded; drug dependent persons are under constant long-term surveillance. These factors allow implementing the consistent transition from forced remission to stable therapeutic remission. Concurrently, education of juvenile and adult convicts at a comprehensive secondary school and acquisition of a profession at a vocational school are conducted. Rise of educational level of convicts promotes formation of habits of work, adoption of new socially accepted patterns of the behavior. Proposed multistage system of medico-psychological and social rehabilitative activities allows complex resolution of problems of re-adaptation and re-socialization of the convicts. Use of differentiated therapeutic-rehabilitative and social programmes at penal institutions in combination with protective regimen creates favorable conditions for development of long-term remission in drug dependent adolescents under conditions of full exclusion of possibility of drug use.

Therapeutic and rehabilitative programmes developed and adapted to penal conditions include complex of medical, educative, social, psychological programmes and principles of professional training. Education acquired by convicts broadens substantially possibilities of their employment and social adaptation after discharge. Inclusion of individual and group forms of psychotherapeutic work (Gestalt-therapy, cognitive-behavioral, positive and client-focused psychotherapy) allows achieving the stable remission in the contingent of convicts, heightening the efficacy of rehabilitation, excluding breakdowns and relapses of the illness under conditions of penal institutions and creating the possibility of further rehabilitation. After therapy and rehabilitation during three-year follow-up period (87,0% of convicts) in the period of service of term, breakdowns and relapses occurred in 1,6% and only in adult convicts. Among discharged convicts according to obtained data, breakdowns have been noted in 18,4% of adolescents and 33,3% of adults.

As a whole, introduction of effective programmes of revealing the drug dependent persons, therapy and rehabilitation at institutions of The Federal Penal Service has allowed achieving the improvement of quality of rendering the specialized psychiatric and narcological care for special contingent. In the process of work with convicts, drug addicts, issues of improvement of social adaptation of these persons after service of term require an essential attention. The most considerable difficulties arise namely after discharge, these are problems with family, housing, employment that frequently can provoke the breakdown of disease. It is necessary to create transitional centers (like "Half-Way Homes"), development of social programmes and funding for programmes of initial adaptation of such persons. Combination of state social programs, active participation of non-governmental organizations without doubt will have a positive effect namely at final stage of rehabilitation. Key direction in reforming of the system of psychiatric, narcological and medical-psychological service is creation of therapeutic-rehabilitative (post-prison) centers of care for persons after discharge from penal institution with rendering of real social and medico-psychological help.

REFERENCES

Bravender, T., Knight, J. R. (1998) Recent patterns of use and associated risks of illicit drug use in adolescents. *Current Opinions in Pediatrics*, 10(4), 344-349.

Egorov, V. F., Koshkina, E. A., Korchagina, G. A., Shamota, A. Z. [Narcological situation in Russia (according to data of official medical statistics]. *Rossijskij medicinskij zhurnal* [*Russian Medical Journal*]. 1998; (2): 109-140. (In Russ.).

Garcia, L. M., McGeary, K. A., Shultz, J. M., et al. (1999) The impact of insurance status on drug abuse treatment completion. *Journal of Health Care Finance*, 26:40–47.

Igonin, A. L., Tuzikova, Yu. B., Irishkin, D. A. [Substance abuse and asocial behavior]. *Narkologija* [*Narcology*]. 2003; (3): 50-58. (In Russ.).

Pyatnitzkaya, I. N., Naidenova, N. G. [*Adolescent narcology*]. Meditsina, Moscow, 2002. 256 p.

In: Antisocial Behavior
Editor: Justine H. Gallo
ISBN: 978-1-63321-521-4

Chapter 7

What Is the Link between Antisocial Behavior of Adolescents and Parenting: A Systematic Review of Parental Practices to Manage Antisocial Behavior

Anja R. Human-Hendricks and Nicolette V. Roman*
Department of Social Work, University of the Western Cape,
Bellville, Cape Town, South Africa

Abstract

Background: Parents play a central role in the lives of their children. Parent-child interaction is a central variable in the etiology of antisocial behaviour. Research suggests that families of antisocial individuals are characterized by harsh and inconsistent discipline, little positive parental involvement and poor monitoring and supervision. Thus parents could create environments for unhealthy parent-child relationships with subsequent antisocial behaviour of their adolescents.

Aim of the study is to systematically appraise studies which seek to examine the link between antisocial behaviour of adolescents and parental practices to manage the antisocial behaviour of their adolescents.

Methods: A comprehensive search was conducted to extract information regarding the topic. Ebscohost (Medline, CINAHL, PsycArticles), JSTOR and Pubmed for the period of 2003-2014. Two reviewers independently evaluated the methodological quality of the studies reviewed. Data was be extracted independently by two reviewers using the 'JBI data extraction tool'. The findings are summarized in narrative form.

Results: Eight studies were eligible for inclusion in this study. The majority of studies were longitudinal and included a study in Taiwan, New Zealand and the remainder in the USA. Parenting, in relation to antisocial behaviour of adolescents, was examined both genetically and environmentally. Parenting practices have an effect on the antisocial behaviour of adolescents. These parenting practices may also be transferred across generations. In particular, harsh, inconsistent parenting as well as low attachment levels between parent and adolescent, low parental control, low monitoring and low

* Corresponding author: Email: nicoletteroman@gmail.com.

guidance all encouraged antisocial behaviour of adolescents and in some studies into young adulthood.

Conclusion: Positive and consistent parenting, father involvement and good parental role models reduced antisocial behaviour of adolescents.

Keywords: Adolescence, parenting, parent-child interaction, antisocial behaviour, Systematic Review

INTRODUCTION

A 'parent' in essence is defined as a person who provides significant care for a child in a home or family context (Moran, Ghate & Van der Merwe, 2004). As Baumrind (1994) suggests parenting emphasizes the responsibility and qualities of exemplary behavior of the parent.

Parenting, as a concept, provides a very broad perspective of a bi-directional reciprocal relationship between two human beings. This relationship is between an older (parent) and younger person (child). The reciprocity is seen when the parent is the catalyst for a response from the child, but it also occurs that the child is a catalyst for a response from the parent. Regardless, the term parenting, in its simplest form, is a verb encompassing many facets of nurturing, caring, growing and learning. It directly relates to the dynamics of child-rearing, childcare functioning and the developmental factors or influences thereof. Ultimately, it includes the approaches (styles and practices), which influence the behaviour of the child (child, adolescent, young adult and adult). Research suggests that by its very nature, when parenting is positive, a positive response from the child is experienced (Baumrind, 1978), but this may not always be the case because parenting is not 'cast in stone' and may not necessarily be a 'one size fit all'.

As we know human development is affected by 50% genes and 50% environment. Interestingly, parents not only provide the 50% genes but also provide the environment for development. The parental environment is part of a larger environment or social context, which consists of other family members, the circumstances or environments in the home, the schools children attend, church, peers, parents' work, any other person in the community or society in which the child lives and interacts. Each of these societal contexts has many other factors which reflect back to people/parents/children.

Parents often have challenges which they face. *Firstly*, the family structure could provide a challenge for the parent-child relationship (Hoque & Ghuman, 2012; Westbrook & Harden, 2010). For example being in a one or two-parent family environment makes a difference to the parent-child relationship as there are different types and levels of support and resources. *Secondly*, the influence of work could be a challenge. For example, a parent may need to travel for the purposes of work and would therefore not be a very present parent, which means that the child may not be monitored or may be allowed to his or her own devices. *Thirdly*, being part of a particular culture could provide a challenge. For example, the parent may hold very traditional or patriarchal beliefs and practices, but the child may be educated differently in school and this then could strain the parent-child relationship. These challenges are acknowledged as being possible confounders for or influences on the parent-child relationship, but the fact of the matter is that children, regardless of age, need to be parented.

Parents change and adapt according to the developmental needs or requirements of their children and therefore change their approaches accordingly. For example, a parent often uses a different approach when raising a toddler than with an adolescent. While no one is the perfect parent, there are certain parenting approaches that can have serious negative effects on children with subsequent maladaptive behaviour such as antisocial behaviour. The behavioural outcomes of children are often associated with the way children were raised by their parents, either on a basis of love and discipline or limits or within an environment with a lack of love, lack of discipline or a lack of limits. It is the purpose then of this chapter to explore the link between parenting and the behaviour of their adolescent children, specifically antisocial behaviour, by means of a systematic review.

THEORETICAL UNDERPINNING

For the purposes of this chapter Self-Determination Theory and the Ecological Systems Theory are used to understand the dynamics in a challenging parent-child relationship.

Self- Determination Theory

Self- Determination Theory (SDT) posits that human beings are motivated to a sense of well-being as well as being self-determined in their behavior. In order for this to evolve, SDT posits that there are three basic psychological needs which need to be satisfied. These needs include the need to be competent, autonomous and related (Deci & Ryan, 1985; Ryan & Deci, 2000; Van Steenkiste, 2005). If these three needs are met the individual will be adjusted and emit healthy behavior. If these needs are unmet, individuals are at-risk and would potentially then engage in health risk or antisocial behavior (Deci & Ryan, 2000). In addition, the environment needs to be supportive in order for the individual to be well and self-determined (Chirkov, et al., 2003). According to Guardia and Patrick (2008), SDT offers a broad perspective on the mechanisms through which relational processes are related to personal well-being and relational functioning, for example the relationship between the parent and the child (or adolescent). In order to achieve self-determination, individuals need to exist and interact in an environment which is constructive, positive and supportive (Deci & Ryan, 2000). When environments are contrary, in other words controlling or non-supportive, well-being and healthy behavior are hindered. Individuals, such as adolescents, may become increasingly frustrated and therefore may react in various ways, an example of which could be antisocial behaviour (Patterson, 1990).

The Ecological Systems Theory

Bronfenbrenner (1977) presents the ecological systems theory as a set of interrelated circles representing interactive systems. According to Bronfenbrenner (1979), the environment is comprised of five layers of systems, which interact in complex ways that can both affect and be affected by the child's development in an ever-changing environment

(Johnson, 2008). These systems include the microsystem, mesosystem, exosystem, macrosystem and chronosystem.

The ecological model clearly shows that these layers are designed in circular motion, indicating that the child is influenced by these layers and that the layers are affected by the child. This means that without environmental influences such as the child's family, parents, peers, school teacher or community, the child cannot develop without knowledge gained from these sources. This implies that children are dependent on their environment and learn on a daily basis, whether it is through observation or experience. Given that humans do not progress in isolation, Bronfenbrenner's ecological model suggests that during the ever-changing environments in which the child is situated, child development requires constructive interactions between these environments (Bronfenbrenner, 1979). This interaction process is necessary for knowledge to be transmitted to the child through the people with whom the child makes contact. The principles of this theory highlight that (1) the child is at the centre of this model; (2) The model acknowledges that a child affects, and is affected by the settings in which he/she spends time; (3) The most important setting for a young child is his/her family, because that is where he/she spends the most time and because it has the most emotional influence on him/her; (4) A child's development is determined by what he/she experiences in these settings he/she spends time in. These experiences called proximal, or near - processes, have implications for child development /outcomes; (5) The number and quality of the connections between the settings in which a young child spends time that is his/her family and preschool also have important implications for the child's development; (6) Other environments where the child does not spend time can also affect the power of proximal processes to influence development. These can include both more immediate factors for example; the parent's workplace or community norms and more remote ones for example state policies and laws. Thus the layers are explained as follows:

The Microsystem Layer

The microsystem is described as a setting of activities that takes place between the developing person and personal associations and interactions (Bronfenbrenner, 1979). The child is socialized through personal engagement with their parents, caregivers or siblings, living together with the child in the same household. Psychological theories highlight that parents have a direct effect on socialising their children (Beaver & Wright, 2007). Louw and Louw (2007: 250) state that, "parents act as role models and educators for their children, as they create home environments that transmit parental values".

The Mesosystem Layer

Bronfenbrenner (1979), states that the mesosystem extends further in terms of the interaction between the developing person, and two or more links, such as the child's relations among their home, school, neighbourhood or friends. The mesosystem is formed when the child moves from the microsystem, to participate with additional networks outside of the family setting, in which interaction exists between the two layers (Bronfenbrenner, 1979). The people with whom the child interacts in the mesosystem, such as the peers, play an important role in socialization and interactions. Often, the experiences the child has at school or in the community becomes part of the family interactions.

The Exosystem Layer

The exosystem layer does not show that the developing person is directly engaging with the events that are happening. According to Bronfenbrenner (1979), the exosystem layer is a setting in the model that represents occurring incidents that influence, or that are influenced by the developing person, in which the individual is not an active partaker. Examples of this layer indicate the wider community, the child's extended family, mass media, the parent's work place, religion, or activities of the local school board (Bronfenbrenner, 1979). In the case of a child, he/ she may cognitively be affected by what they observe on television, or how a caregiver reacts to a parent meeting attended at the school, although the child does not directly participate.

The Macrosystem Layer

Bronfenbrenner, (1979) describes the macrosystem layer as a lower-order system, which interacts with the micro-, meso-, and exosystem layers in the ecology model. This layer depicts sub-culture or culture as a whole, along with any belief systems or ideology underlying such consistencies produced by attitudes, customs, values, and laws transmitted by the State (Bronfenbrenner, 1979). Knowledge is thus transmitted from a top-down process by which the State and parent/s of the child have sole responsibility of influencing their children. Ultimately, children are affected by what they are taught (knowledge), in the manner they receive information (access), and how they use it in their behavior. Cook (2007) indicates that children's participation is an ongoing process of their active involvement in decisions that affect their daily lives, affording children the power and knowledge to shape both the processes and outcomes.

The Chronosystem Layer

The chronosystem occupies time that influences the process of all the layers in the ecological model, and how this affects the child over a short, or long-term period in their existence. Bronfenbrenner's model shows the significance of the developing person in their daily experiences, including how the child is shaped in their development via other events that are linked.

These theories help us to understand that the environment closest to the child plays a very important role in the development of the child. In particular, the behaviour of parents that is their parenting style may aid in encouraging negative child behaviour such as externalising or antisocial behaviour.

PARENTING STYLES AND PRACTICES

Parenting includes care, guidance and love given by the parent, or care giver to a child (Kerby, 2007). Parental involvement, and specifically positive parental participation in the parent-child relationship, reduces the risks of externalizing behaviours of youth (Stolk, et al., 2007). However, destructive parenting increases the risk for the development of adjustment problems in children. Consequently, there is a strong correlation between the early maladaptive parent-child interactions and the development of externalizing problems (Stolk, et al. 2007).

Parents make a lifelong commitment to invest in the rearing and development of a child/ren by being responsible care givers (Brooks; 2011). Parents, as care-givers, then become the providers intended for formulating both internal (emotional, spiritual, mental) and external (social, physical) fundamentals of a child's growth and development. Parents therefore provide both direct and indirect actions with children which manifest in different forms (Brooks; 2011).

According to Brooks (2011:6) responsible care-giving includes:

- An on-going attachment and relationship with the child
- Material resources such as food, clothing and shelter
- Access to medical and dental care
- Responsible discipline, avoiding injuries and cruel criticism and harmful physical punishment
- Intellectual and moral education
- Preparation for taking on responsibilities of adulthood
- Assuming responsibility for child's actions in the larger society.

Parenting is a process of action and interaction between parent and child. The positive and effective development of a child involves reaching social, emotional, cognitive capabilities in childhood and adolescence (Bares, Delva, Grogan-Kaylor, & Andrade, 2011). Thus the way in which parents interact with their children is extremely important. This interaction can be understood in terms of parenting styles and practices.

Parenting styles that include criticism, inconsistency, and harsh parenting, have been associated with adolescents displaying greater levels of aggressive behaviour (Ge, Brody, Conger, Simons, & Murry, 2002; Narusyste, Andershed, Neiderhister, & Lichtenstein, 2007) and delinquent behaviour (Capaldi, Pears, Patterson, & Owen, 2003). Also parenting practices that include unresponsive and non-authoritative parenting are deleterious to the development and functioning of children (Goldstein, Harvey, & Friedman-Weieneth, 2007; Trenas, Cabrer, & Osuna, 2008). These parenting practices displayed may in turn sustain, and over time increase the negative behaviours of the child, causing an increase in future chances of problem risk behaviours of adolescence. Thus, parental negativity appears to precede variation in adolescent antisocial behaviours, a key predictor of which is aggression of antisocial behaviour later in life (Narusyte et. al., 2007).

According to Baumrind (1966, 1967, 1968, 1978), parenting can be divided into different types or styles of parenting. These styles include authoritarian, permissive and authoritative styles of parenting.

Authoritarian Parenting Style

Authoritarian parents set very high standards and rules for their children. The core of the parent-child relationship is that what the parent says is truth and law and cannot be questioned and the child must obey these rules and if they do not then they will experience the wrath of the parent. The child's opinion is not asked nor accepted, which means that the communication between the parent and child is restrictive. The authoritarian parent has low love and high limits for the child. Failure for the child to comply or obey would results in forceful and punitive parenting.

The behavioural outcomes of the child is a delay or stagnation of the child's development, a lack of individualism and autonomy are unhappy, aimless, do not get along with others, low in achievement motivation and social assertion.

Permissive Parenting Style

This parent believes the child must be free – free from discipline, restrictions, rules and structure – and should therefore be left on his/her own to grow and develop as an individual. Permissive parents are therefore very indulgent, accepting, assenting and have a benevolent and compassionate manner towards the child's impulses and actions. The parent becomes a resource rather than a socialisation agent to shape and change the child's continuous behaviour. Baumrind (1978: 255) considers permissive parents to be "self-involved and offer freedom as a way of evading responsibility for the child's development", although they are "loving and protective". Permissive parents are high on love but low on limits. They do not follow through on discipline.

Behavioural outcomes for the child include a lack of impulse control, are self-centred and low in achievement orientation. Furthermore, children of permissive parents are more likely to engage in substance abuse (Tackett et al., 2013).

Authoritative Parenting Style

An authoritative parenting style is considered a more positive approach to managing children. Parents who use an authoritative parenting style provide structure and rules when raising their children. However, children are also part of developmentally appropriate decision-making tasks in the family and the reasons for rules and structures created by parents. Authoritative parenting is warm, supportive, encouraging, accepting and responsive. This means that that the child knows what to expect in the future because there are clear rules for consequences for behaviour. The focus of this parent-child relationship is on the child's autonomy, individualism and behaviour rather than on the child's person. Thus when the child misbehaves, for example, being rude to a parent, the authoritative parent would focus on what the child is doing wrong by saying "Rudeness will not be tolerated because it is disrespectful" rather than saying "You are rude". This relationship also focuses on social competence and ultimately responsible adults. Authoritative parents are highly demanding and highly responsive and successfully protected their adolescents from problem drug use and generating competence.

The behavioural outcomes for children are high achievement orientation, motivation, energetic, socially outgoing, autonomous, friendly, socially receptive; have higher self-esteem and life satisfaction with lower depression for children; secure attachment; academic achievement; maturity and competence. The children become well-adjusted adults.

Rejecting-Neglectful Parenting Style

Rejecting-neglectful parents are linked to permissive parents. This parent is "disengaged" and are "neither demanding nor responsive" to their children (Baumrind, 1991: 62). In addition, these parents do not provide structure in the home nor do they monitor their children. They are not supportive "but may be actively rejecting or else neglect their childrearing responsibilities altogether". This parents has low firmness and low warmth.

The behavioural outcomes for children of rejecting-neglecting parents are the least competent, undisciplined, lack structure and an internal sense of discipline. As they do not receive love and warmth from their parents, these children may not be able to show these feelings to others and will seek other sources to find love and warmth. They may also take on the parents' responsibility of caregiving if they have younger siblings and subsequently miss out on their childhood. These children may continue to be challenged in having and maintain healthy relationships into adulthood.

ADOLESCENCE AND ANTISOCIAL BEHAVIOR

Adolescence

Adolescence is a period of development categorized by the age between 13-17 years. The physical care, play, and day to day cognitive, social and emotional needs of adolescence are unique as it is a stage when adolescents want to make their own choices, develop unique personalities and opinions, want more independence and responsibility and require less day to day physical care and close monitoring by parents (Erickson, 1968;). Arnett (2006) highlights that extremes of behaviour and emotion in adolescents are perfectly normal. This is partly because even though most adolescents do not exhibit serious problems, certain types of behavior, such as conflict with parents and experimentation, are more common during adolescence than at other ages (Arnett, 1990). Deroma, Lassiter and Davis (2004) found that positive outcomes in adolescence were enhanced when parents engage the adolescents to be more involved in the decision making. Adolescents whose parents are warm (accepting), firm and democratic enjoy psychological and behavioural advantages over their peers who did not have this. They are adjusted at school, are more self-reliant, report less psychological distress and engage in less delinquent activities (Steinberg, Mounts, Lamborn & Dornbusch, 1991). Parents are the first significant figures in a child's life, therefore the dynamics between the parent-child relationships could influence their choices (Kasser, et al., 1995) which could be to engage (or not) in antisocial activities. Regardless of the independence adolescence obtain at this developmental stage, parents remain a continual source of influence (Baumrind, 1994).

Antisocial Behavior

Patterson (1990) defines antisocial behaviour as a developmental trait that begins early in life and often continues into adolescence. Antisocial behaviour of adolescence may be associated with youth, who engage in bullying others and criminal behaviour (Rigby, 2003; Sourander et al., 2007). Furthermore, it is associated with poor academic achievement, school failure and conduct problems (Fergussion & Horwood, 1995; Nelson, Benner, Lane & Smith, 2004). Antisocial behaviour, including aggression and attention problems shown during childhood, may hinder the development of children into adolescence and carried further into adulthood (Hayatbakhsh, et al., 2008). Research suggests that there are child risk factors which predict long term antisocial behaviour. These include stress, caregiver criminal convictions and dysfunctional parenting (McLoughlin, Rucklidge, Grace, & McLean, 2010). In terms of parenting, Narusyte, et al., (2007: 128) state "A traditional notion has been that parents by their behaviour or lack of certain behaviours, directly affect the behaviour of their children". The parent-adolescent relationship becomes a vicious cycle as the aggressive behaviour of children evokes negative and sometimes harsh parenting, which subsequently influences and produces antisocial behaviours of adolescence (Narusyte, et al., 2007).

Clearly, previous research suggests that there may be a particular correlation between the parent and the antisocial behaviour of adolescents (Roman, Human & Hiss, 2012). While this research provides evidence of this relationship, these studies may not necessarily indicate the parental practices used to manage the antisocial behaviour of adolescents. The current study therefore used a systematic review of previous research to systematically appraise studies which seek to examine the link between antisocial behaviour of adolescents and parental practices to manage the antisocial behaviour of their adolescents. Specifically, the objectives of this study were to (1) examine the types of antisocial behaviour of adolescents; (2) examine the parenting styles and practices used in this context of behaviour; (3) explore parental management of antisocial behaviour of adolescents; (4) critically appraise the methodological quality of the studies related to adolescent antisocial behaviour and parenting styles and practices, with a view to identifying opportunities to improve future research quality.

METHODS

A systematic review was conducted in order to extrapolate evidence-based recommendations of how parents manage the antisocial behaviour of their adolescents. The PRISMA Statement (Moher, Liberati, Tetzlaff & Altman, 2009) was used as a guide for the formulation of this study. With the onset of the study, both authors agreed to the terms and definitions used for this study. In addition the roles of each contributor were clarified with ARH-H being the implementer of the study and NVR being the reviewer of all the stages of the process.

The online databases explored were Ebscohost (Medline, CINAHL, PsycArticles), JSTOR and Pubmed. The search period was between 2003 and 2014. In addition, reference lists were manually searched to further explore relevant articles by authors on the topic. Search terms included antisocial behaviour, parenting, parenting styles, parenting practices, youth: adolescent/s/ce, at-risk behaviour. When inserting the term "AND" between concepts the results revealed were less than using the term "OR". There were also instances when no results were revealed by using the term "AND".

The following terms and definitions were applied to this review:

Table 1. The methods of review

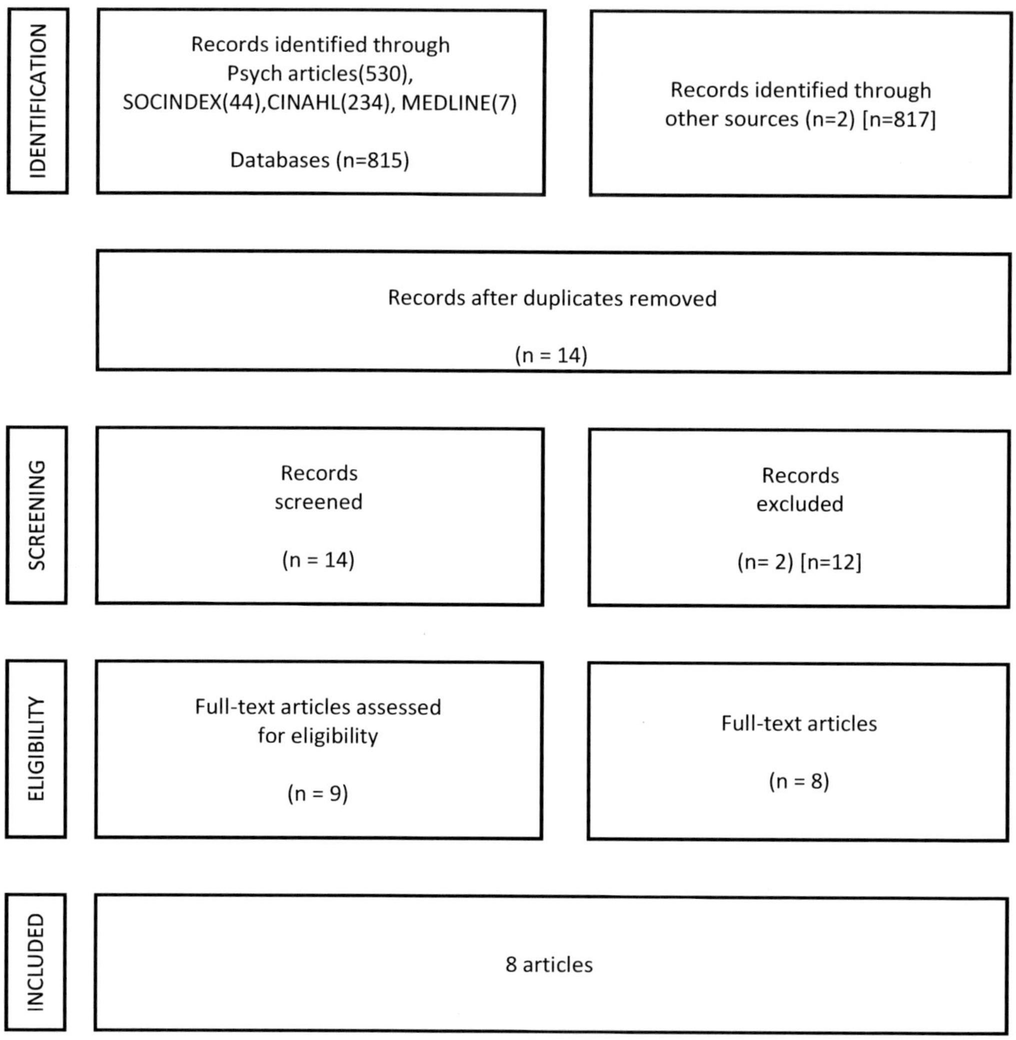

- **Parenting:** has been defined as the rearing of the child or children and includes care, guidance and love given by the parent, or care giver (Kerby, 2007).
- **Adolescents** (youth): 11-18
- **Antisocial behaviour:** According to Baumrind (2005), antisocial behaviour is a form of externalising behaviour where the individual disobeys rules and laws. Additionally, antisocial behaviour can be defined as "[opposition] to society or to existing social organization and moral codes" and "aggressive, impulsive and sometimes violent actions that flout social and ethical codes such as laws and

regulations relating to personal and property rights" (Corsini, 2002: 57). Furthermore, the phenomenon of antisocial behaviour is depicted as strongly inclined toward aggressive encounters, self-will destruction, other troubling behaviours and even minor offences (Reid et al., 2002). Antisocial behaviour in this study is understood as externalising behaviours such as the use of substances, driving intoxicated, unprotected sex, conduct problems and breaking societal rules which are also known as risk-taking behaviours (Arnett, 2000, 2005; Schulenberg & Zarrett, 2006).

This review considered studies that included males and female youth/adolescents. The studies were inclusive of race, education and socio-economic status. These criteria were applied to the parents of the adolescents. The studies which included the parenting styles and practices of the parents were based on Baumrind's parenting styles, which included permissive, authoritarian, authoritative and rejecting/neglectful parenting styles. The criteria for inclusion into the study were that i) publications had to be written in the English language; ii) publication dates were between 2003-2014; iii) quantitative cross-sectional and longitudinal cohort studies were included; iv) studies which focused on the influence of and the relationship between parenting and antisocial behaviour of adolescents. The methodology of these studies examined the variables in terms of associations and predictors. This means then that studies, which assessed parenting styles as predictors of adolescent antisocial behaviour, were included. Studies which were excluded were reviews, randomised control trials and programme interventions and qualitative studies.

All articles obtained for the review were recorded in a table. For tracking purposes, a data storage form was created, which provided details about the article's authors, title and source, as well as the database from which the article was retrieved. Data was extracted independently using the 'JBI data extraction tool' and entered into a data extraction sheet (see Table 4).

The search yielded 815 articles for the relationship between parenting styles and the antisocial behaviour of adolescents. An additional 2 articles were provided by an expert source which increased the articles searcher to 817. After screening the titles and abstracts for eligibility and duplicates a sample of 14 articles was retrieved. Two articles were removed as they were reviews, which then culminated in 12 articles to be methodologically appraised for the study. These 12 articles were read independently by the two authors in order to agree to the inclusion of the articles for the methodological appraisal.

The next stage was the methodological appraisal tool. This tool was adapted from a systematic review conducted by Roman & Frantz (2013). The appraisal tool is indicated in Table 2 and the results from the appraisal process are indicated in Table 3. The methodological quality was based on the sampling method, response rate, measurement tool, data sources, and the inclusion of parenting and further explanation of anti-social behaviour. The final sample consisted of eight articles to be included in the study as they had met the desired criteria (60%-100%). A flow chart (see Table 1) indicates the process of the study.

Table 2. The critical appraisal tool

1.	**Was the sampling method representative of the population intended to the study?** A. Non-probability sampling(including; purposive, quota, convenience and snowball sampling) [0] B. Probability sampling (including; simple, random, systematic, stratified, cluster, two-stage and multi-stage sampling) [1]		
2.	**How was non-response addressed?** A. Reasons for non-response described [1] B. Reasons for non-response not described [0]		
3.	Did the study report any response rate? (If the reported response rate is below 60%, the question should be answered "No.") A. No [0] B. Yes [1]		
4.	Was the measurement tool used valid and reliable? A. Yes [1] B. No [0]		
5.	What was the source of the data? A. Secondary source: survey not specifically designed for the purpose [0] B. Primary source [1]		
6.	Do the authors include the definition of antisocial behavior, adolescence and parenting as used for their study? A. Yes [1] B. No [0]		
7.	Is parenting of antisocial behaviour of adolescence further explored in the study? A. Yes [1] B. No [0]		
8.	Have recommendations and implications for parenting and antisocial behavior of adolescents been included for this study? A. Yes [1] B. No [0]		
Scoring method: Total score divided by total number of all applicable items			
Grading of the QACO score			
0-33%		33%-66%	67%-100%
Bad		Satisfactory	Good

Table 3. Scoring sheet for critical appraisal

		1	2	3	4	5	6	7	8	Score	%
1	Chien & East, 2012	0	0	0	1	1	0	1	1	4	50
2	Bares et al. 2011	0	1	1	1	1	1	1	0	6	75
3	Thornberry et al., 2009	1	1	1	1	1	0	1	1	7	88
4	Narusyte et al., 2007	0	0	1	1	1	0	1	0	4	50
5	McLoughlin et al., 2010	0	1	0	1	1	1	1	0	5	63
6	Klahr et al., 2011	0	1	1	1	1	0	1	0	5	63
7	Harris-Mckoy & Cui, 2013	1	1	1	1	0	1	1	1	7	88
8	Johnson & McGue, 2009	1	1	1	1	1	1	1	1	8	100
9	Bailey, Hill, Oesterle & Hawkins, 2009	1	0	1	1	1	1	1	1	7	88
10	Roman, Human & Hiss, 2012	0	0	0	1	1	1	1	0	4	50
11	Tu, Lee, Chen, & Kao, 2014	0	0	0	1	1	1	1	1	5	63

RESULTS

General Description of the Studies Reviewed

Of the final eight studies included in the systematic review, two were cross-sectional studies (Bares, et al., 2011; Tu, Lee, Chen, & Kao, 2014) and 6 were longitudinal (Bailey, Hill, Oesterle & Hawkins, 2009; Harris-McKoy & Cui, 2013; Johnson, McGue & Iacono, 2009; Klahr, McGue, Iacono & Burt, 2011; McLoughlin, Rucklidge, Grace & McLean, 2010; Thornberry, Freeman-Gallant & Lovegrove, 2009). The studies in the final sample were 1 from Taiwan (Tu, Lee, Chen, & Kao, 2014), one from New Zealand (McLoughlin, Rucklidge, Grace & McLean, 2010) and 6 from the USA (Bailey, Hill, Oesterle & Hawkins, 2009; Bares, et al., 2011; Harris-McKoy & Cui, 2013; Johnson, McGue & Iacono, 2009; Klahr, McGue, Iacono & Burt, 2011; Thornberry, Freeman-Gallant & Lovegrove, 2009). Data was collected by means of survey questionnaires in all the studies. The longitudinal studies were conducted at different ages and therefore spanned from children to young adulthood. The sample sizes for the studies ranged from 117 to 13 358. The sample studies also included participant children who were adopted, twins and who were children of biological parents. This meant that the association between parenting and antisocial behavior was examined both genetically and environmentally. Studies reported ethnicity and the gender of participants were variable (see Table 3).

Defining Antisocial Behaviour (ASB)

Eight of the studies provided a definition of antisocial behaviour (ASB). The definitions of ASB, also known as problem behaviours, risky behavior, externalizing behavior and conduct problems were all encompassing, in defining ASB as associated with delinquency, substance abuse, poor family relationships (especially with parent), aggression, poor academic achievement, poor impulse control, disruptive behavior, unemotional behavior, low emotional intelligence, human assaults, child abuse and attention problems. ASB was also indicated by a disregard for rules and laws portraying vandalism, setting fires, theft and crime (Tu, Lee, Chen & Kao, 2014).

In particular, for studies which reported gender differences, these studies found that more males than females engaged in ASB (Harris-McKoy & Cui, 2013; Klahr, McGue, Iacono & Burt, 2011) but in addition studies in the sample also over sampled on males due to previous studies which suggest that more males than females engage in ASB (McLoughlin, Rucklidge, Grace & McLean, 2010; Thornberry, Freeman-Gallant & Lovegrove, 2009). The majority of the studies identified ASB as early as 9 years of age until age 27 years in longitudinal studies. Studies in the sample also suggest that children who engage in ASB also have additional environmental factors such low educational levels of parents (McLoughlin, Rucklidge, Grace & McLean, 2010); below average household income (McLoughlin, Rucklidge, Grace & McLean, 2010); single parents or parents who were in a relationship with the child's non-biological parent (McLoughlin, Rucklidge, Grace & McLean, 2010); lived in communities where crime was relatively high (Johnson, McGue & Iacono, 2009; Thornberry, Freeman-Gallant & Lovegrove, 2009); had minimal contact with a biological father (Thornberry,

Freeman-Gallant & Lovegrove, 2009); heads of households were unemployed or receiving welfare (Thornberry, Freeman-Gallant & Lovegrove, 2009); had a parent using substances or engaging in criminal activity (Bailey, Hill, Oesterle & Hawkins, 2009; McLoughlin, Rucklidge, Grace & McLean, 2010; Thornberry, Freeman-Gallant & Lovegrove, 2009).

Parenting and Antisocial Behavior (ASB)

Parenting is depicted as the styles, practices and influential roles that impact on their children's behaviors, whether adopted or biological, throughout the sample of studies. Thus all studies reported a relationship between parental influence and antisocial behavior of adolescents.

In terms of describing parenting the following were found: high parental monitoring and positive parenting (Bailey, Hill, Oesterle & Hawkins, 2009; Bares, et al., 2011; Harris-McKoy & Cui, 2013); low parental monitoring (McLoughlin, Rucklidge, Grace & McLean, 2010); psychological control (Tu, Lee, Chen, & Kao, 2014); harsh discipline (Bailey, Hill, Oesterle & Hawkins, 2009); level of attachment (Thornberry, Freeman-Gallant & Lovegrove, 2009); parental control and guidance (Harris-McKoy & Cui, 2013); time out (McLoughlin, Rucklidge, Grace & McLean, 2010); inconsistent parenting (McLoughlin, Rucklidge, Grace & McLean, 2010); low levels of emotional awareness and empathetic concern (McLoughlin, Rucklidge, Grace & McLean, 2010); conflictual parenting (Klahr, McGue, Iacono & Burt, 2011)

Relational aspects between parenting and ASB of adolescents suggest that parenting is transferred across generations (Bailey, Hill, Oesterle & Hawkins, 2009; Johnson, McGue & Iacono, 2009; Klahr, McGue, Iacono & Burt, 2011; Thornberry, Freeman-Gallant & Lovegrove, 2009); fathers play a very important role in reducing ASB in terms of rule breaking and aggressive behavior for their adolescent sons, while mothers are important for their daughters (Bares, et al., 2011); harsh parenting had an effect on ASB (Bailey, Hill, Oesterle & Hawkins, 2009); parental engagement in ASB was transferred to the child when attachment was low (Thornberry, Freeman-Gallant & Lovegrove, 2009); maternal psychological control was a stronger predictor of ASB than paternal psychological control (Tu, Lee, Chen, & Kao, 2014); low parental control were associated with delinquency during adolescence and criminal behavior during young adulthood (Harris-McKoy & Cui, 2013); parent-child conflict, as a shared environmental influence, was related to ASB (Klahr, McGue, Iacono & Burt, 2011). In terms of genetics, one study suggests that the parent -child relationship and adolescent maladjustment are influenced by genetic effects (Thornberry, Freeman-Gallant & Lovegrove, 2009), where the parent had also previously engaged in ASB during adolescence.

Table 4. Data extraction sheet

no.	Author	Country	Study Design	Instruments	Sample	Definition of ASB and/or Parenting	Parenting- to reduce antisocial behaviour of adolescence	Type of parenting
1	Bares et al., (2011)	Santiago - Chile, USA	Cross-sectional study from longitudinal data	Youth Self Report [Rule Breaking Behavior, Aggressive Behavior, Attention Problems], Behavioral Approach-Drive, Behavioral Inhibition Scale, Parental Monitoring, Mother and Father Parenting Behaviors	884 participants chosen out of a total from 1,100 families	Problem behaviours including aggression and attention problems.	As a whole, parents who properly attend to their children's needs and who engage in positive parenting are more likely to be successful in guiding adolescents to engage in less rule-breaking and aggressive behaviours and develop less attention problems. Young and older male adolescents benefitted more than girls if they had a positive relationship with the father resulted in less rule-breaking.	Protective Relationship; Parental monitoring, positive parenting by both mothers and fathers;
2	Tu, Lee, Chen, & Kao (2014)	Taiwan	Cross-sectional	The Chinese Paternal Psychological Control Scale	The final sample consisted of 377 participants. 134 boys, 239 girls;	Antisocial behavior is defined as external	Prevention and interventions targeting adolescents who are	Psychological Control; mothers are perceived as
				(CPPCS) and Chinese Maternal Psychological Control Scale; The Children's Depression Inventory; Antisocial Behavioral Scale	35.9% adolescent males; Age ranged from age 15 to 17 years old (M = 15.30); Grade ten through twelve (M =10.40)	behavioral traits with regard to not obeying rules and laws. These behaviors include assault, vandalism, setting fires, theft, crime and other delinquent acts which conform to social norms.	at high risk for the development of such behaviors is of the utmost importance for the well-being of the adolescents themselves, their families, and the community at large. The convergence of traditional Chinese culture and modern western values in the 20th century in Taiwan had a significant effect on family structures and processes	significantly more psychologically controlling than fathers

Table 4. (Continued)

no.	Author	Country	Study Design	Instruments	Sample	Definition of ASB and/or Parenting	Parenting- to reduce antisocial behaviour of adolescence	Type of parenting
3	Bailey, Hill, Oesterle & Hawkins (2009)	Seattle, USA	Longitudinal	Parent externalizing behaviour in adolescence; Child Behaviour Checklist; Parental monitoring; Harsh discipline; Grandparent and parent substance	808 participants; 771 parents; 86% of parents were female with a Mean age of 39 years; 9% of parents were males with a Mean age of 42 years. Interviews	Externalizing behaviour: Poor impulse control and oppositional, aggressive or delinquent behaviour	Some parenting practices are integenerationally continuous. Harsh discipline had an effect on externalizing behaviour. Intervention targets should be	Parental monitoring and harsh discipline
				use; Conflict Tactics Scale; Sociodemographic risk	were conducted at 10 to 16 years, 18 and every 3 years after including age 27.		implemented to reduce intergenerational discontinuity in parenting.	
4	Thornberry, Freeman-Gallant & Lovegrove, (2009)	USA [New York, Rochester]	Longitudinal	*Parent antisocial Behavior *Hudson Index *Life Stressors *CES-D Scale *Child Behavior Checklist	Mother (137) Supervisory Father (155) Child [9 years] Sample was over represented on males (75%) and poor families; included 68% African American, 17% Hispanic and 15% White; 33% HH were unemployed and 40% received welfare	No definition but discusses its attributes	Childhood antisocial behaviour has deep roots extending back to the parents adolescent antisocial behaviour. Parent-child attachment is central to reduce the possibility of the intergenerational transference of antisocial behaviour from parent to child. In this study attachment is a mediator of intergenerational continuity.	Level of attachment
5	Harris-McKoy & Cui	USA	Longitudinal study	Adolescent delinquency (Wave 1); Young	Wave 1: 17 636 adolescents; Wave 2: 13 358.	Risky behaviour: such as	Parental control is still influential through the period	Parental control: providing
	(2013)			adult criminal behaviour (Wave III) – 7 items summed for each wave; Parental Control – 6	Based on attrition analysis, male adolescents, African Americans and those with lower levels of	delinquency. Adolescence: time of transition, called period of storm and stress.	of adolescence and early young adulthood. Low parental control is positively associated with delinquency and criminal	guidance and monitoring

no.	Author	Country	Study Design	Instruments	Sample	Definition of ASB and/or Parenting	Parenting- to reduce antisocial behaviour of adolescence	Type of parenting
				items.	education dropped out of the study.	Also a stage of autonomous seeking and independence.	behaviour in young adulthood. Too much autonomy can result in negative outcomes such as delinquency. Although adolescents must have a say in decision-making, parents should have the final say for healthy adolescent development. To limit or reduce adolescent delinquency, parents should continue to control what adolescents watch on television,	
							who they associate with, and how much unsupervised time they are allowed out of the house. Parental control should be applied to young adults as well in order to reduce criminal activities.	
6	McLoughlin, Rucklidge, Grace & McLean (2010)	New Zealand	Longitudinal study- cohort study	ICU-24 item questionnaire derived from the Anti-Social Processing Screening Device (APSD). Child Behavior Checklist. Conners' Parent Rating Scale Revised. Child Social Behavior Scale. Alabama Parenting Questionnaire. Parent's or Caregivers' Criminal History. Antisocial Process	Children aged 10 and 11 years. 94 children and their parents/caregivers were selected from an original sample of 117. Phase 1: 70 boys, 47 girls. 50.3% New Zealand European/Pakeha, 32.5% Maori, 10.3% Pacific Islan and 6.8% European or Asian. Phase 2: 74 Low CU/Agg children and 20	Disruptive behaviour: aggressive behaviour and poor school achievement; unemotional, behaviours are linked with psychopathology in adulthood; significantly lower emotional intelligence, low scores for stress management.	Parents with children in the High Callous unemotional aggression group: the ways in which parents interact with their children in terms of upholding rules and social norms eventually relates to the development of delinquency and problem behaviour. Consistently it has been shown that the most powerful and consistent predictor of juvenile	Parenting techniques used with the High group included time out, lower levels of monitoring and inconsistent discipline. Also included low levels of emotional awareness and empathic concern.

Table 4. (Continued)

no.	Author	Country	Study Design	Instruments	Sample	Definition of ASB and/or Parenting	Parenting- to reduce antisocial behaviour of adolescence	Type of parenting
				Screening Device. BarOn Emotion Quotient Inventory	High CU/Agg children. Parents of the high group – 50% had no qualifications or school leavers certificates, below the average household income (35%), 30% were married to or in a de facto relationship with the child's biological parent; 25% were married to or in a de facto relationship with the child's non-biological parent, 45% were single parents. Low group had 40%, 28.4% had below average		offending is poor inconsistent parenting. Parental criminality is also a major contributory factor to the development of anti-social behaviour in children.	
					for the household income, 43.8% were married to or in a de facto relationship with the child's biological parent, 15.1% were married to or in a de facto relationship with the child's non-biological parent, 41.1% were single parents. SES was not significantly different.			
7	Klahr, McGue, Iacono & Burt, (2011)	Miinnesota, USA	Longitudinal study cross-lagged model	Delinquent Behavior Index, DSM-IV, Parental Environment Questionnaire	672 adopted adolescents in 405 families. 63.7% of fathers were college graduates. Mean age of adolescents was at intake	Antisocial behaviour associated with destruction of property, human	Parent - child relationship influences the development of conduct problems during adolescence and early adulthood via shared	Parent-child conflict; Conflictual parenting styles

no.	Author	Country	Study Design	Instruments	Sample	Definition of ASB and/or Parenting	Parenting- to reduce antisocial behaviour of adolescence	Type of parenting
					14.1 years and 18.2 years at follow-	assaults, child abuse, disregard for personal and	environmental mechanisms but not vice versa. Family.	
					up. 55% of adolescents were female. 95% of adoptive parents were Caucasian with 67% of adopted adolescents being Asian American and 21% were Caucasian.	property rights.	or parent level interventions are reasonably effective treatments for behaviour of adolescents rather than individual-level interventions. In this study genes do not play a role and therefore the environment (family, parents) in totality provide a an explanation for the maintenance of problem behaviour over time. Conflictual parenting styles alienate adolescents from their parents and inspire increased rebellion	
8	Johnson, McGue & Iacono, (2009)	Minnesota, USA	Longitudinal twin study	Academic achievement, Educational attainment, Antisocial	Participants were male and female twin pairs. Male sample: 578	Anti-ocial behaviour associated with poor academic	At age24 association between educational attainment and environmental	none
				behaviour (DSM- III – R), Socio-economic status.	twins (289 pairs). Female sample 674 twins (337 pairs). 98% were Caucasian	achievement and school failure. Childhood disruptive behaviours defined and linked.	influences is related to acceptance and responsibility vs parents ability to support them financially. Environmental influences experienced before the age of 24 were carried into the homes they moved into.	

Parental Practices to Manage ASB of Adolescents

The studies in this systematic review suggest that positive parenting and higher levels of attachment are all encompassing for managing and reducing ASB across the lifespan. Antisocial behaviour is a negative behavioural trait and is associated with negative parenting practices. By inference then, one could assume that positive parenting should be used to manage and possibly reduce antisocial behaviour. Specifically, in order to manage antisocial behaviour, the following strategies should be implemented: (1) parents should properly attend to their children's needs (Bares, et al., 2011); (2) fathers should be more present and more involved with their adolescent children (Bares, et al., 2011); (3) intervention and prevention strategies should focus on parents and families rather than the child or adolescent (Bailey, Hill, Oesterle & Hawkins, 2009; Klahr, McGue, Iacono & Burt, 2011; Tu, Lee, Chen, & Kao, 2014); (4) attachment between parent and child should be strengthened (Thornberry, Freeman-Gallant & Lovegrove, 2009); (5) higher parental control and guidance should continue into young adulthood (Harris-McKoy & Cui, 2013); (6) autonomy in adolescence and young adulthood should be developmentally managed (Harris-McKoy & Cui, 2013); (7) parents should be empowered and have the final say in decision-making (Harris-McKoy & Cui, 2013); (8) parents should assist their adolescents to improve their (adolescents) emotional intelligence (McLoughlin, Rucklidge, Grace & McLean, 2010); (9) parents should be good role models by not engaging in criminal activity and substance abuse (Bares, et al., 2011; McLoughlin, Rucklidge, Grace & McLean, 2010; Thornberry, Freeman-Gallant & Lovegrove, 2009); (10) parenting should be consistent (McLoughlin, Rucklidge, Grace & McLean, 2010); (11) parents should try not to use conflictual parenting practices as this approach alienates adolescents and increases rebellion (Klahr, McGue, Iacono & Burt, 2011); (12) parents should be supportive (Johnson, McGue & Iacono, 2009); (13) parents should monitor television time, friendships and unsupervised time outside of the house of their adolescents (Harris-McKoy & Cui, 2013).

Discussion

This systematic review sought to answer the question: *What is the link between antisocial behaviour of adolescents and parenting practices?*

The findings in our systematic review suggest that negative parenting has implications for antisocial behaviour from childhood to young adulthood. These forms of parenting included harsh, inconsistent, conflictual and low attachment parental practices. These practices together form particular parenting styles as highlighted by Baumrind (1978). For example, negative parenting styles such as authoritarian and permissive parenting have been linked to negative outcomes or maladaptive behavior for children (Brooks; 2011; Stolk, et al. 2007). In particular children of permissive parents show a lack of impulse control and low achievement oriented, which is similar to some of the current findings. The results in this systematic review are consistent with other studies which have linked particular parenting practices such as criticism, inconsistent and harsh parenting specifically with aggressive behaviour (Ge, Brody, Conger, Simons, & Murry, 2002; Narusyste, Andershed, Neiderhister, & Lichtenstein, 2007) and delinquent behavior (Capaldi, Pears, Patterson, & Owen, 2003). In addition, the studies in this systematic review indicate that there is the possibility of transference of parental practices and a continuation of antisocial behavior across generations either by genes or by shared environmental factors. Similarities were found in other research studies (Narusyte et. al., 2007). The results of this systematic review highlight the risk factors or challenges within the parent-adolescent environment, which include family structure such as being a single parent. These risk factors were found to be challenging in other research studies as well (Hoque & Ghuman, 2012; Westbrook & Harden, 2010).

While adolescence is identified conceptually as a period when young people do not require parents to monitor them as avidly as when they were younger (Arnett, 2006; Erickson, 1968), the current research propose that parents continue with their control and guidance strategies during adolescence as these strategies reduce engagement in antisocial behavior. These strategies of course need to be accompanied by parenting which is nurturing, warm, accepting and firm (Deroma, Lassiter and Davis, 2004) in order to aid adjustment and adaptive behavior (Steinberg, Mounts, Lamborn & Dornbusch, 1991).

The underlying thread across the studies, especially the longitudinal studies, suggests that the earlier antisocial behaviour is identified and dealt with, the better the outcomes will be as the child becomes older. If this is not done timeously and left to develop, the types of misbehaviour would increase to the level of criminal activities. From a preventative perspective, fathers should be more involved with their children, especially with their sons. In fact, Carlson (2006) suggests that when fathers live with their adolescent children it is more beneficial for the adolescent. In addition, these studies also suggest that if the role models are positive, engagement in antisocial behaviour will be reduced. The results of this review highlight particular parental strategies which could aid in the reduction of antisocial behavior. These results are similar to those identified by Brooks (2011). In particular *parental monitoring* such as parents' knowledge of their adolescent*'s* activities and friends; *parental involvement (and in particular fathers)* such as doing activities together including chores, playing games, watching television or having a meal together; *good parental modeling* such as not engaging in any behaviors which the child would mimic such as drinking alcohol or engaging in criminal activities; *parent-adolescent attachment* indicated by bonding, warmth, acceptance and nurturance, if consistent, all contribute to reducing negative child behaviour.

The majority of the studies scored above average on the study quality score. Our review highlights limitations of the studies reviewed. Studies were excluded due to limitations in the methodology, such as not reporting response rates, excluding information regarding measurement tools and lack of/not any recommendations made. Limitations of studies in this review are also noted by a lack of relevant demographic data (such as gender of the adolescent, educational levels of the parents) which could be considered as additional risk factors for antisocial behavior of adolescents as they provide additional challenges for parents to manage their children. The role of the father is also not very clear in certain studies as in contrast to those which compare mothers and fathers, which indicate the very positive contribution of fathers in possibly reducing antisocial behavior of adolescents. The definition of antisocial behavior, also indicated as problem behaviour, risky behaviour and conduct problems were all encompassing in this systematic review as associated with delinquency, substance abuse, poor family relationships, aggression, depression, poor academic achievement and attention problems (Fergussion & Horwood, 1995; Nelson, Benner, Lane & Smith, 2004Rigby, 2003; Sourander et al., 2007).

Conclusion

This systematic review shows that antisocial behaviour is generally a concern internationally. Clearly, parents play role both in terms of parenting their children and modeling appropriate behavior for their children. Generally, studies show mothers as ever present; this systematic review highlights the need for father-child studies. These studies should include comparative studies between involved or uninvolved fathers and the effects on the behavior of their children. Across the current sample, it is evident that antisocial behaviour is experienced at the young age of 9 years and progresses into emerging adulthood as late as 27 years. This implies that there is a need for intervention and preventative strategies to address these externalizing behaviours as early as possible.

References

Arnett, J. (1990). 'Drunk driving sensation seeking, and egocentrism among adolescents'. *Personality and Individual Differences*, *11*(6), 541-546.

Arnett, J. (2000). The Theory of Development from the Late Teens through the Twenties. *American Psychological Association*, *55*(5), 469-480.

Arnettt, J. J. (2004). *Emerging adulthood: the winding road from the late teens through the twenties.* New York: Oxford University Press.

Arnett, J. (2007). Suffering, Selfish, Slackers? Myths and Reality about Emerging Adults. *Journal of Youth Adolescence*, *36*, 23-29.

Bailey, J. A., Hill, K. G. Oesterle, S., & Hawkins, J. D. (2009). Parenting practices and problem behavior across three generations: Monitoring, harsh discipline, and drug use in the intergenerational transmission of externalizing behavior. *Developmental Psychology*, *45*, 1214-1226.

Baradon, T., Sinason, V. & Yabsley, S. (1999). 'Assessment of parents and young children: a child psychotherapy point of view', *Child Care Health and Development*, *25* (1) 37-53.

Baumrind, D. (1966). Effects of authoritative parental control on child behaviour. *Journal of Child Development*, *37*, 887-907.

Baumrind, D. (1967). Child care practices interceding three patterns of preschool behavior. *Genetic Psychology Monographs*, *75* (1) 43-88.

Baumrind, D. (1968). Authoritarian vs authoritative control. *Adolescence*, *37*, 255-272.

Baumrind, D. (1971). Current patterns of parental authority. *Developmental Psychology*, *4* (1), 1-103.

Baumrind, D. (1978). Parental disciplinary patterns and social competence in children. Journal of Youth & Society, *9*, 239-276.

Baumrind, D. (1987). A developmental perspective on adolescent risk taking in contemporary America. New Directions for Child Development, *37*, 93-125.

Baumrind, D. (1989). Rearing competent children. In W. Damon, (Ed.), *Child Development Today and Tomorrow*, (349-378). San Francisco: Jossey-Bass.

Baumrind, D. (1991). The Influence of parenting style on adolescence competence and substance use. *Journal of Early Adolescence*, *11*(1), 56-95.

Baumrind, D. (1997). Necessary distinctions. *Psychological Inquiry*, *8*, 176–182.

Bares, C.B., Delva, J.Grogan-Kaylor, A., Andrade, F. (2011). Personality and Parenting Processes Associated with Problem Behaviors: A Study of Adolescents in Santiago, Chile. *Social Work Research.*, *35* (4), 227-240.

Beaver, K. M., and Wright, J. P. (2007). The stability of low self-control from kindergarten through first grade. *Journal of Crime and Justice*, *30*, 63-86.

Brooks, J. (2011). *The Process of Parenting.* Eighth Ed. New York: McGraw Hill.

Bronfenbrenner, U. (1977). Toward an experimental ecology of human development. American *Psychologist*, *32* (7), 513-531.

Bronfenbrenner, U. (1979). *The Ecology of Human Development: Experiments by Nature and Design.* Cambridge, MA: Harvard University Press.

Bronfenbrenner, U. (1985). *Freedom and discipline across the decades.* In G. Becker, H. Becker, &Huber (Eds), Sonerducke aus: Ordung und undordunung (326-339). Berlin, Federal Republic of Germany: Beltz Verlag, Weinheim, und Basel.

Bronfenbrenner, U. & Morris, P. A. (1998). *The ecology of developmental processes.* In W. Damon (Series Ed) & R.M. Lerner (Vol. Ed), Handbook of child psychology: Vol. 1: Theoretical models of human development, (993-1028). New York: Wiley.

Bronfenbrenner, U. (2004). *Making Human Beings Human: Bioecological Perspectives on Human Development.*

Capaldi, D. M., Pears, K. C., Patterson, G. R. & Owen, L. D. (2003). Continuity of parenting practices across generations in an at-risk sample: A prospective comparison of direct and mediated associations. *Journal of Abnormal Child Psychology*, *31*, 127-142.

Carlson, M. J. (2006). Family structure, father involvement and adolescent behavioural outcomes. *Journal of Marriage and Family*, *68* (1), 137-154.

Chirkov, V., Ryan, R. M., Youngmee, K. & Kaplan, U. (2003). Differentiating autonomy from individualism and independence: A self-determination theory perspective on internalization of cultural orientations and well-being. *Journal of Personality and Social Psychology*, *84*, 1, 97-110.

Cook, L. J. (2007). *Postcommunist Welfare States: Reform Politics in Russia and Eastern Europr.* Ithaca, NY: Cornell University Press.

Corsini, R. J. (2002). *The dictionary of psychology.* New York: Brunner-Routledge.

Deater-Deckard,K., Malone,P., Sobring,E., Bombi,A., Chang,L., Dodge,K., Pastorelli,C., Tapanya,S., Zelli,A., Lansford,J., Alampay,L., Bacchin,M., Bornstein,M., Giunta,L., Oburu,P., Skinner,A., Tirado, L. & Al Hassan,S. (2011). The Association Between Parental Warmth and Control in Thirteen Cultural Groups. *Journal of Family Pscyhology.*, *25* (5), 790-794.

Deci, E. L. & Ryan, R. M. (1985). Intrinsic motivation and self-determination in human behavior. New York: Plenum Press.

Deci, E. L. & Ryan, R. M. (1985). *Intrinsic motivation and self-determination in human behavior.* New York: Plenum Press.

Deci, E. L. & Ryan, R. M. (2000). The "what" and "why" of goal pursuits: Human Needs and the self determination of behaviour. *Psychological Inquiry*, *11*, 319-338.

Deroma, V. M., Lassiter, K. S. & Davis, V. A. (2004). Adolescence involvement in discipline decision-making. *Behaviour modification*, *28*(3), *420-437.*

East, P. L., Chien, N. C. (2012). The Young Siblings of Childbearing Adolescents: Parenting Influences on Their Academic and Social-Emotional Adjustment.

Eaves, L. J., Prom, E. C. & Silberg, J. L. (2010). The mediating effect of parental neglect on adolescent and young adult anti-sociality: A longitudinal study of twins and their parents. *Behavior Genetics*, *40*, 425-437.

Fergusson, D. M. & Horwood, L. J. (1995). Early disruptive behavior, IQ, and later and achievement and delinquent behavior. *Journal of Abnormal Child Psychology*, *23*, 183-199.

Gershoff, E. T., Grogan-Kaylor, A. Lansford, J. E. Chang, L. Xelli, A., Deater-Deckard, K. & Dodge, K. A. (2010). Parent discipline practices in an international sample: Associations with child behaviours and moderation by perceived normativeness. *Child Development*, *81*, 487-502.

Ge, X. J., Brodu, G. H., Conger, R. D., Simons, R. L. & Murry, V. M. (2002). Contextual amplification of pubertal transition effects on deviant peer affiliation and externalizing behavior among African American children. *Developmental Psychology*, *38*, 42-54.

Goldstein, L. H., Harvey, E. A. & Friedman-Weieneth, J. L. (2007). Examining subtypes of behavior problems among 3-year old children, part III: Investigating differences in parenting practices and parenting stress. *Journal of Abnormal Child Psychology*, *35*, 125-136.

Gliem, F. & Glem, R. (2003). *Calculating, Interpreting and Reporting Cronbach's Alpha Reliability Coefficient of Likert Type Scales.* Conference in Adult, Continuing and Community Education.

Guardia, J. & Patrick, H. (2008). Self – Determination Theory as a Fundamental Theory of Close Relationships. *Canadian Journal of Psychology*, *49* (3), 201-209.

Hayatbakhsha, M. R., McGeeb, T. R., Borc, W., Najmana, J. M., Jamrozika, K. & Mamuna, A. A. (2008). Child and adolescent externalizing behavior and cannabis use disorders in early adulthood: An Australian prospective birth cohort study. *Addictive Behaviors*, *33* (3), 422-438.

Harris-McKoy, D. & Cui, M. (2012). Parental Control, Adolescent Delinquency, and Young Adult Criminal Behavior. *Journal of Child and Family Studies*, *22*, 836-843.

Hoque, M. E. & Ghuman, S. (2012).Contraceptive practices in the era of HIV/ AIDS among University students in South Africa. *Journal of Social Aspects of HIV/AIDS*, (In Press)

Human, A. (2010). *An examination of the relationship between psychologically controlling parenting and anti-social behaviour of emerging adults in the Faculty of Community and Health Science (CHS).* South Africa: University of the Western Cape.

Johnson, W., McGue, M. & Iacono, W. G. (2009). School Performance and Genetic and Environmental Variance in Antisocial Behavior at the Transition From Adolescence to Adulthood. *Developmental Psychology*, *45* (4), 973-987.

Kasser, T. & Ryan, R. M. (1996). Further examining the American dream: Differential correlates of intrinsic and extrinsic goals. *Personality and Social Psychology Bulletin*, *22* (3), 280-287.

Kerby, D. B., Laris, B. A. & Rolleri, l. A. (2007). Sex and HIV education programs. Their impact on sexual behavior of young people throughout the world. *Journal of Adolescent Health*, *403*(3), 206-217.

Klahr, A. M., McGue, M., Iacono, W. G. & Burt, S. A. (2011). The Association Between Parent-Child Conflict and Adolescent Conduct Problems Over Time: Results from a longitudinal adoption Study. *Journal of abnormal psychology*, *120*, 46-56.

Louw, D. A. & Edwards, D. J. A (1998). *Psychology: An introduction for students in Southern Africa*. Johannesburg: Heinemann Publishers.

Mc Loufhlin, N., Rucklidge, J. J., Grace, R. C. & McLean, A. P. (2010). Can Callous-Unemotional Traits and Aggression Identify Children at High- Risk of Anti-Social Behavior in a Low Socio-economic Group? *Journal of Family Violence., 25*, 701-712.

Moher, D., Liberati, A., Tetzlaff, J., & Altman, D.G. (2009). Preferred reporting items for systematic review and meta-analyses: the PRISMA statement. British Medical Journal, 339:b2535.

Moran, P., Ghate, D. & Van der Merwe, A. (2004). What Works in Parenting Support? *A Review of the International Research Literature.* Research Report RR574. London: Department of Education and Skills.

Narusyte, J., Andershed, A., Neiderhiser, J. M. & Lichtenstein, P. (2007). Aggression as a mediator of genetic contributions to the association between negative parent-child relationships and adolescent antisocial behavior. *European Child and Adolescent Psychiatry, 16*(2), 128-137.

Nelson, J. R., Benner, G. J., Lane, K. & Smith, B. W. (2004). Academic achievement of K-12 students with emotional and behavioral disorders. *Exceptional Children, 71*, 59-73.

Patterson, G., Debaryshe, B. & Ramsey, E. (1990). *A developmental perspective on anti-social behaviour. American Psychologist, 44*, 329-335.

Reid, J., B Patterson, G. R. & Snyders, J. J. (2002). *Antisocial behavior in children and adolescents: A developmental analysis and model for intervention.* Washington, D. C.: American Psychological Association.

Renda, J., Vassallo, S. & Edwards, B. (2011). Bullying in early adolescence and its association with anti-social behaviour, criminality and violence 6 and 10 years later. *Criminal Behaviour and Mental Health., 21*, 117-127.

Rigby, K. (2003). Consequences of bullying in schools. *Canadian Journal of Psychiatry., 9*, 583-590.

Roman, N. V. (2008). *Single and married mother-preadolescent relationships: Understanding and comparing the interaction between self -esteem and family functioning.* Unpublished Doctoral Thesis, University of the Western Cape.

Roman, N. V., Human, A. & Hiss, D. (in press). Young South African adults' perceptions of parental psychological control and antisocial behavior. *Social Behavior and Personality: An International Journal.*

Ryan, R. M. & Deci E. L. (2000). *Self -determination theory and the facilitation of intrinsic motivation, social development, and well-being. American Psychological Association, 55* (1), 68-78.

Schulenberg, J. E. & Zarrett, N. R. (2006). *Mental health during emerging adulthood: continuity and discontinuity in courses, causes, function.* In J. J. Arnett & J. L. Tanner (Eds). Emerging adults in America: Coming of age in the 21st century (1913-218). Washington DC: American Psychological Association.

Soenens, B. (2006). *Psychologically Controlling Parenting and Adolescent Psychological Adjustment.* University of Leuven.

Sourander, A., Jensen, Ronning, J. A., Niemela, S., Helenius, H., Sillanmaki, L., Kumpulainen, K., Piha, J., Tamminen, T., Moilanen, I. & Almqvist, F. (2007). What is the early adulthood outcome of boys who bully or are bullied in childhood? The Finnish 'From a Boy to a Man' study. *Paediatrics., 120*, 397-404.

Steinberg, L., Lamborn, N. D., Mounts, N. S. & Dornbusch, S. M. (1994). Over-time changes in adjustment and competence among adolescents from authoritative, authoritarian, indulgent and neglectful families. *Child Development*, *65*, 3, 754-770.

Steinberg, L., Mounts, N. S., Lamborn, S. D. & Dornbusch, S. M. (1991). Authoritative parenting and adolescent adjustment across varied ecological niches. *Journal of research in Adolescence*, *1* (1), 19-36.

Stolk, E. H. (2007). Spatial quality in the policy of the province of North-Holland: some recommendations for a better implementation with regard to design review and design process', PHD proceedings Urbanism 2006-2007 F. D. van der Hoeven (Delft) IOS press.

Stolz, H. E. & Barber, B. K. (2005). Toward Disentangling Fathering and Mothering An Assessment of Relative Importance. *Journal of Marriage of Family*, *67*, 1076-1092.

Vansteenkiste, M. Simons, J. Lens, W. Soenens, B. & Matos, L. (2005). Examining the motivational impact of intrinsic versus extrinsic goal framing and autonomy-supportive versus internally controlling communication style on adolescents' academic achievement. *Child Development*, *76* (2), 483-501.

Thornberry, T. P., Freeman-Gallant, A. & Lovegrove, P. J. (2009). The Impact of Parental Stressors on the Intergenerational Transmission of Antisocial Behavior. *Journal of Youth Adolescence.*, *38*, 312-322.

Trenas, A. F. R., Cabrera, J. H. & Osuna, M. J. P. (2008). Parenting styles and their relationship with hyperactivity. *Psicothema*, *20*, 691-696.

Tu, Y. C., Hung-Chang Lee, H-C., Chen, H-Y. & Kaod, T-F. (2014). A study on the relationships among psychological control, adolescent depression and antisocial behavior in Taiwan. *Procedia - Social and Behavioral Sciences*, *122*, 335 – 343.

Van Steenkiste, M. (2005). Intrinsic versus extrinsic goal promotion and autonomy support versus control. Unpublished doctoral dissertation, University of Leuven, Belgium.

Van Steenkiste, M., Zhou, M., Lens, W. & Soenens, B. (2005). Experiences of autonomy and control among Chinese learners: Vitalizing or immobilizing? *Journal of Educational Psychology*, *97* (3), 468-483.

Westbrook, T. R. & Jones Harden, B. (2010). Pathways between exposure to violence, maternal depression, family structure and child outcomes through parenting: A multi-group analysis. *American Journal of Orthopsychiatry*, *80*(3), 386-400.

INDEX

#

A

B

C

D

E

I

J

K

L

P

Q

R

S

T

U

V

W

Y